Dover Opera Guide and Libretto Series

CARMEN

By

GEORGES BIZET

Translated and Introduced

By

ELLEN H. BLEILER

DOVER PUBLICATIONS, INC.

New York

Published in Canada by General Publishing Company, Ltd.,
30 Lesmill Road, Don Mills, Toronto, Ontario.

Published in the United Kingdom by Constable and Company, Ltd.,
10 Orange Street, London WC 2.

This Dover edition, first published in 1970, contains the
following material:

The French libretto of *Carmen*, as published by
G. Schirmer, Inc.

A new English translation of the libretto and supplemen-
tary material by Ellen H. Bleiler.

Standard Book Number: 486-22111-3
Library of Congress Catalog Card Number: 68-10868

Manufactured in the United States of America

DOVER PUBLICATIONS, INC.
180 Varick Street
New York, N.Y. 10014

CONTENTS

GEORGES BIZET

Why Georges Bizet was registered at birth as Alexandre-César-Léopold Bizet is no longer remembered, but it was with this legal name that his birth certificate was filled out on October 26, 1838. About a year and a half later in 1840 he was christened Georges Bizet, the name that he used for the rest of his life except in legal documents.

Georges Bizet was born on October 25, 1838 into a family that was musical on both sides. His father, Adolphe Bizet, was a native of Rouen who had come to Paris as a young man, and after working for a time as a wigmaker and hairdresser, had become a teacher of voice, specializing in coaching opera singers. Georges Bizet's mother was a Delsarte, one of a musical family that claimed a remote Spanish ancestry. Bizet's maternal uncle, François Delsarte, was a well-known singer of the day. He had lost his voice, however, and had become a performer for connoisseurs only, who were willing to forgive his shadowy whisper of a voice for his flawless artistry. Great singers like Malibran and Viardot rated him highly, and at least twice in his life French rulers summoned him to court performances. Delsarte was also a musical scholar who edited and published early music; his tastes, however, were reactionary, since he felt that everything that had happened since Mozart (whom he called "the great betrayer") was musical treason. He was also something of a crank who spent years trying to become a homeopathic doctor and often embarrassed his family with extravagant behavior. Despite Delsarte's obvious musical achievement, Georges Bizet, always a modernist, rated Adolphe Bizet as much the better musician.

Georges Bizet showed an early talent for music, and the family seems to have found it fitting that he become a professional composer. In Paris, unlike some other parts of Europe, no social stigma was attached to being a musician, and a successful composer could make a very good living.

At this time in France there was an established and recognized life-history for a professional musician. First, he must attend the Paris

Conservatoire, and since the Conservatoire did not accept pupils until
they were ten years old, it was a standard coup if the admissions committee could be persuaded to take the student at an earlier age. When
Georges was nine, the Bizets and Delsartes started to pull strings in the
musical world, and Georges was examined for admission. He passed
his interviews brilliantly: he performed spectacularly on the piano, of
which he was already an excellent player; and he demonstrated his
gift of absolute pitch and his knowledge of harmony by first identifying
complex chords that were played for him, and then discussing their
function in music.

The Conservatoire had long been the heart of musical study in
France, but during Bizet's time it had fallen upon tired days. Daniel
Auber, composer of the opera *Fra Diavolo*, was director, but he was a
laissez-faire administrator who was willing to wink at inefficiency as
long as he was not bothered. Fromental Halévy, who wrote the opera
La Juive, taught composition, harmony and counterpoint. A mild-
mannered eccentric who suffered from a melancholy that often
rendered him incapable of working, Halévy carried Roussellian educa-
tional theories to an extreme. He never assigned work to his students or
criticized their music in a larger sense, but simply quietly corrected,
from a grammatical point of view, whatever they happened to turn in
to him. As he said to Sainte-Beuve on one occasion: "I make no
demands. I am working with mature young people who have reached
the age of reason and should know what they need. I am always ready
to listen ... but I have made it a point of duty never to thwart their
inclinations." Halévy's deficiencies were not wholly of his own making:
his wife suffered from periodic attacks of insanity, and the entire
routine of the family was structured around her current mental condition. It was the daughter of Fromental Halévy that Bizet was to
marry many years later.

Bizet was a very successful student at the Conservatoire, and his
school career was marked by a succession of musical prizes. Some of his
music from these early days survives: a few songs, some piano music, and
an *opéra bouffe*, *La Maison du docteur*, the manuscript of which is still
preserved at the Conservatoire. This earliest of his operas, probably
written for the amusement of his fellows, has never been printed, but
it is said to be somewhat reminiscent of Weber. Much the most important
of these fledgling efforts, however, is the Symphony in *C*, which he
finished in 1855 at the age of 17. This symphony, which was discovered
only in the 1930's, is a remarkably precocious work, and in the opinion

of many musicians shows a quality which disappeared from Bizet's work and did not reappear again until his last few years. It is derivative, of course, but it contains a wealth of delightful music.

The next step in the ideal musical life-history now came within possibility of attainment. This was the Prix de Rome, an institution founded by Louis XIV and Colbert in 1666. Although it has taken many forms during its long existence, basically it has always been a scholarship awarded each year after competitive examinations to outstanding young painters, sculptors, architects, musicians and sometimes other artists. During the 1850's winners would live for two years in Rome, spend one year in Germany and then two years in Paris on a living allowance. Among the Prix de Rome in music have been such men as Fromental Halévy, Berlioz, Thomas, Gounod, Guiraud, Massenet and Debussy.

Bizet first competed for the Prix in 1856, but the judges did not award a first prize in music that year, and Bizet had to be satisfied with a second prize. This consolation prize, however, enabled him to attend the lyric theatres of Paris without having to pay an admission fee.

In 1856 Bizet also entered a contest which Jacques Offenbach was conducting for his new theater, the Bouffes-Parisiens. Offenbach supplied the libretto, an *opéra bouffe* in the Italian style, prepared by Ludovic Halévy and Léon Battu and called *Le Docteur Miracle*. Bizet tied for first place with another young musician, Charles Lecocq, and they divided the prize of 1,200 francs between them. Since there were two winners, Offenbach's organization performed both their operas, eleven times each. This success unquestionably helped Bizet, but Bizet and Lecocq were enraged at having to divide the prize and the glory. According to Lecocq, who later became a close friend of Bizet's, it was only due to the influence of Fromental Halévy that Bizet's score was awarded the prize. Be this as it may, Bizet's *Docteur Miracle*, which has been characterized as a capable attempt at light Italian *opera buffa*, has never been published and remains in manuscript in the Paris Conservatoire.

In the following year, 1857, Bizet again competed for the Prix de Rome, and submitted a cantata entitled *Clovis et Clotilde*. Based upon the required text for the competition, this work described the conversion of the pagan king of the Franks to Christianity. This time Bizet was successful—though he loathed religious music—and he won the coveted first prize. In December, 1857 he left Paris for Rome, taking the long journey by stagecoach with the winning contestants in painting and architecture. He left Paris as a juvenile celebrity, a young man whom many felt it would be well to remember. Through the Conservatoire he had become acquainted with most of the important French musicians—Auber, Thomas and Halévy—and he had become a close friend of Charles Gounod's. During his last year there he had helped Gounod to orchestrate his work and had prepared piano renderings of Gounod's unsuccessful opera *La Nonne sanglante*. Bizet had also attended many of the brilliant soirées given by Rossini, and was acquainted with the international world of music that was represented there.

In Bizet's time the young Prix de Rome were housed in the splendid Villa Medici in Rome. In theory the Prix sounds very impressive, but like its modern counterparts, its value depended much upon the recipient. Certain winners have sneered at it as years wasted out of their lives; others have praised it as very fruitful. Bizet's opinion of it seems to have varied depending upon his mood and his current level of acceptance. Less relative advantages were the factor of reputation associated with the prize and the provision that certain licensed musical establishments of France had to perform at least one work by a Prix each year.

It is difficult to say how much Bizet learned at Rome. At this time Italian music instruction was at a low ebb, and it was generally conceded that the Prix would be better constituted if the students spent one year in Italy and two years in Germany. Bizet was very contemptuous of the level of musical studies and performance; as he put it, anyone who could play a scale with both hands was considered a piano virtuoso. Bizet did not work very hard—very few of the scholars did—but he did manage to see the wonderful landscape and ancient cities of Italy, and to saturate himself in Italian culture. From this period, too, dates his interest in literature and art, which made him one of the best-rounded of French musicians. His enthusiasm, intelligence and bonhomie made him some firm friends, while his impatience, excitability, disdain for time-serving and sharp tongue made him permanent enemies. Yet despite intense social activities and considerable time lost through his chronic throat ailment, he studied musical scores exhaustively and mastered an enormous amount of music. As he half-seriously announced, he alternated at this period between Mozart and Verdi. When the weather was pleasant, he preferred Mozart or Rossini; when the weather was hot and sultry, he preferred Verdi. In later life he lost much of his enthusiasm for Verdi.

At the end of the first year, according to the conditions of the Prix, Bizet was to submit a mass, cantata or some other form of religious music to the Académie des Beaux Arts in Paris. He hesitated, for he disliked religious music and felt that it would be hypocritical for him to write such music, since he was an atheist. He also felt bitter at having failed badly in a contest at the Villa for a Te Deum. Most of all, probably, his interests really lay in operatic music.

Bizet thereupon won permanent fame in the anecdotology of music by becoming the young man who dared to submit an *opéra bouffe* instead of a Mass for his first-year qualification. He looked hard for a libretto, and finally, in a second-hand bookshop, came upon *Don Procopio* by Carlo Cambiaggio, a play very similar to Donizetti's opera *Don Pasquale*. A foolish old man wishes to marry off his pretty young niece to an elderly miser, since he fears that the young man she herself favors is a fortune-hunter who will squander her money. The young people rig a plot that includes a pretended marriage, and the girl behaves so outrageously to the miser that he breaks the engagement and the girl can marry her young man.

Bizet submitted his entry and waited impatiently. The receiving committee, headed by Thomas, must have been remarkably tolerant, for they accepted the work without demur—undoubtedly because it was a very capable piece of work. Frankly Italian in style, *Don Procopio* had considerable spirit and wit, and if it was not especially original, it was very professional. It might have been a minor work by one of the better Italian composers.

The result of *Don Procopio* was two official letters to Bizet. The first, the public letter, praised the work and called attention to some of its good points. It was one of the most laudatory reports that the committee had issued for many years. The second, the confidential report, scolded Bizet for not having followed regulations and urged him in strong terms to learn to write serious music, since all music was deepened by serious study.

For many years it was believed that the manuscript of *Don Procopio* was lost, but in the last decades of the nineteenth century it was unexpectedly found among Auber's papers. It was first published in 1905, in a heavily edited version, and performed the following year. In 1958 it was performed in Strasbourg in Bizet's original form, and was considered very amusing.

During his second year at Rome Bizet worked fairly conscientiously at his required exercise, a cantata entitled *Vasco de Gama*, based upon

Camões's *Lusiads*. This was accepted by the committee and was performed in Paris several years later, in 1863, without arousing much critical enthusiasm. For the symphonic music required for his third year Bizet worked upon a program symphony based upon the cities of Italy; part of this, the "Roma" section, later was included in his unsuccessful *Roma* Symphony. He should have spent his third year in Germany, but he petitioned the Académie to let him stay in Italy, and with his close friend Guiraud he saw the sights there.

In September, 1860, almost twenty-two years old, Bizet returned to Paris, and entered upon the mode of life that he was to follow until his early death. He supplemented his Prix de Rome allowance by writing piano transcriptions of other men's work, eventually including operas by Gounod and Mozart; gave piano lessons to children; served as a music doctor and orchestrator for composers who were either too pressed or too unskilled; and wrote operas upon commission for the various opera-performing media.

Bizet also moved in the musical world of the time, and his gift for company and his wit made him a valued member of many of the best cultural circles. It was at a reception given to Liszt in 1861, at Fromental Halévy's house, that Bizet demonstrated his remarkable abilities as a pianist and sight-reader. According to Pigot, one of the earliest biographers of Bizet, Liszt had just played a fantastically difficult piece of his own composition, and had then stated in his grand manner, "A difficult piece. Indeed, I account it extremely difficult. There are only two men who can play it properly—myself and Hans von Bülow." Halévy, knowing Bizet's remarkable memory for music, turned to him, and asked him if he remembered the passage that went so-and-so. Bizet thereupon sat down and played the difficult passage through, to perfection. Liszt, astonished, gave Bizet the manuscript, which Bizet played very brilliantly. Liszt's generous comment was, "I was wrong. There are three of us. And I must admit that the youngest of us is perhaps the boldest and most brilliant." From this occurrence and others in Bizet's life, it seems clear that Bizet could have been enormously successful as a concert pianist. But he was afraid of being labeled a performer instead of a creator and believed that he could serve his gifts better by remaining solely with composition.

As the final obligation to the Académie des Beaux Arts Bizet was commissioned by the Opéra-Comique to write a one-act comic opera, *La Guzla de l'Émir*, upon a libretto by Jules Barbier and Michel Carré. Bizet finished the opera and the committee accepted it, though they

Georges Bizet.

Caricature of Bizet in the magazine *Diogène*, September 28, 1867.

Fromental Halévy, composer of *La Juive* and father-in-law of Bizet. Lithograph after a photograph by Carjat. (*Cabinet des Estampes, Bibliothèque Nationale, Paris; photo courtesy Bibliothèque Nationale*)

Léon Carvalho, manager of the Théâtre-Lyrique and later director of the Opéra-Comique.

criticized it for stylistic affectation and over-instrumentation. *La Guzla de l'Émir* went into production, but Bizet suddenly withdrew it because of a better opportunity offered by the Théâtre-Lyrique. What then happened to the música for *La Guzla* is now unknown; the best guess is that Bizet destroyed it many years later when he burned his juvenilia.

The Théâtre-Lyrique, which was an independent house without state subsidy, was often the stormy petrel of the operatic world. It was willing to take chances upon unknown composers. Its manager, Léon Carvalho, was the nineteenth-century equivalent of a Hollywood producer in sensuality, vulgarity and egotism; but he was also the most daring and imaginative showman in the Parisian world. At this time the Théâtre-Lyrique had received a large financial bequest on the condition that the theater perform one new three-act opera each year, by a Prix de Rome. Carvalho, who knew Bizet's work and rated it highly, offered him the contract. But a further condition of the bequest was the Prix de Rome should never have had an opera performed. It was for this reason that Bizet withdrew *La Guzla*.

The opera which Carvalho assigned to Bizet was *Les Pêcheurs de perles*, libretto by Eugène Cormon (pseudonym of Pierre-Étienne Piestre) and Michel Carré. Bizet worked conscientiously at the music from 1862 to 1863, though the labor must at times have been frustrating. The impossible libretto was still in process of composition as Bizet worked; originally set in Indian Mexico, it was shifted to Ceylon because Carvalho insisted upon an Oriental background. It was cynically written by Cormon and Carré as a potboiler likely to strike the public fancy. Later both men admitted that if they had been aware of Bizet's talent, they would have done a better, more responsible job.

A contemporary anecdote, which may or may not be true, illustrates how the management felt about *Les Pêcheurs*. Until about two weeks before the première, Cormon and Carré had not decided how to end the opera. Carvalho said to Cormon, "Throw the whole thing in the fire," and this became the solution: to break the plot crisis and release the hero and heroine the librettists decided to burn down the fishing village.

In plot *Les Pêcheurs de perles* is almost a parody of a romantic opera. Two Singhalese fishermen, Nadir (tenor) and Zurga (baritone), while visiting Kandy, quarrel over a woman, Leila. They agree to return to their village and resume their friendship. Some time later Nadir discovers that the local veiled temple virgin is Leila. When Leila reciprocates Nadir's love, Zurga denounces them to the priesthood, and they are condemned to death. At the last moment, however, Zurga repents, and to distract the priests and villagers, sets fire to the village. Nadir and Leila escape; Zurga may or may not survive, depending upon which version of *Les Pêcheurs* one sees. There are, of course, many other complications. Bizet, who came to loathe both the opera libretto and his own music to it, later called his dog Zurga.

Les Pêcheurs de perles had its première on September 20, 1863. It received some applause from the audience, but it was not really successful financially. All in all, it was performed eighteen times up through November, and then it was taken off the stage until 1886, eleven years after Bizet's death. Since that time it has become part of the standard French repertoire, and it is one of Bizet's two operas that are still alive in France and Italy. Its success elsewhere, however, has not been marked, either in the original version or an abridged one entitled *Leila*. It has been occasionally performed in the United States, with Jean de Reszke and Emma Calvé in the 1890's, and in the early part of the twentieth century with Enrico Caruso and Frieda Hempel. Its high points, which are occasionally sung as concert arias, are the soprano aria "Comme autrefois dans la nuit sombre," which has been brilliantly sung by Galli-Curci and Tetrazzini, and the tenor aria "Je crois entendre encore," which the reader, if he is very fortunate, can best hear in Caruso's brilliant version on the rare Opera Society 78 rpm disk.

In later life Bizet came to dislike *Les Pêcheurs de perles* intensely, and this is not surprising. The music is very uneven, all too often descending into a banal saccharine manner reminiscent of Gounod and Meyerbeer at their worst. Its strongest features are an occasionally successful evocation of strange atmosphere, but even this is just anticipation of Bizet's later, better work. Most of all, *Les Pêcheurs de perles* is simply dull.

Most contemporary critics attacked Bizet's opera. A review in *Le Figaro* commented, "Neither fishermen in the libretto nor pearls in the music," while Bertrand, one of the more important reviewers, called it a "weak imitation of the funeral march in *La Juive*, with the shocking, violent effects of the latest Italian school—and much too much screaming." On the other hand, Hector Berlioz, the foremost French musician of the older generation, praised it: "[The music is] quite successful. It contains many beautiful, expressive pieces, full of fire and color. ... M. Bizet ... took the journey to Rome; he has come back without having forgotten what music is. Since his return to Paris, he has rapidly acquired the unusual reputation of an incomparable score reader. His talent as a pianist is also great enough that no technical difficulty can stop him in his transcriptions of orchestral music, which he can do at sight. ... He must be recognized as a composer in spite of his rare talents as a sight reader." We can judge from the "in spite of" in this review (and its implied evaluation of pianists vs. composers) why Bizet did not yield to the temptation of becoming a concert pianist.

At the time Bizet felt sufficiently satisfied with *Les Pêcheurs de perles* to finish an opera entitled *Ivan IV* for the Théâtre-Lyrique; he had been working upon it desultorily for some time. But after his labor was finished, he discovered to his dismay that the Théâtre-Lyrique was in financial difficulties and could not stage it, while the other opera houses were either unwilling or forbidden by governmental regulations to perform it. The score went into Bizet's trunk, and was never performed during his lifetime. It was long believed to be lost, but it turned up in Paris in the 1920's, with a few orchestral pages missing from the last act, and received its first performance in Germany in 1946 with a new libretto. Musicologists have agreed in considering it a derivative work, perhaps stronger dramatically than *Les Pêcheurs de perles*, but weaker musically.

The years immediately following the fiasco of *Les Pêcheurs de perles* were lean for Bizet. He continued to make a bare living at musical hackwork, preparing piano transcriptions of orchestral and operatic scores, teaching, directing rehearsals and doing miscellaneous small jobs. Socially, he stood in the middle of the French musical world, and he was generally recognized as one of the "up-and-coming" French musicians. He took part in the musical battles around Hector Berlioz, whose music he enthusiastically admired; in 1862 he had even been provoked to a duel for his fervor. The duel, however, did not occur, since the letter which had insulted Bizet was declared to be a forgery. He continued intimate with Gounod, who stood in some measure as his patron as well as his friend; he performed on the piano for the highest soirées in Parisian society, including the salons of Princess Mathilde at the Louvre; yet he was never able to transform his great musicianship and social successes into any sort of financial security. His own answer to this situation was a statement which he often repeated and took quite seriously: "I am the victim of a persecution, of a conspiracy against me." Considering the state of French public life and personalities in the decadent days of the Emperor Louis Napoleon's reign, Bizet may not have been entirely wrong.

Bizet's financial situation was eased a little in 1854 when he moved out of Paris to a suburban real estate development called Le Vésinet. Here Adolphe Bizet, his father, had purchased about an acre of land and had built two small cottages at opposite ends of the plot, one for himself and one for Georges. Paris was easily accessible, because the railroad, to stimulate the development, offered a free three-year pass to commuters. This retreat may well have saved Bizet from serious financial trouble, and for several years it was here that he entertained his friends, conducted his affairs and wrote his music.

In 1866 Carvalho of the Théâtre-Lyrique offered Bizet a new commission: an opera based upon Sir Walter Scott's *Fair Maid of Perth*. The circumstances of the offer are not completely clear, but it would seem that Carvalho, who was almost two million francs in debt, thought that Scott might save him, since Donizetti's *Lucia di Lammermoor* (taken from Scott's *Bride of Lammermoor*) had been such a remarkable success. Bizet finished his score by the end of 1866, but financial and production delays postponed the appearance of the opera until 1867, at which time it was a failure. The libretto, by J. H. Vernoy de Saint-Georges and Jules Adenis, was inane, and the performance was not the best. Yet the critical consensus (such as was not deliberately hostile because of feuds) was favorable. Bizet was complimented upon his progress since *Les Pêcheurs de perles*, although he was also blamed for pandering to the worst extravagances in unnecessary vocal coloratura. Bizet had to admit that this criticism was just, since he had written the coloratura deliberately for Christine Nilsson, who had been intended to create the title role. Another soprano, less capable, eventually sang the part. *La Jolie Fille de Perth* closed after eighteen performances. It has been revived a few times since 1867, but it has never shown enough vitality to hold the stage. Musically it is said to be in advance of Bizet's earlier work, with much of Meyerbeer's influence eradicated, but with considerable similarity to aspects of Verdi and Gounod.

These last years of the 1860's, difficult enough to Bizet, were the final flash of glory for the Second Empire. Life was gay, money flowed easily, and the Parisian Exposition of 1867 drew crowds from all over Europe and America. Bizet's connections with the Exposition afforded a typical story of musical and political intrigue. The Committee for the Exposition had announced a competition for a cantata and a hymn for the Exposition, to specified texts. The prizes were large —10,000 francs and a medal worth 1,000 francs for the hymn, and a medal of equal value for the cantata and a fee of 5,000 francs for each time it was performed. The committee of judges included Auber, Thomas, Verdi, Théophile Gautier, Rossini and Berlioz. Needless to say, most of the musicians of France competed, submitting over a hundred cantatas and eight hundred and fifty hymns. The judges soon decided that the hymn competition was impossible to resolve and canceled it. Meanwhile, as was customary, each contestant tried to influence the judges, while disguising his entry so that his enemies on the board could not identify it. Saint-Saëns, who won the cantata prize, went to the length of using German paper, with the result that some of the judges (it has been claimed) thought the entry was by Wagner and voted for it. Bizet used a pseudonym and a Provençal address, but did not win even an honorable mention. His failure, he was sure, was due to the hostility of the judges, who had recognized his entry. Saint-Saëns never collected his prize money for the cantata, for the committee simply never performed it, thereby saving 5,000 francs per possible performance. All of these machinations, however, were surpassed by those of Rossini, who was on the committee. Rossini did not sit with the other judges and examine manuscripts. He wrote a hymn of his own and took it to Louis Napoleon, who commanded that it be accepted and performed.

Bizet's next opera was doomed from the time that he started to work on it. The Paris Opéra had staged a contest for a libretto, and had awarded its prize to *La Coupe du roi de Thulé* by Louis Gallet and Édouard Blau. This contest was followed by a contest for music to the libretto, in which many of the foremost French musicians competed. Bizet was torn between opposing forces: he wanted to enter the competition, especially since the Director, Perrin, had taken him aside and assured him that his winning the contest was a certainty; on the other hand, he did not trust Perrin and was afraid of jeopardizing his future with another failure. He also expected another large contract to be proffered in the very near future. Bizet temporized, helped his friend Galabert, who had entered the competition, and worked intermittently at a score. It is not certain just how much he finished, though it seems to have been at least two acts. In any case, he never submitted his entry, and most of his manuscript has been lost. About one sixth of his music for this opera survives, in fragments, though these fragments are claimed to be among his best music.

Other events of importance took place during this feverish period before the Franco-Prussian War. Bizet's sponsor, Carvalho, and the Théâtre-Lyrique went into bankruptcy in 1868. Bizet wrote some hack operatic work anonymously and under pseudonyms, so that his exact compositions during this period are questionable. And in June, 1869 he married Geneviève Halévy.

Geneviève Halévy (1849–1926) was the second daughter and only surviving child of Bizet's old composition teacher and friend at the Conservatoire, Fromental Halévy. Bizet had come to be on very friendly terms with him, and became Halévy's musical executor. In 1868 and 1869 Bizet had completed Halévy's unfinished opera *Noë* and had hoped to see it through performance. Geneviève Halévy and Bizet had announced their engagement earlier, 1867, but this engagement had been broken almost immediately by Geneviève. The reasons for the broken engagement are not definitely known, but two grounds emerge. While the Bizets were not religious, the Delsartes, Bizet's mother's family, were fanatically religious, and objected violently to the marriage because the Halévys were Jewish. The Halévys and their associated families, who were mostly wealthy bankers associated with the Rothschilds and Pereiras, disapproved of Bizet for religious reasons, but even more because of his personal life. He was financially irresponsible and he was disorderly and Bohemian. The fact that he had an illegitimate daughter and perhaps an illegitimate son (though this son was at the time considered the mistake of Adolphe Bizet, and was only later attributed to Georges) may well have been held against him by the ultra-respectable, ultra-conservative Halévys. By 1869, however, all objections seem to have vanished, and Bizet and Geneviève Halévy were married by the mayor of their *arrondissement* with a very formidable French contract.

That their marriage could not be completely successful must have been obvious to many of their friends. Bizet was not a strong man physically, but suffered from a recurrent throat infection; he was also extremely excitable and incapable of tolerating any restraint. Geneviève, who had inherited her mother's personality, was equally difficult. Frequently overcome by imaginary illnesses, she was capricious, demanding and often not in sympathy with Bizet's work. (After Bizet's death she married a banker named Straus, conducted a brilliant salon, which included Proust, and according to Proust's notes she was the prototype of the Duchess of Guermantes.) There are indications that at the time of Bizet's death in 1875 they were already close to estrangement.

Meanwhile, an unforeseen event interrupted Bizet's career of musical drudgery and failure. This was the Franco-Prussian War, which broke

Mme. Geneviève Halévy-Bizet-Straus. (*Cabinet des Estampes, Bibliothèque Natio-nale, Paris; photo courtesy Bibliothèque Nationale; used with the kind permission of Mme. Louis Joxe [Françoise Joxe Halévy]*)

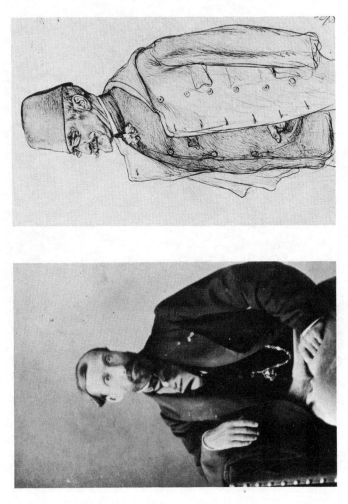

Adolphe de Leuven (*left*; *photo by Nadar*) and Camille du Locle (*right*), co-directors of the Opéra-Comique. (*Courtesy Bibliothèque et Musée de l'Opéra, Paris*)

out in July, 1870. The Prussians won the war almost immediately, with the battle of Sedan on September 2 and the capture of Louis Napoleon and most of his army. Paris declared itself a republic on the following day and in about two weeks the Prussians had surrounded Paris and started to besiege it. The initial mood of optimism which had inspired the French at the beginning of the war was now gone. The opera houses were closed, except for an occasional concert, and the musicians, like most other healthy, adult males, were either in military service or had fled. Gounod had escaped to England; Massenet was in the infantry; and Saint-Saëns and Bizet went into the non-mobile National Guard. Bizet at times was assigned to guard fortifications, and at other times served in a first-aid station. He saw no action. A photograph of him survives from this period: a small bearded man, grinning in amused embarrassment, wrapped in an ill-fitting uniform, dwarfed by a gigantic rifle.

This period of the war was uneventful for Bizet, and the hardships of the siege do not seem to have affected him and his wife too greatly. When the siege was lifted, just before the emergence of the Commune, Bizet and Geneviève fled to his cottage at Le Vésinet and escaped the brief but bloody civil war, during which the Opéra was used as a prison and execution ground.

When peace came and musical life arose again in Paris, the artistic situation was very different from earlier days. The musical temper had changed, and Offenbach's frothy satire was no longer in favor. To sound the new temper, the directors of the Opéra-Comique, Camille du Locle and Adolphe de Leuven, commissioned Bizet to write a one-act comic opera upon an Arabian Nights situation. This was *Djamileh*, based upon a poem by Alfred de Musset, with a libretto by Louis Gallet. The plot is a far-fetched fantasy: Haroun, a rakish prince of medieval Cairo, is accustomed to buy a new girl as his concubine each month, and then discard her. When he purchases Djamileh, however, it is his undoing, for Djamileh is determined to become permanent. She bribes the prince's purchasing agent into disguising her so that Haroun will think she is a different girl, and she succeeds in convincing Haroun that constancy is better than variety.

The opera had its première in May, 1872, quite disastrously, when the heroine suddenly skipped thirty-two measures in an aria and the orchestra had to race to catch up with her. The audience was cold. As Gallet relates in his memoirs, Bizet leaned toward him and said, "You can hear the thud. It's a failure." Later Bizet said to Gallet, "See how it happens? You kill yourself, you do the best you can, and you still don't succeed. If you're going to make good, you've got to be dead— or a German."

Financially *Djamileh* was a failure, since it lasted only ten performances, but it was a failure with a difference. Bizet's music was praised by almost everyone, and it was now recognized that he had arrived musically. As he wrote three weeks after the first performance:

> It is not a success, [but] I am still extremely satisfied with the results. The press has been very interesting; never before has a one-act comic opera been so seriously, and I may add, so passionately argued. ... Reyer, Weber, Guillemot of the *Journal de Paris* ... that is to say more than half of the daily press—have been very warm. De Saint Victor, Jouvin, etc. have been favorable in the sense of conceding me talent and inspiration—all corrupted by Wagner.

Bizet's evocation of an oriental atmosphere was almost universally praised. Modern critics have agreed with the favorable contemporaries, and Bizet has been praised for making a silly libretto come to life. His musical techniques had improved, his dramatic abilities had grown. *Djamileh* contains some of the most imaginative music that he wrote. It is usually considered Bizet's first mature work.

Du Locle and de Leuven showed their faith and satisfaction by authorizing Bizet to work on a three-act opera, the libretto to be provided by Ludovic Halévy (a cousin of Bizet's wife) and Henri Meilhac. Bizet, however, was quite wrong when he wrote, "I've been commissioned to do a three-act opera for the Opéra-Comique. Meilhac and Halévy are doing the book. It is going to be *gai*, but the sort of *gaîté* that will permit *le style*." It eventually turned out to be *Carmen*.

Before *Carmen* appeared Bizet had a second qualified triumph with the performance of *L'Arlésienne*, a play by Alphonse Daudet, to which Bizet wrote the incidental and background music. *L'Arlésienne*, technically classified in French dramatic theory as a *mélodrame*, had been commissioned by Carvalho, who was now managing the Vaudeville in Paris. It is a semi-naturalistic story of strong emotions in Provence— a young man's infatuation with a heartless coquette from Arles (who never appears on the stage), his attempt to escape from her, his discovery that she has a lover, and his suicide.

L'Arlésienne opened on October 1, 1872, to a very unfriendly house, and survived only twenty-one performances. Many reasons are given for its failure: resentment at the experimental nature of the play, which was not only sordid in subject matter but too daring in technique; bad scheduling, for it appeared without adequate publicity and with inadequate claquing, since it was pushed up in schedule because of the unexpected banning of another play by the censor; poor integration between music and drama, for Bizet's twenty-seven numbers were usually played between scenes, and when they took place during the scenes they interfered with the performance.

Despite the failure of *L'Arlésienne* as a whole, Bizet's music received serious praise from the outstanding critics and musicians of the day, and Bizet himself was satisfied with the outcome of the performance. He had been limited by the budget to a small, somewhat motley orchestra, which included a saxophone and a piano, and he worked wonders with what he had. He was remarkably successful in evoking the atmosphere of Provence, and his music was daring and original. As a result his music was not allowed to die and Bizet revised and pieced together an orchestral suite from the more significant numbers. This suite was first performed in November, 1872 at a concert given by Pasdeloup, and has remained a favorite. At a later date, Ernest Guiraud pieced together a second suite from the remains of *L'Arlésienne*, *La Jolie Fille de Perth* and other early work. The full *L'Arlésienne melo-drame* at this time is apparently almost never performed outside Paris.

The circumstances surrounding the selection of *Carmen* for Bizet's next opera are not known, and one can only speculate on the reasons that led two veteran librettists and a composer most of whose previous work was very romantic, to the first naturalistic opera. The original *Carmen* by Prosper Mérimée had been accepted as a modern classic by this time, but there seems to have been no immediate reason that it should have been selected as material for a libretto. Perhaps the influence of Zola was making itself felt. Perhaps Bizet and his librettists wanted to make capital out of Bizet's remarkable skill at creating musical landscapes, and his melodies, harmonies and devices of orches-tration that evoked all the flavor and strangeness of other lands and times. It was this ability that enabled Bizet to create the coloring that makes *Carmen* the great Spanish opera, even though Bizet had never been to Spain, knew very little about Spanish music and used only a few Spanish sources in *Carmen*.

The composition of *Carmen* was filled with difficulties. The manage-ment of the house was afraid of it. Although du Locle was at first not unfriendly to the project, the other director of the Opéra-Comique, de Leuven, was violently opposed to *Carmen*'s melange of Gypsies, prostitutes, murderers and thieves. De Leuven's point, which was not without some justice, was that the Opéra-Comique was a family theatre, catering to the bourgeoisie on its night out, in which entertainment consisted of amusing, innocuous trifles. There had never been a death in an *opéra comique* and never a brothel. The librettists promised to "sanitize" *Carmen*, but de Leuven was not convinced and early in 1874 he sold his share of the Opéra-Comique to du Locle and left in protest.

The Opéra-Comique, meanwhile, was in financial trouble and the première of *Carmen* was postponed several times. Maria Roze, who was first approached to create the role of Carmen, rejected it as "scabrous." The management could not afford to pay first-line salaries to the singers, so that negotiations between the house and Marie Galli-Marié, the mezzo-soprano who was next approached to create the title role, continued interminably. Rehearsals were often postponed because of lack of cash.

Very few details are known about the collaboration between Bizet and his librettists, since most of their work was done together in Paris, and was not recorded in correspondence. Halévy alone kept a journal, but in his ultra-respectable old age he destroyed most of the entries from this period. But enough of the original manuscript and working drafts survives to show that Bizet was not simply a passive musician; he took a very active part in preparing the libretto.

The present words to the "Habanera" were written by Bizet, perhaps in despair at Halévy's artificial, stilted phrases. The differences can be seen at a glance:

HALÉVY	BIZET
Illusion et fantaisie,	L'amour est un oiseau rebelle
Ainsi commencent les amours,	Que nul ne peut apprivoiser,
Et voilà pour la vie,	Et c'est bien en vain qu'on l'appelle
Ou pour six mois ou pour huit jours;	S'il lui convient de refuser.
Un matin sur sa route	Rien n'y fait, menace ou prière;
On trouve l'amour—Il est là.	L'un parle bien, l'autre se tait;

Bizet's revision of Halévy's card song increases the depth of the characterization of Carmen:

HALÉVY	BIZET
Mais qu'importe après tout si par cette menace	En vain pour éviter les réponses amères,

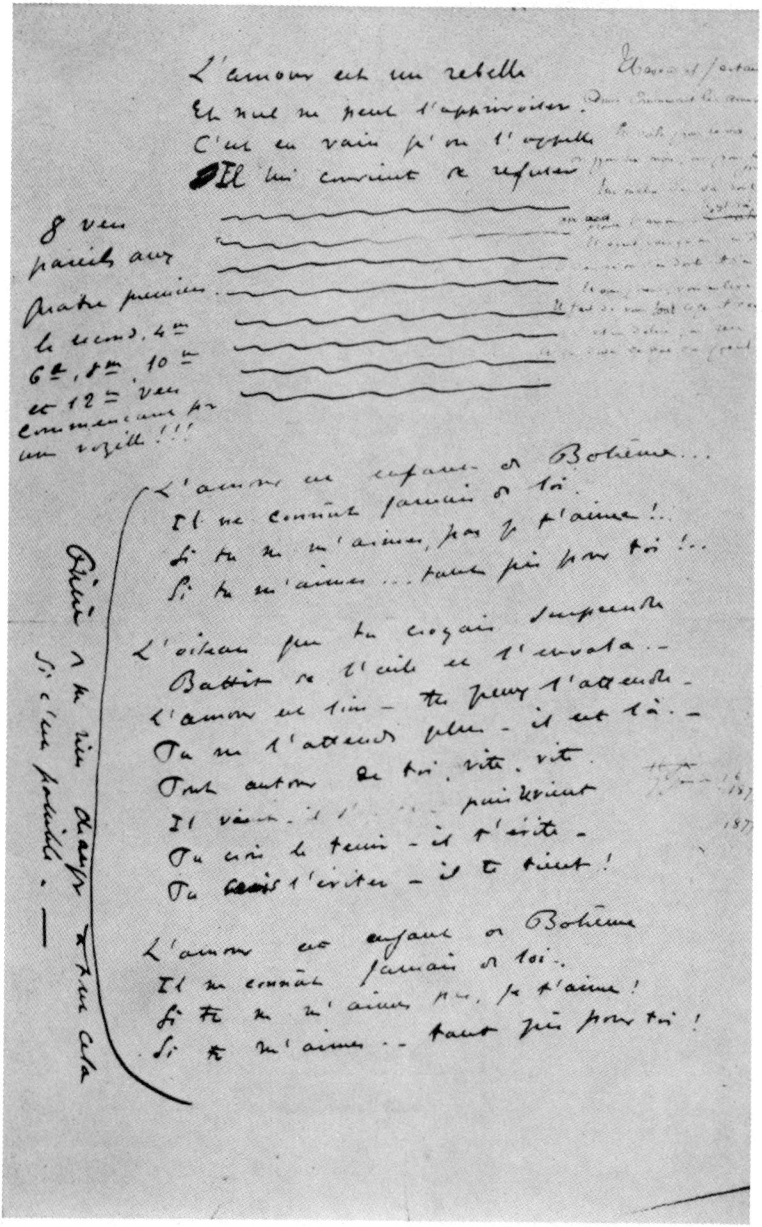
L'amour est un rebelle
Et nul ne peut l'apprivoiser.
C'est en vain qu'on l'appelle
Il lui convient de refuser
8 vers pareils aux quatre premiers le second, 4me 6e, 8me, 10me et 12me vers commençant par un
L'amour est enfant de Bohême...
Il ne connaît jamais de loi.
Si tu ne m'aimes, pas je t'aime!..
Si tu m'aimes... tant pis pour toi!..
L'oiseau que tu croyais surprendre
Battit de l'aile et s'envola.-
L'amour est loin - tu peux l'attendre-
Tu ne l'attends plus - il est là.-
Tout autour de toi, vite, vite
Il vient ... puis revient
Tu crois le tenir - il t'évite -
Tu ~~crois~~ l'éviter - il te tient!
L'amour est enfant de Bohême
Il ne connaît jamais de loi.
Si tu ne m'aimes pas, je t'aime!
Si tu m'aimes.. tant pis pour toi!

The draft of the text of the "Habanera" in Bizet's hand.

Bizet toward the end of his life. Photograph by Carjat.

Cover of the original piano score of *Carmen*.

Mon cœur n'est pas troublé?
Cette mort qui m'attend je la re-
    garde en face,
Carmen n'a pas tremblé.

En vain tu mêleras,
Cela ne sert à rien, les cartes
    sont sincères
Et ne mentiront pas.

Halévy's first line for the "Seguidilla" was "J'irai dimanche en voiture," which Bizet with considerable pain managed to have changed to "Près des remparts de Séville." When Halévy and Meilhac reproduced the book in their collected works, they still stubbornly refused to go along with Bizet and quoted "Près de la porte de Séville."

During the rehearsals of 1874 it soon became evident that de Leuven's timidity had been contagious. Du Locle obviously worried more and more about repercussions and began to urge that the ending be changed to a happy one. Bizet and Galli-Marié managed to stave him off, although Du Locle is known to have advised a government official to attend the dress rehearsal rather than bring his family to the première. The librettists, too, beginning to fear for their future, pressed the toreador to stop chucking the chorus girls under the chin and tried to persuade Galli-Marié to interpret Carmen in a more restrained, more refined manner. In the latter endeavor they were unsuccessful, for Galli-Marié was artist enough to recognize the necessities of the story. Even the outside world was caught up in the dissension. Mysterious comments began to appear in the newspapers saying that the Opéra-Comique could no longer be considered a family theatre if *Carmen* was performed. Several hours before the première the Government awarded Bizet the Legion of Honor—why, no one now knows. As a contemporary wit said of this decoration, "They were just in time, because it won't be possible to decorate him after *Carmen* hits the stage."

There were also musical difficulties in preparing the opera. The chorus, which was accustomed to enter in a body, assume statuesque postures and point their voices at a particular place, complained that it could not conceivably sing if members had to enter as individuals and move around the stage. After all, they were singers, not actors. And the music was unsingable, anyway. Du Locle agreed about the music; he called it Indochinese music. Galli-Marié did not like the music that Bizet had written for the "Habanera." Bizet, to be obliging, rewrote it thirteen times, then gave up in despair and adapted Yradier's "El Arreglito," which he apparently thought was a Spanish folksong. This music pleased Galli-Marié. Escamillo felt that his big aria was unworthy of him; Bizet, muttering, "They want ordure and they'll get it," took the offensive aria and wrote in the present toreador bombast. And the orchestra had to be led by the nose through the strange music.

On March 3, 1875 the première of *Carmen* took place at the Opéra-Comique. The audience was remarkable: Gounod, Thomas, Delibes, Offenbach, Massenet, Daudet, Dumas *fils*, Prince Troubetskoi, d'Indy and most of the musical world of Paris. As an audience it was not unfriendly, although, on the other hand, it was not exactly enthusiastic.

The performance itself was mediocre. Galli-Marié was excellent, although her interpretation, as will be seen, was considered scandalous. Lhérie, the tenor, did reasonably well, apart from being unable to maintain the pitch on the unaccompanied "Soldier's Ballad" in Act Two. For the second performance Bizet engaged d'Indy to play the harmonium softly offstage to help Lhérie, who, according to Bizet, was likely to start in *G* and finish almost anywhere around *E*. The other singers were only fair. The orchestra was correct, but somewhat flaccid, completely ignoring Bizet's dynamics. It is true that the tympanist miscounted measures and enthusiastically thumped his kettledrum in the middle of the duet between José and Carmen in Act Two, when Carmen is singing pianissimo, but this caused only a few smiles. The chorus, however, was quite bad. The singers could not manage Bizet's rhythms and the cigarette girls, unaccustomed to the cigarettes they carried, gasped and choked through their most important piece. The stage hands, too, seemed to have trouble, since the first intermission lasted twenty-three minutes, the second forty-two minutes and the third again twenty-three.

According to legend *Carmen* was a complete failure and Bizet died of a broken heart. As with many legends, this is partly true and partly false. The first act received enthusiastic applause; the second was applauded mildly; the third less, and the fourth not at all. At the end of the opera the house was silent; indeed, many of the audience had already left. A few of Bizet's personal friends congratulated him, but everyone knew that the opera was really a colossal failure. After the house was empty, Bizet and his faithful friend Guiraud walked the streets of Paris in depression until dawn.

The press was incredibly savage to *Carmen*. Reviewer after reviewer either sneered at the music or hysterically denounced the immorality of the libretto:

> "Let an author once become fouled in the social sewer, and he is forced to descend ... to the lowest levels for his models. ... [Carmen is] a savage; half Gypsy, half Andalusian; sensual, sacrilegious, without shame

... a true prostitute of the gutter and the streetcorner ... the music written for a small coterie who alone pretend to understand him," Achille de Lauzières in *La Patrie*.

"Friends of uninhibited Spanish licence must have been highly pleased. Andalusians whose breasts are sunburnt, the sort of women to be found only in the lowest cabarets in Seville ... a madhouse of castanets, of leers à la Congreve, provocative hip-swinging, of knifings distributed impartially among both sexes ... to preserve the morality and the actions of the impressionable soldiers and bullfighters who surround this 'lady,' she should be gagged, a stop put to the unrestrained twisting of her hips; she should be straitjacketed and cooled off with a pitcher of water over her head. The pathological condition of this unfortunate woman, devoted without cessation to the burning of the flesh ... is more likely to inspire the solicitude of medical men than to interest the decent audience who come to the Opéra-Comique with their wives and children ... fed on the enharmonic succulences of the seekers of the music of the future [a slam at Wagnerism] Bizet has fed his soul on this diet that kills one's heart ... ingenious details in the orchestra, dangerous dissonances, instrumental subtleties cannot portray the uterine madness of Mlle. Carmen and the wishes of her ribald followers ... unfortunately [the music] lacks novelty and ... distinction. There is no plan, no unity in its style ... it is neither dramatic nor scenic ...," J. P. O. Comettant, in *Le Siècle*.

"The orchestra was perpetually babbling and saying interminable things that were not needed," *Le Monde Illustré*.

Bizet's music was damned as unmusical and undramatic; un-Spanish and un-French; the music of anarchy and irresponsibility, the music of routine and opportunism.

Much analytical power and ingenuity have been expended in trying to explain, after the fact, why the première was so outrageously attacked, when a few years later the same hostile critics made a complete *volte-face* and praised Bizet and *Carmen* as fulsomely as they had damned both before. The answer is probably complex, with parts of the answer arising from many domains of French life.

The French, first of all, were not prudish or Puritanical about literary matters at this time, but *Carmen* happened to come along just when Zolaism was a living controversy. The Parisians apparently held to the opinion that life should be compartmentalized: what is permitted in one place is regarded with aversion in another. Certainly the very critics who condemned *Carmen* often took bribes and kept mistresses. They would probably have excused their conduct by saying that they kept such affairs private and did not invade the sanctity of the family with prurience. Bizet and his colleagues, on the other hand, were dragging the bordello into a theatre that was a family institution, where perhaps a fourth or a fifth of the box office income came from marriage interviews in the loges. There was also some resentment at Bizet's naturalistic treatment of the *canaille*, without Hugoesque romanticization; after the Commune and its terror and the Versailles government and its terror, intelligent Parisians may not have been happy to find reminiscences of the mob in an opera. And there was also the easily aroused sadism of the French mob-spirit, the same frenzied, misunderstanding hatred that had met Wagner's *Tannhäuser* some fourteen years earlier.

Bizet probably contributed to the debacle with his music, since it was obviously music that could displease many parties. The traditionalists were driven into paroxysms of rage at Bizet's unorthodox modulations and harmonies; they bitterly resented his violation of the generally accepted structure and orientation of the comic opera. They immediately identified Bizet with Wagner, by now a symbol of Teutonism. The Wagnerites were annoyed because Bizet went along his own path, paying no heed to the dramatic theories emanating from Bayreuth. The French modernists were angry with Bizet for what they felt were opportunistic concessions to outmoded forms and foolish traditions. The performance, too, left much to be desired: a forty-two-minute intermission is enough to destroy anyone's empathy, and the opera was quite a bit longer, in this first version, than the present *Carmen*.

Personal factors also entered the picture. Bizet had many close friends, but he also had many bitter enemies, for he was a singularly tactless and passionate man. And of course, last, simplest, and perhaps most correct of all, is the reason suggested by Berton, a librettist who knew well the operation of a theatre. Du Locle had simply neglected to "sweeten" the critics, as was the custom. In his memoirs Berton states that he knew which reviewers should be approached, and how much should be given to each. Berton's reasons may sound silly and spiteful at first, but they should not be dismissed lightly.

Carmen languished on at the Opéra-Comique through the spring of 1876; it was discontinued in May, and revived briefly in November, 1876. All in all, it had forty-six performances. It has been claimed that forty-six performances indicate success, and that the story of the failure of *Carmen* is only legend. It has also been pointed out with more justice

Exterior view of the second Salle Favart (built 1840), the Opéra-Comique building in which *Carmen* was created, shown after the fire that destroyed it in 1887. Pen drawing by A. Deroy. (*Courtesy Bibliothèque et Musée de l'Opéra, Paris*)

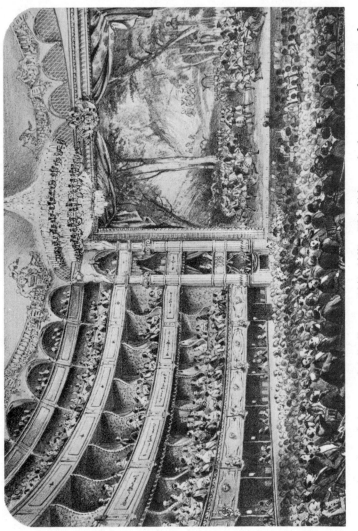

Interior view of the second Salle Favart (1840–1887). This lithograph shows a performance of Meyerbeer's opera *L'Étoile du Nord*, 1854. (*Courtesy Bibliothèque et Musée de l'Opéra, Paris*)

(since box office receipts were recorded) that forty-six performances before gradually decreasing audiences (many of whom had free passes), to half-empty houses that did not meet production costs, eventually to a nearly empty hall, do not indicate success.

Performances elsewhere, however, soon showed that the Parisians were wrong. In the fall of 1875 the grand opera version of *Carmen* was a success in the Vienna Opera House, as it was the next year in Brussels. The judgment of the early French reviewers was also soon reversed, and the opera was very highly rated by contemporary and later composers. The first well-known composer to praise *Carmen* was Tchaikovsky, who said that he had never been carried away so completely by any other modern work and prophesied that *Carmen* would soon be the most popular opera in the world.

Both Wagner and Brahms, representing antithetical schools of music, were delighted with *Carmen*. Wagner, who saw it in 1875 in Vienna, considered it the beginning of a new school of French opera. His comment after the opera was, "At last, someone with ideas in his head." Brahms, who took Debussy to see *Carmen* in Vienna some years later, called it the finest piece of operatic music since the Franco-Prussian War, and declared that he had seen it twenty-one times. The great conductors Bülow, Mottl and Weingartner all rated it very high.

The moderns showed themselves equally enthusiastic. Debussy, even though his followers did not always agree, stated that Bizet's death was the greatest disaster to French music in a hundred years. Busoni considered *Carmen* "almost perfect," and thought the last act one of the greatest achievements in music. Stravinsky called it one of his favorites.

All this, however, did not help poor Georges Bizet. Greatly discouraged, he lingered around Paris for a short time, quarrelled with his critics, then withdrew, on doctor's orders, to the country at Bougival. His health began to fail rapidly; attacks of his throat infection recurred; he was beset by rheumatic fever, and on June 2, 1875, he died, apparently of a heart attack. By a strange coincidence Galli-Marié collapsed at the Opéra-Comique probably at the moment when Bizet lost consciousness; she had been obsessed with the notion that something was badly wrong, and was barely able to finish her performance.

Bizet's life had a tragic element even beyond financial difficulties and ill health, lack of recognition and critical abuse. Mozart died at about the same age as Bizet, but Mozart had long been a mature musician and left behind him many unsurpassable works. Bizet, on the other hand, attained his full talents very late; he was struck down almost as soon as he had crossed the threshold of maturity.

*　　　*　　　*

The following selection from Stuart Henry's *Paris Days and Evenings* has been included here to show how Bizet impressed a perceptive student who studied piano under him. It is probably the only picture of Bizet which shows him as a living person rather than as a subject for biography.

It was a delightful American lady who used to tell us of Bizet June evenings in her salon on the crown of the Champs-Elysées, and was wont to intersperse our entertainment with impetuous excursions to the piano to dash off some strain of "Carmen." Educated in Europe, and particularly in Paris, she displayed such a mixture of French elegance and Spanish fire, that some one remarked on one occasion: "I know now where Bizet got his 'Carmen'—he got it from his third pupil!"—for his "Carmen," every one knows, does not stop with that of Mérimée. ...

Doubtless you, too, are a lover of "Carmen," and are as curious as were we to get a glimpse of the man Bizet, since Marmontel, Galabert, and even Pigot have written little of him. So, without prelude or exercise, I score here in an informal key some fragments of our hostess's impromptus about him.

"Let me see! Was it in '72 or '73? It must have been '73, for I was twelve years old—1861 and twelve—yes, '73. I remember I was twelve, for I was just then the pride of our family—*enfant prodige*—because I could play Dussek's 'Twelfth Concerto.' We had come from the Isle of Wight, and had taken apartments in the Faubourg Saint Germain for a long stay. My sister and I were to finish our education here. ...

"M. Bizet only had two pupils then, my friend and another Russian girl, a sister of the celebrated General S——. She is a famous princess nowadays. M. Bizet did not seem to want pupils, and only took those two because they interested him. Mamma was very anxious that I should take lessons of him, so my friend got his permission to let me go with her one day and play before him. I remember it as if it were yesterday. I was so frightened I didn't see a key from beginning to end. But I had been pretty severely put to it down at the Conservatory of Lausanne. It had quite a reputation in those days, and then too I played my Dussek 'Concerto,' and that happened to be a great favourite of M. Bizet. He had won his *prix de Rome* on it.

"He appeared to be somewhat surprised to see a child—I was not yet even a little 'cornette au bout d'un cotillon,' as Musset would say— tackling that Concerto under such refrigerant circumstances. When I had finished, he said he thought I had done very bravely with it. Mamma asked him if he would take me. He gave an impetuous toss of his head, with an 'Ah!' as if annoyed by such a question. 'Oh, well, I'll try her for a while; you know I haven't much patience with pupils.' And that's how I became his third pupil, for he had no one but us— three girls—during the last two years of his life.

"At first he used to come to our place. They were half-hour lessons and 20 francs. He was supposed to come at three o'clock. You never saw a more irregular man. We would wait, wait, wait; and I was always glad if I thought he was not coming, for I was afraid of him, and naturally dreaded the severe lessons. Not that he ever scolded, but the way he would look at you through those eyeglasses! Our apartments had several rooms strung along one after the other. When M. Bizet arrived, he would often have to knock at all the doors and hunt us up, for sometimes it would happen that everybody would be here and there and nowhere, and my sister and I would be hanging out of the balcony at the end room of the suite, I revelling in the prospect of having no lesson. One day he became impatient at finding no one, and we heard him stop in the room adjoining the one where we were, and rap on the floor with his cane, exclaiming: 'Est-ce qu'on m'entend? Qu'est-ce que je viens faire ici? Est-ce qu'on croit que j'ai du temps à gaspiller comme ça!'

"And of all the absent-minded persons! He was not conscious of time, place, anybody, or anything but music and *petits fours* at four o'clock. He was always dreaming; up in the clouds—*loin*. He would usually go away and leave something in the room—often left on the piano the banknotes that mamma had paid him; always forgot his overcoat on the rack in the hall, and once in a while the maid would run after him with his hat. He did not appear to relish the idea of receiving pay; apparently disliked to handle money or think of it; treated my lessons as if they were a favour to us. Yes, an ideal artist to the tip of his fingers, to the ends of his hair; hating the material, prosaic world; always keyed up to the last notch in a realm of his own. He never seemed to realise that I existed in flesh and blood; scarcely ever looked at me or touched me; could not have told whether I was blond or dark. I was merely a sort of concept taking a music lesson! He was as economical of his compliments as, I imagine, Saint-Saëns is; always left me feeling that no one could be doing more wretchedly; that I was utterly stupid, hopeless. Once in a great while, though, he would say: 'Pas mal, pas trop mal,' and then I felt elated.

"I was afraid of him; yes, but then I was over my head in love with the man too—he was so handsome. The result was, of course, that I could never play my best before him. I would practise and work over my lessons, and they were hard ones. Think of Chopin's 'Second Scherzo' all at a clip, fifteen or twenty pages—yes, here it is, sixteen pages! I would think my lesson was going to be perfect, and then when he would come in, in his handsome, restless way, it was all up with my playing for the day. I was not unconscious and I was considered quite a goodlooking girl—old for my age—looking nearer twenty than twelve. I had a wealth of chestnut hair reaching to my ankles. It somewhat offended my pride—grieved me not a little—to see that M. Bizet took no notice of me, while my singing teacher, an Italian, was always holding my hands and kissing them, and proposing all kinds of delicious romances to me. M. Bizet considered me a child. He apparently liked mamma very much. She was a beautiful woman, with a tasteful, *distingué* way which probably interested him. He always seemed to want to talk with her, and frequently would ask: 'Est-ce qu'on ne voit pas madame aujourd'hui?'

"He was as uneasy as a lion in a cage during the lesson; moved about the room, sitting down and getting right up again, looking everywhere but at the piano. I often thought he was paying no attention to my playing, and sometimes I would begin to grow careless, and make little slips in fingering, and then he would say savagely: 'Je ne dors pas! Je ne dors pas!' It has been a marvel to me to this day how he could detect the slightest error in fingering, and be looking at a picture on the other side of the room. He never touched my piano, never played a lesson through for me at our house; said that he did not want to make apes of his pupils.

"Brimful of music, bubbling over with it, as he was every moment, I do not remember that he ever whistled a note, but he hummed. He had no voice—no, not a bit of voice; said that if he had had one, he would have been a great singer. He hummed, always getting tremendously excited when the music became triumphant. When I would come to the crowning passage in Chopin's 'Second Scherzo,' he would become half mad. He would rush up and down the room, crying out to me: 'This is the climax! Throw your whole soul into it! Don't miss a note! Play as if you were saying something!'"

"Oh, but I haven't told you how handsome he was. He was very plump and vigorous—a very showy, attractive man, without ever thinking that he was, or seeming to care what his effect was on other people. He had light brown hair, and a full beard almost russet or reddish-brown. His eyes were dark gray or dark blue. He dressed with extreme care and for his own personal satisfaction. It was one expression of his thoroughly artistic nature, and seemed to him as natural a need as any other. There was not a hint of a dandy about him. He did not act as if he were conscious that any one was to look at him.

"He wore the finest linen I ever saw. His gloves were *gants de Suède*—ladies' gloves—very long, soft, light brown, with no buttons. And when he would come in and strip off his gloves, throw them on the piano, and reveal those beautiful hands! They were hands of shell—the palms all shelly, with pearly layers of flesh and bluish traceries between. They were chubby, white, soft—not large; he always said one must have large hands for the piano. He seemed proud of them, and careful as a rule to keep them covered up—gloved. He had a lovely complexion—pink and white. But with all his dreaminess—his nonchalant, artistic temperament —he did not impress one at all as being an ethereal person. He was too healthy, too thoroughly rammed with life, for that.

"And what a gormand for sweets! He was crazy for bonbons, cakes, *friandises*. He always had *petits fours* at four o'clock. He was everywhere and at all times stuffing himself with confectionery. As soon as he saw the bonbon dish at our house, he would make for it and eat what there was in it. He once nearly lost his life when indulging his sweet tooth. There used to be a *pâtisserie*—very likely it's there yet—on the corner of the boulevard right across from the old Opéra-Comique—Place Boïeldieu. M. Bizet was there one day when the ceiling suddenly fell in, or a part of it. I think one or two persons were killed. He barely escaped, for a great piece of the plaster struck him on the shoulder, just missing his head.

*   *   *

"After about a year, M. Bizet said one day: 'I am too busy to be giving lessons. If you are to keep on, you will have to come *chez moi* hereafter." And so I went regularly to his apartment in the Rue Saint Georges. M. Bizet did not appear to have money, but Madame Bizet had. She was the daughter—the second daughter, I think—of Halévy, the composer. Their apartment was on the third floor—very artistic, with pictures and bronzes. I remember particularly the heavy *portières* with deep fringes.

"At home M. Bizet seemed a different man. When he was *chez nous*, he was ill at ease—*gêné*—evidently annoyed, displeased at the thought of giving lessons, so he rarely stayed longer than the half-hour. *Chez lui* he seemed glad to see us, and wanted to visit, especially when mamma happened to go with us. He would frequently be half the afternoon giving me my half-hour. He talked, showed his pictures, and would bring in his beautiful baby. He was very proud of it. Madame Bizet would almost always come in, and altogether it was very hospitable—neighbourly.

"Here he was interested, enthusiastic—seemed to have a wealth of leisure, and made us feel as if no one was in a hurry or had anything important to do; and still he worked to excess as everyone knew. Here we discovered, too, how he loved to play the piano. He would play this and that piece, and was apparently very fond of matching his hands against the cold, white ivory of the key-board. He was a pianist of the

highest order—superb and brilliant, full of sentiment—*entrain*, fire—
spontaneous, colourful, yet having all the technique and precision of the
Conservatoire.

"This was in the salon—I took my lessons there. His studio was
adjoining, and he had in it a piano and a little pipe organ. Once he had
me sing Gounod's 'Ave Maria,' and he accompanied on the organ.
Sometimes he would excuse himself during the lesson, and go in to the
piano in the studio, close the door, and work over some strain that would
be running in his head. This proved to be 'Carmen.' He was full of the
airs of 'Carmen' at this time, so I heard most of them sooner than almost
anyone, but of course I did not know what they were. We only knew he
was at work on an opera. He would hum the melodies and develop them
on the piano. I recall particularly the toreador song, and—

> 'J'irai danser la séguidille,
> Et boire du Manzanilla!'

"Oh, how he threw his soul into all these strains! Yet he did not
appear to harbour any illusions about the fate of the opera, for one day
some one asked him, 'Well, do you think your new opera is going to be a
success?' 'Grand Dieu, no!' replied M. Bizet, with an impatience which
revealed the deep undercurrent of sadness and disappointment within
him; 'it will fall flat like the others,' or words to that effect. He was
really a sad man in spite of all his vigour, robustness, and love of music.
He had been deeply wounded by the critics and the public. He felt that
people persisted in misinterpreting his art—in sacrificing him on the
national altar of race prejudice. He was accused of being Wagnerian.
Whether the failure of 'Carmen' at the Opéra-Comique hastened his
death, I cannot say. It was given the third of March, and he died the
third of June 1875. At any rate, he was putting his full energy into it,
and giving it scrupulously the best within him. You know that Carmen's
chanson d'entrée was rewritten or remade thirteen times!

"It was in March that I last saw him. Mother had suddenly died, and
we were all torn up and being bundled off to America. My sister and I
were on the boulevard near the Madeleine with the governess one
afternoon, and we happened to meet him. It must have been in the last
days of March, for I remember we were to sail April second. He stopped,
patted my sister on the back, took us both by the hands. He seemed
just the same—as well as ever. Of course I was too young to know about
the 'Carmen' fiasco, and then we were having so much grief and trouble
of our own. This was the first time he ever appeared to take any notice of
me. I was wearing my first long dress, and he remarked it. He looked at
me and said 'Tiens! la petite va être très jolie.'

"We were astounded to hear a few weeks later of his death—and it
happens that mother's tomb looks right down over his at Père-Lachaise."

THE OTHER MEN IN "CARMEN"

In all probability Georges Bizet considered it an honor when the Opéra-Comique contracted with his friends Ludovic Halévy and Henri Meilhac for the work that eventually turned out to be *Carmen*. Halévy and Meilhac were the foremost librettists of the day, the heroes of many spectacular successes both on the stage and in the Offenbachian music hall.

Ludovic Halévy, the nephew of Bizet's teacher, friend and father-in-law, Fromental Halévy, was born in 1834; he was the son of Léon Halévy, a moderately successful dramatist and literary man. What with the family connections in music and the stage, it is not surprising that Ludovic Halévy gravitated toward the theatre, although he worked in the civil service from 1852 until 1865, at which time he was successful enough in letters to retire. At the time of his withdrawal from the government, he was *secrétaire-rédacteur* for the Corps Législatif.

Halévy's entry to the French stage came as something of an accident. Jacques Offenbach, operating as both composer and impresario, had just managed to acquire a license to operate the Bouffes-Parisiens, a small theatre near the Parisian Universal Exposition of 1855. He was having trouble in getting a librettist to prepare a program, since all the librettists he knew refused the work. Finally, in last-moment despair, Offenbach thought of Ludovic Halévy, a young man whom he had met socially. Halévy accepted the commission, which incidentally was studded with all sorts of conditions and complications, and a collaboration began that turned out to be among the most successful in French culture.

With Offenbach's brilliant music and Halévy's ironic wit, the stock of the Bouffes-Parisiens kept mounting, until in October, 1858 a climactic moment arose: *Orphée aux enfers* (Orpheus in the Underworld). This was the first of the really great Offenbach operettas, with a script prepared by Halévy and Hector Crémieux. Gay, witty, irreverent, suggestive—it was both a parody of the old Orpheus myth in a very improper way and a satire on French manners and morals. It was an enormous success, and is still well remembered.

Offenbach, Crémieux and Halévy continued together for a few more years, but in 1860 Crémieux withdrew from the team and a new man entered: Henri Meilhac. Henri Meilhac (1831–1897), a friend of Halévy's, had been doing very well on his own as a playwright and humorist. Unlike the family man Halévy, Meilhac was a happy Parisian bachelor, whose chief aim in life apparently was to be the ideal *flâneur*. Halévy and Meilhac worked together until 1880. Just what each contributed to the collaboration has never been known apart from generalities: Meilhac, who was the more imaginative of the two, seems to have provided broad plot outlines and to have sketched out important scenes; Halévy, whose forte was more in the polished urbane line, restrained Meilhac's exuberance and wrote scenes in detail. This is said to have been their general pattern, but there seem to have been many exceptions to the pattern, and Offenbach often worked at the piano with both men when the actual composition was taking place.

Three great works emerged from this triumvirate of Offenbach, Halévy and Meilhac: *La belle Hélène* (1864), *La Vie parisienne* (1865), and *La Grande-Duchesse de Gérolstein*, which came as close to being an international sensation as any work of art ever has. *La Grande-Duchesse*, it has been maintained, was really the attracting force that drew much of Europe to Paris in 1867, not the highly touted exposition. It was to see Hortense Schneider, the marvelous musical comédienne, that the Prince of Wales went backstage; it was Hortense Schneider that drew Czar Alexander of Russia to Paris. Bismarck, King Wilhelm of Prussia and Moltke came to Paris, and were delighted to see signs of French "decadence" in the operetta; and the Sultan of Turkey, and the Kings of Portugal, Sweden and Bavaria were all on hand to delight in Offenbach's irony on militarism and autocracy.

Yet *La Grande-Duchesse*, despite its fantastic success, was really the swan song for the Offenbachian comic opera. Within a year or two the moral, cultural and military climate had changed enormously, and Offenbach and his librettists were at times in public disfavor. By the end of 1870 France had lost a major war and its government had been toppled. Within another few months monarchist feelings had been crushed; Paris had known a brief Communist state and had been besieged by the Prussians; Communists and Moderates had slaughtered one another when each was in power. The breezy internationalism of the prewar period was dead, and Offenbach's work was now considered somehow unpatriotic, immoral and frivolous.

This meant that the collaboration of the three men was at an end, and although things dragged on for a time, the two librettists presently moved on to other areas and types of entertainment. Among their dealings was the arrangement made with the Opéra-Comique for an opera with Bizet.

Not much is known about the circumstances of writing *Carmen*, since Halévy, who alone kept a diary, destroyed the entries in his stuffy old age. But it seems that Meilhac, who was best at broad humor, did the spoken sections, especially the comic scenes of the original libretto. Halévy presumably handled the sentimental sections and the musical verse. Bizet himself, however, wrote the final words for the "Habanera" and the "Card Song," in both cases much better than Halévy's versions. Both Halévy and Meilhac seem to have mingled in the battle over staging *Carmen*; at first they were enthusiastic, but du Locle's timorousness proved to be contagious, and eventually it came to a battle, with Bizet and the cast on one side and the producers and librettists on the other. When *Carmen* was publicly denounced in practically every reviewing medium in Paris, Halévy and Meilhac again proved to be timid, and assailed Galli-Marié for the fiasco. During the first revival of *Carmen* in Paris, in 1883, they supported the bowdlerized version that the Opéra-Comique staged, and intermittently for the remainder of their lives both librettists asserted that their Carmen was not the Carmen of Mérimée, but a person somehow purer and more moral.

Carmen was not the first Mérimée work that Halévy and Meilhac had done together. They had previously adapted Mérimée's play *Le Carrosse du Saint-Sacrement* for Offenbach under the new title of *La Périchole*, with Hortense Schneider as star. *La Périchole* is still played; in New York it is given in an English adaptation.

Around 1880 Halévy and Meilhac struck out into different paths. Meilhac continued in the theater and had the honor of seeing his collected works brought out just before his death. Halévy concentrated more upon prose fiction. Both men were elected to the French Academy, Halévy in 1884, Meilhac in 1888. Meilhac died in 1897, Halévy in 1908. Meilhac's work is now forgotten (apart from the great Offenbach librettos), Halévy is still remembered for a study of the French bourgeoisie, *Monsieur et Madame Cardinal* (1873), and most of all for *L'Abbé Constantin* (1872), a saccharinely pleasant *nouvelle* which is still read each year by thousands of American high school students.

A third man is also to be associated with *Carmen*: a man whose important share is seldom recognized by the audiences. This is Ernest

Guiraud, whose recitatives are practically always included in the opera.

Ernest Guiraud (1837–1892) was born in New Orleans, the son of a French émigré who seems to have left France for either political or economic reasons. When the situation changed, the Guirauds returned to France, and Ernest, then fifteen, entered the Paris Conservatoire. In 1859 he won the Prix de Rome. His father had also been a Prix de Rome winner, and this is said to be the only instance when both father and son won the award.

Guiraud and Bizet had known each other from their classes in the Conservatoire, but a real intimacy arose between them in Rome, where their scholarships overlapped. While Bizet felt that Guiraud's music was often dull and flaccid, he still admired Guiraud's warmth of personality and amiability. The two men remained close friends for the remainder of Bizet's life. Bizet attempted to invigorate Guiraud's work, defended him against personal enemies, and was often recklessly honest about Guiraud's music when they were among friends. Guiraud, on the other hand, sometimes served as the force that restrained Bizet from verbal and physical attacks upon enemies, and was a staunch support during Bizet's depression at continued failures.

After returning to Paris Guiraud continued to pursue music as a livelihood, but he was never markedly successful. He was inclined to be lazy and to procrastinate, and his work lacked imagination and depth. All in all he was much more suited to be an academician or a teacher than a successful composer. He wrote several operas, some of which were performed and then forgotten, and a fair amount of orchestral work, which was somewhat more successful, but is now equally forgotten. Perhaps his greatest operatic triumph came post-humously when his opera *Frédégonde*, completed by Saint-Saëns, aroused some interest in Paris in 1895.

In 1876 Guiraud became professor of harmony and composition in the Conservatoire, where he taught for the remainder of his life; among his pupils were Debussy and Satie. Guiraud recognized Debussy's genius and guided him toward the Prix de Rome, providing encouragement and assistance when Debussy was in trouble at the Conservatoire because of his revolutionary concepts of harmony. Guiraud was elected to the Institut in 1891; he died the following year.

Today Guiraud is heard only in the works of other composers, and his share is seldom popularly known. He orchestrated Offenbach's *Tales of Hoffmann* and prepared the recitatives for the grand opera

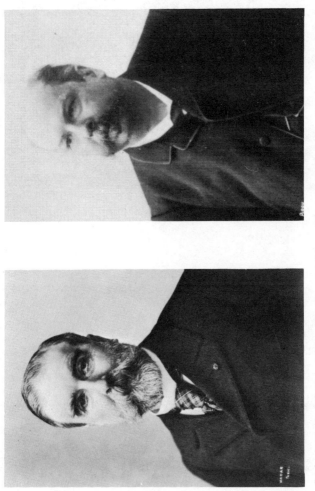

Ludovic Halévy (*left*) and Henri Meilhac (*right*), co-librettists of *Carmen*. (*Courtesy Bibliothèque et Musée de l'Opéra, Paris*)

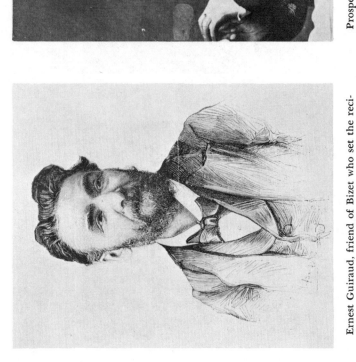

Ernest Guiraud, friend of Bizet who set the recitatives of the grand opera version of *Carmen*. Wood engraving after a photograph by Camus. (*Cabinet des Estampes, Bibliothèque Nationale, Paris; photo courtesy Bibliothèque Nationale*)

Prosper Mérimée, author of the *nouvelle* on which the opera *Carmen* is based. Photograph by Emile Robert. (*Cabinet des Estampes, Bibliothèque Nationale, Paris; photo courtesy Bibliothèque Nationale*)

version of *Carmen*. As Bizet's musical executor and the musician most intimate with him, Guiraud was the logical choice for this work, which has held the stage since the autumn of 1875 in Guiraud's version. Guiraud can be criticized for the severity with which he abridged the spoken sections that later became his recitatives, but his music has seldom been criticized beyond the truism that Bizet probably would have done it better. It is a measure of his success that only musicologists have been aware that another man's work is mixed with Bizet's in *Carmen*.

GYPSIES, PROSPER MÉRIMÉE
AND "CARMEN"

I. THE GYPSIES

The Gypsies first appeared in Europe in the late fourteenth and early fifteenth centuries, when mysterious caravans filled with a strange dark folk emerged from the Byzantine world and wandered across Europe, even to Scotland. They were called Gypsies in English, because early chroniclers believed that they had come from Egypt. They called themselves Romani, however; some scholars derive this from their stay in the Roman Empire of the East, others, with more likelihood, equate the name Romani with the tribal names of Rom or Dom in medieval India, where the Gypsies certainly originated. Beggars, dancers, musicians, thieves and often criminals, they were legislated against, tortured by the Inquisition and executed just for being Gypsies, but they still remained the terror of rural areas, especially in Spain and East Central Europe.

It was not until the early nineteenth century, though, that the Gypsy assumed importance in literature. His ways were examined with sympathy, his language and songs recorded, and his steps were dogged by enthusiastic collectors and dilettantes. This was mostly due to George Borrow, the eccentric Englishmen who lived on the road for years and described his experiences with Gypsies in such a strange mixture of truth and exaggeration that one is often tempted to believe what is fiction and disregard what is truth.

Borrow described his adventures among the British gypsies in two remarkable books, *Lavengro* and *The Romany Rye*, and for the first time it was seen that the Gypsies were human beings, susceptible to literary treatment, and very interesting in their ways. A few years after his adventures on the road in England, Borrow obtained a position with the Bible Society and from 1835 to 1839 distributed Bibles as a *colporteur* in Spain and Portugal. His experiences among the Spaniards and the Spanish Gypsies are described in *Zincali, or the Gypsies of Spain* (1841) and *The Bible in Spain* (1843).

In a relatively short time Borrow had established something like a cult of the Gypsy, and it became as modish for a literary man to know something about Gypsy ways and vocabulary as it was a few years ago to join the Baker Street Irregulars and write about the real life of Sherlock Holmes. Toward the end of the century, indeed, it must have been ludicrous to see elderly literary men who believed themselves to be linguists, harassing and browbeating the poor Gypsies of England and America.

One of George Borrow's stepchildren emerged in French literature when the French essayist and man of letters Prosper Mérimée wrote *Carmen* in 1845. *Carmen* is in part derived from Mérimée's travels in Spain, incidents and personalities that he observed there, and stories that he was told. But its Gypsy lore, its Gypsy vocabulary, and much else are frankly borrowed from George Borrow, the original Romany rye. Since it is from *Carmen*, written by Mérimée, adapted by Bizet and his librettists, that the type image of the Spanish Gypsy has emerged, it is to George Borrow that the ultimate ancestry must be traced.

II. PROSPER MÉRIMÉE

Prosper Mérimée (1803–1870) was one of the most noted French authors of the nineteenth century. During his lifetime and shortly thereafter, his work was rated very high, since it furnished a peculiar amalgam of qualities which appealed to post-Romantic French taste: violence of action, urbanity and simplicity of diction, local color and strange settings, and over everything a cloak of sometimes cruel cynicism. Perhaps one of the causes of his success was his reason for invoking violence and bloodshed—not for the sake of thrills per se as with Dumas *père*; not for the sake of pathos, as with Hugo; but apparently for the sake of showing how a cultivated *boulevardier* can mock the forces of terror.

Mérimée was the son of Léonor Mérimée, permanent secretary of the École des Beaux Arts, a noted art historian. Léonor Merimée, like his British counterpart Sir Charles Eastlake, spent his life tracking down the technical methods of the premodern painters, and his books are still inexhaustible for scholars in this area of art history. Léonor Mérimée was also a man of culture and counted among his friends not only most of the celebrities of Paris but also men of letters in many other countries, including England. It is in part at least to the international background of the Mérimée family that Prosper Mérimée owed his wide range of travel and the linguistic gifts which made him one of the best linguists of his day.

When it was observed that Prosper Mérimée had little talent as an artist, it was decided that he would become a lawyer and enter the service of the government. In 1823 he took a law degree and entered the civil service, in which he remained for most of his life. At first he worked at drafting the language of legal documents for the government; then he became administrator of the semaphore and the payroll; from 1834 to 1853 he served as inspector general of historic monuments and antiquities. In the last position he served well and happily, since he was an antiquary by hobby, and he undertook many expeditions to remote parts of France to examine discoveries or to conduct investigations.

His greatest love, after the life of the *boulevardier*, was literature, at which he worked diligently. It is perhaps characteristic, however, that his entry into literature was by means of a hoax. In 1825 there appeared a book titled *Théâtre de Clara Gazul, comédienne espagnole*, which contained six plays, supposedly written by a Spanish actress then in exile in England. The book was received with great enthusiasm, and it was not known until several years later that the plays had been written by Prosper Mérimée, and that his close friend Henri Beyle (later known as Stendhal) had helped by correcting proofs. The plays were translated into English and German, and achieved a European reputation.

The *Gazul* plays were followed in 1827 by a purported collection of Serbian ballads, gathered from folk singers in the mountains of Illyria: *La Guzla, par Hyacinthe Maglanovitch*. Once again Europe was fooled, and scholars later congratulated Mérimée on his achievement. Only the aging Goethe in Weimar penetrated the hoax and declared that the poems were fraudulent and by the same hand as the previous plays of "Clara Gazul." It is significant that Mérimée's first literary ventures should be a cynical fraud.

For the remainder of his life Mérimée devoted himself to letters, but now on a serious level. He wrote many excellent historical and literary essays, much poetry and a fair amount of prose fiction. His best work consists of collections of his own letters. Among his stories that are known in the English-speaking world are the short story *Mateo Falcone*, a story of family honor in Corsica; *Colomba*, about romance and feuds in Corsica; *La Vénus de l'Ille*, about a demonic statue of Venus which murders a man; and, of course, *Carmen*. Most of his other work is not known outside France, although he was an accomplished stylist with a pure mode of writing that contrasted greatly with the romantic styles of his contemporaries Gautier and Hugo.

Mérimée travelled extensively, visiting Spain in 1830, England several times, the Turkish Empire and Greece and even the little-known areas of the Western Slavic world. He was an excellent linguist, going to the lengths of learning Lithuanian for purposes of comparative studies. He prepared the first French translations of Pushkin and Gogol. He was also the confidant and close correspondent of Stendhal. The two men were intimate enough to exchange mistresses whenever either felt that the calls of romance were becoming too heavy. When Stendhal died, he appointed Mérimée his literary executor, and Merimée wrote his authorized biography.

Little of event happened in Mérimée's life. He remained a bachelor, lived as a *bon vivant*, and was renowned as a dandy. Most people found his cynical sneer difficult to tolerate, with the result that he was often considered to be a monster of selfish egotism. To his intimate friends, however, he could be charming and affable. In later life he declared that his natural warmth had been quenched so often when he was a child that he had adopted the armor of cynicality and aloofness for protection.

Mérimée was a political aristocrat by inclination, and had little regard for France's perpetual attempts to establish a democracy. He was also a close friend of Eugénie de Montijo, whose family he had known in Spain. When Louis Napoleon III took Eugénie for his Empress, one of his first acts was to create Mérimée a lifetime senator, with a large permanent income. Mérimée remained an intimate of the Napoleonic circle as a combination of poet laureate and court jester, and probably had much to do with diplomatic and political policies of the unfortunate empire. During this period he wrote little.

When 1870, the year of the Franco-Prussian War, came, Mérimée was prematurely old and sick, and his prediction that he could not survive another invasion of France came true. He died shortly after the defeat of the French armies in 1870, killed in part at least by a broken heart. It is somewhat ironic that he is now remembered either for a high-school classic in *Colomba* or for Georges Bizet's opera *Carmen*.

III. CARMEN

Carmen owes its origin to Mérimée's trip to Spain in 1830. Here, as a young man of twenty-seven, he spent much of his time riding aimlessly around the barren countryside, attended by a Spaniard who served as guide, servant and bodyguard. On one of his expeditions in Andalusia, near Murvieda, he chanced upon a small, isolated inn, where he was served water and gazpacho (a cold vegetable soup) by a darkish girl named Carmencita. He soon observed that his guide was ill at ease and eager to leave, though unwilling to give his reasons. Upon being pressed, the guide finally revealed that Carmencita was a witch. Mérimée sketched the girl in his notebooks, and then moved on.

A little later, back in Madrid, Mérimée struck up an acquaintance with the Montijo family. This family of grandees was one of the strange results of Britain's historical links with Spain. The present count, Mérimée's friend, had married a girl named Kirkpatrick, who was descended from Jacobite exiles. Among their children was a little girl, who was later to become the Empress of the French as consort of Louis Napoleon.

Mérimée owed the second portion of the *Carmen* situation to the Montijo family, for while he was visiting them, the Countess Montijo told him the story of a local Gypsy girl who had been killed by her jealous lover. This was the kernel of *Carmen*, and when Mérimée was writing *Carmen* in 1844 he wrote to the Montijos for more details.

The incidents of his own Spanish trip and the story of the murdered Gypsy girl became blended in his mind, and when to this were added his antiquarian lore and Borrow's Gypsy material, there emerged the *nouvelle, Carmen*. It was published in 1845 in the *Revue des Deux Mondes*. It has been accepted as a modern classic and has long been available in English translations.

Mérimée's *Carmen* differs in many respects from the libretto of the opera. It is told in fragments through the personality of an English traveler and archeologist, who learns the story of Carmen and Don José in pieces, and later puts them together.

The Englishman, as Mérimée tells the story, is traveling in the wastes of Cordova, when he falls in with a stranger, who is obviously not a native Andalusian, and is just as obviously a *bandido* of distinction. Hospitability, however, is invoked, and the Englishman manages to save the life of the stranger (Don José Lizzarrabengoa, known locally as Don José Navarro) when José is betrayed to the authorities.

Some time later the Englishmen is in Cordova, idly watching sights upon the famous mole, when the girl Carmencita, obviously a Gypsy sorceress, approaches him and engages him in conversation. She is petite and dark, with "a wild and savage beauty, a face which astonished you at first, and was never to be forgotten. Her eyes, especially, had an expression at once voluptuous and fierce that I have never met since in any other human being." He offers to accompany her home, ostensibly to have his fortune told, and is taken to a hovel across the river. They are just beginning, when the door bursts open and Don José bursts in, furious with rage. He recognizes the English-man, however, and turns his wrath solely upon Carmencita. But Carmencita merely urges Don José, in Basque, to murder the English-man, who has no difficulty in following her conversation "only too well from seeing her pass and repass her little hand under her chin." José refuses, and escorts the Englishman politely back to the bridge. Some time later, the Englishman discovers that his watch, whose repeating chimes Carmen had admired, has disappeared.

Several months later, the Englishman is in Cordova again, and is told by the authorities that his watch has been found, and that the thief is about to be garroted. He visits the thief, Don José (who had re-ceived the watch from Carmen). The Englishman agrees to have Masses said for Carmen's soul, and learns the tragic story of Don José and Carmen.

Don José Lizzarrabengoa, a Basque from the Northern provinces, had been a corporal in the army, one of the guards assigned to the tobacco factory in Seville. One day, while he was fixing his gear, Carmen came along and began to flirt with him. "She had a cassia-flower in the corner of her mouth, and she came prancing along like a thoroughbred filly from the stud of Cordova. In my country, such a woman in such a costume would have made everyone cross himself. At Seville, however, everyone paid her some bold compliment upon her figure. She answered them all with side glances, her hand on her hip, as bold as the true Gypsy she was. At first she did not please me, and I resumed my work; but she, after the custom of women and cats, who come not when called, but only unasked, stopped in front of me and addressed me."

They converse, though Carmen pokes fun at José. Carmen enters the factory, and a riot soon breaks out. It is discovered that Carmen has slashed one of her fellow workers. José is in charge of the guard to take her to prison. She has apparently discovered his origin, for she addresses him in Basque, claiming that she is not really a Gypsy, and begs him to let her escape. In a moment of weakness at hearing his native tongue, Don José complies, Carmen escapes, and José is broken to private and sent to prison for a month.

After his prison term is over, José again sees Carmen when she comes to dance at an officers' party where he is standing guard. She manages to whisper to him, "If you want good fried fish, come to Lillas Pastia's in the Triana." When his tour of duty is over, he goes to visit her, and with the money which she had previously smuggled into his cell, they feast and make love. Carmencita, who is José's evil genius, wants him to desert and join her, but he still has a sense of honor, even though his chances of a future in the army have been destroyed. Yet when she later approaches his post at night and asks him to permit smugglers to pass, he yields.

The end to this double life comes when José returns to Lillas Pastia's, and sees Carmencita enter with one of his officers. He and the officer fight, and José kills him. It is now impossible for José to return to the army, and he joins her band of smugglers. Together they wander over Spain, here smuggling silk, there plundering, there robbing tourists: Carmen entices rich travellers into lonely places, and José robs them. During this life José learns that she is married to a member of the band, a one-eyed cutthroat named Garcia, and he decides that he alone must have Carmen. He kills Garcia in a knife-fight, and Carmen, who is quite indifferent about such matters, with a shrug becomes his wife.

But with marriage, fate divides the Gypsy and the deserter. José, despite the depths to which he has sunk, is still motivated by the Basque peasant sense of honor, and wishes his marriage to be honorable. He wants to escape to America, and begin a new life, since they have plenty of cash. Carmen, on the other hand, has "no wish to grow cabbages," and reveals that marriage has destroyed her love for Don José.

The inevitable crisis between the promiscuous Gypsy slut and the weak, yet passionate and idealistic Basque comes when Carmen is about to desert José for a picador named Lucas. José takes Carmen to a lonely spot, and demands that she be true to him. She refuses with a sneer, tells him that she will no longer live with him, and says, "You wish to kill me, I can well see. It is decreed, but you shall never make me yield. ... All is over between us. As my rom you have the right to kill your romi; but Carmen will always be free. Calli [Gypsy] she was born, and calli she will die." After further argument Don José stabs her. He then goes to the guardhouse and turns himself in. His final words to the Englishman, as he narrates this story, are, "Poor girl. Blame the Gypsies for rearing her as they did."

Mérimée's own sketch of Carmen and Don José.

THÉÂTRE DE L'OPÉRA-COMIQUE. — Carmen, OPÉRA-COMIQUE EN QUATRE ACTES, PAR MM. MEILHAC ET HALÉVY; MUSIQUE DE M. BIZET.

Sketches made by Lamy at the première of *Carmen*, March 3, 1875. *(Courtesy Bibliothèque de l'Arsenal, Paris)*

As can be seen, this story differs considerably from the Meilhac-Halévy-Bizet libretto. Bizet's librettists removed the extraneous frame and the unnecessary Englishman, unified the plot, made the characters less shadowy, and heightened the drama. Besides clearing the plot line, Meilhac and Halévy enlarged the episode of the bullfighter (who is a matador now, rather than a picador), changed his name to Escamillo, and created a new major character in the girl Micaëla. Needless to say, it is the Meilhac-Halévy version of *Carmen* that is most widely known.

PLOT SUMMARY*

The story of Carmen and her lover Don José Lizzarrabengoa takes place in and around Seville, about 1820. Carmen is a Gypsy girl who is currently working in the tobacco factory in Seville, she also belongs to a band of Gypsy smugglers and criminals who live in the infamous Triana section of Seville. Don José, a corporal in the Dragoons, is a Basque from Navarre, who was forced to take refuge in the army after either killing or badly injuring an enemy in a fight.

Act One

The play begins in the square in front of the tobacco factory in Seville, where a squad of soldiers occupies a guardhouse. It is almost time to change the guard when Micaëla, a young peasant girl with a blue skirt and long blonde braids, timidly approaches Morales, the cynical corporal of the guard. She asks him if he knows Don José; Morales replies that he does, but that José is in another company and is not on duty. After some attempts at flirtation on Morales's part, and some goodnatured horseplay by the soldiers, Micaëla runs away, saying that she will return when José is on duty.

The relief arrives, led by Lieutenant Zuñiga and Corporal Don José. Morales describes the girl to José, who recognizes Micaëla, an orphan whom his mother, now living close by, had taken into her care. The old guard marches out and José seats himself outside the guardhouse, busying himself at twisting a wire chain for his firing pin.

Zuñiga expresses considerable interest in the girls who work in the factory, since he has just been assigned to this regiment. After some conversation José recommends that Zuñiga look at the girls for himself when they return to work. It is noon at present, and the girls are home at lunch.

The factory bell sounds and hordes of mashers line the square waiting

* This plot summary occasionally contains matter from the 1875 full *Carmen* to explain background, motivations and characters.

for the cigarette* girls who gradually come in. The men and women flirt together, and then notice that Carmen is not there. There is some comment, and Carmen appears, dressed in slatternly Gypsy attire, with a cassia-flower between her teeth. The various men try to pick her up, complimenting her upon her beauty, but Carmen merely turns them away with jests. Her attention, instead, is fixed upon Don José, the only man in the gathering who is not openly admiring her; she acts "in the fashion of women and cats, who come only to those who pay no attention to them." José, who has glanced at her and has been repelled and somewhat frightened by her brazen antics, is concentrating upon his work with the wire. Carmen prances over to him "like a filly from the finest Cordoban stables" and coarsely asks him what he is doing. When he replies that he is making a chain for his *épingle*, she laughingly answers with a double entendre and throws her flower at him like a dart, striking him on the chest. José leaps to his feet in confusion while the onlookers shriek with laughter. The factory bell sounds again, the girls hurry back to the factory, and the soldiers, except José, enter the guardhouse.

While José is meditating upon his strange experience, thinking that in the Basque country Carmen would have been burned as a witch, Micaëla return with her message. The message, from José's mother, is in two parts: a kiss, which Micaëla transmits to José and José returns, and a letter, which José reads as Micaëla leaves. The letter urges José to marry Micaëla. José is just swearing that he will do so and is about to throw Carmen's flower away when an uproar breaks out in the factory.

The workers stream out into the square and the soldiers rush out of the guardhouse, Zuñiga in command. From the confused reports of the opposing factions of the workers Zuñiga can tell only that there has been a quarrel in the factory, that blood has been shed, and that Carmen is involved. He orders José into the factory, and José, taking another soldier, dashes into the cutting room.

After a brief time, during which Zuñiga has been torn back and forth by the factions of girls, José emerges with Carmen as his prisoner. He reports to Zuñiga that Carmen and a girl named Manuelita had been chaffing one another until Carmen, losing her temper, had seized Manuelita, thrown her to the floor and slashed her cheeks. Carmen neither admits nor denies it.

---

* This is an anachronism, of course, since cigarettes were not manufactured in Seville in the 1820's, but it is an accepted part of *Carmen*.

Zuñiga tries to question Carmen, but she simply replies with fragments of Gypsy ballads. He is about to order her to the prison when she
breaks away for a moment and assaults one of the girls nearby.
Zuñiga thereupon comments that it is a shame to tie up such a goodlooking girl, but she must learn; and he orders her wrists tied while he
goes into the guardhouse to write a prison order for José.

Carmen and José are alone when, to José's utter astonishment, she
tells him to release her. Why? He loves her; she has worked the Gypsy
magic upon him. José scoffs mildly, but when Carmen sings of the
delights of love at Lillas Pastia's and indicates that she has just kicked
out her lover and needs a new one, José's resistance collapses very
rapidly. It is agreed that Carmen will knock José down, that he will
impede the pursuit, and let her escape. José unties her hands.

Zuñiga comes from the guardhouse with the prison order. José
moves off with Carmen, and to the cheers and jeers of the crowd she
escapes as planned.

Act Two

The second act takes place one month later,* on the day that Don
José is due to be released from prison for his connivance in letting
Carmen escape; his part was apparently obvious to his superiors. He
has been reduced to the rank of private.

The Gypsies are gathered in Lillas Pastia's squalid establishment,
which is a mixture of brothel, boozing ken and tavern. Gypsy girls are
dancing to entertain a group of soldiers (including Zuñiga), while Gypsy
men madly strum guitars. Carmen joins the dance after the act begins.

The soldiers try to pick up the Gypsy girls, but upon a signal from
Pastia the girls refuse. Zuñiga, who has been flirting with Carmen,
hints that she bears him a grudge for the clash of a month ago, but
Carmen laughingly denies it. She seems pleased when she learns from
him that Don José's imprisonment has ended. Zuñiga then promises
to return to her after roll call, though Carmen does not encourage him.

Just as the soldiers are ready to leave, shouts and cheers from
outside indicate that a procession honoring the toreador Escamillo is
passing by. The soldiers, who are of course ardent devotees of the ring,
invite Escamillo in to drink a toast with them. He complies, and
during the toast is obviously attracted to Carmen. He asks her
whether she will be his mistress; she refuses, but, as she makes clear,
only for the time being, since she is currently taken.

* Guiraud's recitative places this as two months later.

Escamillo and the soldiers leave the tavern, and the Gypsies are then joined by the leader of their band, El Dancaïro, and his comic henchman, El Remendado, who have been out planning a job. They intend to smuggle some textiles from Gibraltar, convey them inland and sell them. The Gypsy leader indicates that he wants Carmen and her two friends Mercedes and Frasquita to come along in the event that women will be needed to carry through their plans. Frasquita and Mercedes raise no objections, since it is all business, but Carmen refuses to leave. When pressed for her reasons, she says that she promised to wait for a soldier who did her a favor, and she cannot go. The Gypsy leader is first enraged, but then scoffs at Carmen's story, prophesying that her soldier will not come.

At this point a voice is heard from outside, singing a soldier's ballad, and the Gypsies see that it is José approaching. They urge Carmen to induce him to join their band; they then leave. Carmen greets José and asks him why he did not escape from prison with the file and gold piece that she had sent him. José replies that he could not desert. The two prepare to make love, and when Don José becomes violently jealous because Carmen had previously danced for the soldiers, she offers to dance for him alone.

Carmen is dancing for José when, at a most inappropriate moment, the bugles sound retreat. He stops Carmen, who is momentarily bewildered but resumes her dance. Don José stops her again, and tells her that he must return to the barracks for roll call. Carmen flies into a passion at finding her charms rejected. José tries to assure her that he really loves her, and producing from his tunic the flower she had thrown to him, tells her how he had treasured it during his imprisonment. But when Carmen urges him to desert, he refuses. As José is about to leave, a knock is heard at the door.

The door bursts open and Zuñiga enters to keep the assignation he had tried to make with Carmen. Zuñiga orders José to leave, but José refuses. A quarrel breaks out when Zuñiga strikes him. The Gypsies separate the two men and decree that Zuñiga shall be held prisoner until they have had time to make their getaway. Since José has struck an officer, he is left no choice but to agree, however unenthusiastically, to join the Gypsy band.

Act Three

Act Three is set in the desolate mountains, probably not too far from Seville, perhaps a couple of months later. Time is not specified, but Carmen and Don José have had enough time to become tired of one another: Don José of Carmen's uncontrollable temper and flirtatiousness and Carmen of José's rigidity and peasant values.

As the act begins, the smugglers, laden with bales of merchandise, have halted temporarily before beginning the last march to the city where they intend to deposit their spoils. El Dancaïro and El Remendado go on ahead to see whether they can get past the guards, while the others remain temporarily encamped. José and Carmen are in the middle of a quarrel.

It is now becoming obvious that it is only a matter of time before Don José and Carmen will separate, and their separation is likely to be perilous, since José has claimed he will kill Carmen rather than lose her. He has told Carmen this, but with the fatalism that is an important part of her character, she accepts her destiny with resignation.

While José stalks away, Carmen goes over to the campfire where her Gypsy friends Frasquita and Mercedes are half-seriously telling their own fortunes with cards. The two other girls manage to get themselves fantastically favorable futures, and laugh about it, but when Carmen joins in, she deals herself only death.

The Gypsy chief returns and reports that the gap in the city wall is well guarded by three customs officers. It is now up to the Gypsy women to distract the guards, and the three girls merrily go forward to seduce them. Needless to say, this is salt upon the jealous José's wounds, and he is almost overcome with shame and fury. El Dancaïro tells him to remain behind and cover their rear while the others carry away the merchandise.

José climbs upon a high pinnacle of rock and stands watch. Off to one side Micaëla appears, looking for José. She is alone, since her guide has left her; frightened by the wild countryside, she prays that Heaven will protect her. She sees José and shouts to attract his attention, but apparently he does not hear her, for he leaps up and fires his musket in another direction at a stranger. The stranger turns out to be Escamillo, who had been purchasing bulls in the neighborhood, when he heard that Carmen was nearby, and decided to see her. He tells this to José, unaware that José himself is Carmen's lover. José thereupon challenges Escamillo to a knife-duel, and the two men fight. Escamillo's knife breaks, and just as José is about to kill him, the Gypsies, attracted by the shot, rush back in. The Gypsies know Escamillo and permit him to leave, and he in turn invites all of them, especially Carmen, to witness his next fight.

One of the Gypsies then happens to see Micaëla, who is hiding among the rocks, and drags her forth. José recognizes her, and she appeals to him to give up his life of crime and return to his mother. The Gypsies, including Carmen, urge José to leave, since he is obviously not suited to being a smuggler, but he stubbornly refuses because of his love for Carmen. He is about to turn Micaëla away, when she tells him that his mother is dying. This moves José, and he leaves with Micaëla, telling Carmen he will return. Carmen, however, now considers their affair at an end, and listens with interest as Escamillo's song is heard in the distance.

Act Four

The fourth act of *Carmen* is set in Seville, in front of the entrance to the bull arena. It is not certain how much time has elapsed since the previous act, but a reasonable estimate might be a month. In the meanwhile Carmen has taken Escamillo as her lover and has returned to Seville; Don José has visited his mother's village to be at her death-bed, and has managed to evade the soldiers sent out to capture him.

It is the day of the great bullfight, and the ceremonial procession of the *cuadrilla* is enthusiastically watched by the audience. The crowds cheer or hoot as particular favorites or enemies march by. Zuñiga is in the audience with Mercedes and Frasquita.

Escamillo and Carmen enter together, Carmen dressed in meretricious finery. They declare to each other the ardor of their present love, and Escamillo then enters the arena, while Frasquita and Mercedes approach Carmen and warn her that José is in the crowd. Carmen is indifferent, for she believes that what is fated will happen.

The crowd pours into the arena, leaving just two persons outside, Carmen and Don José. José intercepts her and demands that she return to him. As they talk, shouts indicate the progress of the bullfight. First José pleads with her to go away with him to start a new life, an honest life, somewhere else. Carmen scornfully refuses. José in desperation offers to go back to the smugglers and to live according to their ways, if only Carmen will stay with him. Carmen again refuses. José asks her if she still loves him. Carmen says no. José, stating that he still loves her and will not release her, then threatens her, but Carmen remains unmoved. To indicate that their affair is over, she throws back at José a ring that he had given to her.

José draws his knife, and though Carmen tries to get away, stabs her. As she falls lifeless to the ground, the final *corrida* in the bullring has

been run and Escamillo appears at the entrance to the arena to gaze
with horror at Carmen's corpse. José, now overcome with remorse,
makes no attempt to escape, but throws himself upon Carmen's body
and calls to the soldiers to arrest him, since it was he who killed
Carmen.

Marie Galli-Marié, who created the role of Carmen. *(Courtesy Bibliothèque et Musée de l'Opéra, Paris)*

Paul Lhérie, the original Don José.

Joseph Bouhy, the first Escamillo.
(*Courtesy Bibliothèque de l'Arsenal, Paris*)

THE PERFORMANCE HISTORY
OF "CARMEN"

I.

As is well-known, the first production of *Carmen* was a failure. The reasons, of course, were many. In fact, in retrospect, it is astonishing that du Locle, with his excellent showman's instinct, ever went ahead with it. There were political reasons, moral reasons, personal and musical reasons that it would fail. But all of these reasons were transitory reasons, which were bound to vanish, and Bizet's less time-bound instinct as a musician had necessarily to outweigh du Locle's pessimism. After all, the music of *Carmen* is for the most part very great, and is set to a generally excellent libretto.

After the first few performances the opera *Carmen* began to undergo the strange internal metamorphoses which are still going on. First of all, Bizet dropped the dumb show that Morales had in Act One, since the pantomime did nothing for the opera except impede the action and implant a wrong mood. Authorities who have examined the music for this section, which is not generally available, are inclined to agree that it was weak. One authority, indeed, would like to believe that this music was not really Bizet's, but had simply been lifted from some forgotten comic opera of the past, but this is going too far. Bizet also shortened the confrontation of Don José and Escamillo in the third act, omitting the section where Escamillo has José at his mercy, but spares him. This omission was less fortunate, since it pared a dimension away from Escamillo's personality and lost some excellent music. But the management of the Opéra-Comique seems to have believed that a prolonged knife-battle was pushing luck too far.

Bizet died very shortly after he signed the contract for the Vienna production, and his friend Guiraud was entrusted with the revisions. Guiraud (or possibly Halévy and Meilhac, though it seems less likely) cut the spoken sections, omitting much of the background, flattening out many of the minor characters, enfeebling motivations and destroying humorous contrast to the tragic scenes. Guiraud then set what was left of the dialogue to recitative, using themes from Bizet's work. He also prepared a ballet, which was first inserted into the second act in the Vienna performance, but was very soon shifted to the first part of the fourth act. This ballet music consisted of a juxtaposition of the "Bohemian Dance" from *La Jolie Fille de Perth* and a chorus from *L'Arlésienne*. This patchwork concession to vapidity was destined to interrupt *Carmen* almost universally until not too many years ago, but lately the tendency has been to use merely the street scene chorus.

The Vienna Opera House performance, which took place on October 23, 1875, was highly successful. The Brussels première in February, 1876, using the Vienna version,* with Galli-Marié as Carmen, was equally successful. Two years later Minnie Hauk gained stardom as Carmen at Brussels, and in June, 1878, the impresario Colonel James Mapleson presented *Carmen* at Her Majesty's Theatre in London, with Hauk as Carmen and Italo Campanini as Don José. This version was sung in Italian. Difficulties in pleasing singers are well summarized in the Mapleson memoirs:

> Prior to the commencement of the season I had heard Bizet's *Carmen* in Paris, which I contemplated giving; and my decision was at once taken on hearing from Miss Minnie Hauk of the success she was then making in that opera at Brussels. I therefore resolved upon engaging her to appear as Carmen. In distributing the parts I well recollect the difficulties I had to encounter. On sending Campanini the role of Don José (in which he afterwards became so celebrated), he returned it to me stating he would do anything to oblige, but could not think of undertaking a part in an opera of that description where he had no romance and no love duet except with the seconda donna. Shortly afterwards Del Puento, the baritone, entered informing me that the part of Escamillo, which I had sent him, must have been intended for one of the chorus, and that he begged to decline it. In vain did Sir Michael Costa order the rehearsals. Mdlle. Valleria suggested that I should entrust the part of Micaëla either to Bauermeister or to one of the chorus; as on no account would she undertake it. This went on for some time, and I saw but little prospect of launching my projected opera. At length, by force of persuasion, coupled with threats, I induced the various singers, whether they accepted their parts or not, to attend a general rehearsal, when they all began to take a great fancy to the roles I had given them; and in due course the opera was announced for the first representation, which took place on the 22nd June [1878].

* For more about the Vienna version see page 74.

Poster for the first performance of *Carmen*, 1875. The final moment of the opera is depicted.

Poster designed by Bastien Lepage for a touring company of *Carmen* in Cincinnati, showing the "Gypsy Song" in Act 2.

Old *Carmen* poster, with Don José confronting Carmen outside the arena (Act 4).

Carmen came to the United States in 1878, when the Mapleson troupe, with Minnie Hauk and Campanini, and conducted by the composer Luigi Arditi, opened at the New York Academy of Music on October 23. Clara Kellogg, however, always claimed that she had sung *Carmen* in America several months before Hauk. According to such records as have been unearthed, Clara Kellogg's *Carmen* opened in Philadelphia two days later than the New York Mapleson company.

A battle of the stages soon arose between the two productions, with Mapleson and Maurice Strakosch, the impresario of the Philadelphia company, at loggerheads. Mapleson claimed that Strakosch did not have the real *Carmen*, but only a shoddy, feeble expansion of a piano score. Strakosch offered to bet $100,000 (though neither of the two men had ever even seen so much money) that his version was genuine. Both troupes eventually toured the country with *Carmen* in their repertoire.

The New York première paralleled that in Paris, being misunderstood by both audience and critics. But *Carmen* suddenly became popular overnight, and during Mapleson's tour of the United States it was in great demand, leading all other operas in number of performances.

In the same year, 1878, St. Petersburg, Russia, was conquered, as were Marseilles, Lyons and Angers. Florence, Milan, Naples, Chicago and Berlin followed. In a very short time Paris alone among great opera centers remained without *Carmen*. By now, in one of the ironies of history, the audience was mature enough for *Carmen*, and there was a perpetual outcry for a revival at the Opéra-Comique. Carvalho, now Director, resisted the demand as long as he could, for he took the position of du Locle and de Leuven that brothels and murders did not belong at the Opéra-Comique. Meilhac and Halévy, who were now in new careers and had compunctions about seeing their *gaucheries* revived, were also against a revival.

Eventually Carvalho could not refuse any longer, for the press almost all sided against him, and in April, 1883, *Carmen* was again presented at the Opéra-Comique, but in a production which suggests either that Carvalho was badly out of tune with his times or that he wanted to get rid of *Carmen* once and for all by sabotaging it.

The overall impression that emerges from the 1883 revival is that of an unwitting parody. The music was slowed down and liberties were taken with the orchestra. The chorus returned to the statuesque poses that Bizet had fought so violently against. Lillas Pastia's low tavern became a most respectable hotel in which beautifully dressed aristocrats and bourgeois sat with dignity, while a classical ballet paced before their eyes. Don José and Escamillo discussed their differences amicably, instead of fighting with knives, and Carmen herself became amiable and chic. Needless to say, the Carmen was a second-rate soprano (for whom the music had to be transposed), for under no circumstances could the role be repeated by the "scabrous" Galli-Marié.

The performance also left much to be desired. Adèle Isaac, the soprano, was a poor choice, and the rest of the cast was third-rate. The sets were the oldest and shabbiest in the house, and the orchestra had great difficulty with the music. Most of the opera is claimed to have been presented without rehearsals, so that it is not surprising that singers forgot their lines and Don José managed to drop his dagger when about to stab Carmen.

The critical response was an uproar, just as it had been eight years earlier. "Desecration" was the cry. But now it was Bizet who was the hero. Carvalho again had to yield, and in 1883 a true *Carmen* was reestablished, again with Galli-Marié. Since then *Carmen* has been the mainstay of the Opéra-Comique. Its thousandth performance occurred in 1904, with a special cast including Emma Calvé and Edmond Clément. By the hundredth anniversary of Bizet's birth *Carmen* had been performed at the Opéra-Comique some 2,271 times.

II.

Many of the greatest singers of each era have played Carmen, sometimes brilliantly, sometimes regrettably. After Galli-Marié the foremost Carmen of the early period was the American singer Minnie Hauk, whose London and New York premières have been described above. Herman Klein, in *The Golden Age of Opera*, says of her:

> The Gypsy appeared strutting forward with hand on hip and flower in mouth. ... The voice itself was not remarkable for sweetness or sympathetic charm, though strong and full enough in the middle register, but somehow, its rather thin, penetrating timbre sounded just right in a character whose music called for the expression of heartless sensuality, caprice, cruelty and fantastic defiance.

In her memoirs Minnie Hauk tells how she swayed back and forth on her chair in Act One, trying to fascinate Don José as a serpent charms a bird. One evening she fell over.

Minnie Hauk also seems to have used some eccentric tempi, which Bizet might not have sanctioned. "I brought in different tempi from

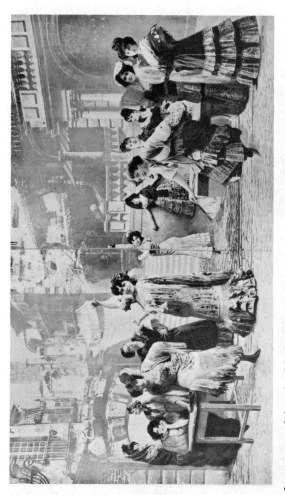

Interpreters of the role of Carmen at the Opéra-Comique. *(From left to right:)* Emma Calvé, Bréval, Delna, Bailac, Chenal, de Nuovina, Maria Gay, Georgette Leblanc, Marié de l'Isle, Deschamps-Jehin, Galli-Marié, Merentié and Vix. From the June 1912 issue of *Musica.*

Galli-Marié as Carmen.

Minnie Hauk as Carmen.

those originally marked in the composer's score, for Bizet only dis-covered his mistakes after the score was printed. Both Maurice Strakosch and Joseph Dupont were intimate friends of Bizet and were familiar with his intended alterations in the score, and with these two men I had studied *Carmen.*"

About Hauk arose one of the strangest legends in operatic history. Perhaps as a planted publicity device, perhaps as a hoax, French periodicals claimed that she was not really American, but Spanish, and that she had been a female bullfighter before turning to opera. The periodical which started the story even gave her "true" name, Manue-lita Cuchares, formerly with the ring-name of "Queen of the Espadas." This unquestionably helped the box office.

Other important Carmens of the early period included Clara Kellogg, who disputed Hauk's première in America; Pauline Lucca, "a very ti-gress with cruel claws ready to dart forth and rend and tear on the small-est provocation. The slightest brush the wrong way turns our fascinating Gypsy into a fiend"; Zélie de Lussan; Mary Garden; and Maria Gay.

Many singers arrived at a position where they considered dramatic mannerisms more important than quality of singing. Mary Garden decided that Carmen was really a *femme fatale*, and slunk around the stage in a most depraved manner. According to her interpretation, Carmen should not dance, since sensuality is better expressed by a pace than a full dance. She did not believe that Carmen should deal out cards in the card scene, carelessly lit a match on the sole of her foot while José was making love to her, and instead of tossing the rose* to José, crushed it into his face.

The greatest Carmen of all, it is generally felt, was Emma Calvé, a soprano of French origin. Those who have heard her early Victor disks can understand her reputation, for in addition to having a dramatic artistry perhaps superior to her rivals, she was also a better singer. As Klein says of her portrayal:

> It had the calm, easy assurance, the calculated dominating power of Galli-Marié's; it had the strong sensual suggestion and defiant resolution of Minnie Hauk's; it had the panther-like quality, the grace, the fatalism, the dangerous impudent coquetry of Pauline Lucca's; it had the spark and vim, the Spanish insouciance and piquancy of Zélie de Lussan's. ... The wonder of the mélange added to exquisite singing made Calvé's assumption from first to last superlative.

---

* Although both Mérimée and the operatic team very specifically mention a yellow cassia-flower, musical folklore and modern performances make it a red rose.

Calvé claimed to have been the first to introduce real Gypsy dancing into her performance. She went to Granada and observed Gypsies for quite a while, and later invited her Gypsy acquaintances to Paris to watch her performance; they thought she was excellent. Needless to say, the press immediately claimed her as a Gypsy in disguise.

Calvé also has the distinction of being the first to introduce the French version of *Carmen* into America, where the Italian translation had hitherto prevailed. At the New York Metropolitan in 1893 she refused to sing the Italian text. Despite the somewhat disingenuous plea by the Metropolitan that no French-singing tenors were available, Calvé managed to come up with no less than the finest tenor of the day, Jean de Reszke, and with him she recreated the role in America.

The most famous Carmen after Emma Calvé was the American singer Geraldine Farrar, who was possibly the first soprano slim enough to look at all the way Carmen should. Miss Farrar accentuated the dramatic possibilities of the role even more than her predecessors, paying a member of the chorus a set fee for each stage assault. She was also the star of the Cecil B. DeMille motion picture *Carmen*.

Yet not all great singers have triumphed in this role; indeed, many singers greater than the successful Carmens have failed in this dramatic role. For the most part these singers have been proponents of the view that Carmen is a refined Spanish girl and not a Gypsy hoyden. Adelina Patti, the greatest female singer of the past century, had her lone failure as Carmen. She had been looking forward to singing the role, since she could play the castanets well, and it was a severe blow when she was hissed at Covent Garden; she later denied ever having sung the part. According to Klein, who witnessed her performance, her faults were that she had (at that time) an insufficient lower register, that she always remained Patti instead of Carmen, and that she insisted upon ornamenting the role with the remarkable coloratura that she alone could manage.

Lilli Lehmann, considered by many the absolute soprano of the late nineteenth century, was also a failure, though it has been claimed that her Carmen was the best sung of all. Lehmann's statuesque, classical style, admirable for Norma or Isolde, proved most unsuitable for Carmen. Olive Fremstad, long a Wagnerian mainstay of the Metropolitan, suffered from the same fault. Within our own time, Rosa Ponselle, the finest recent dramatic soprano, failed at Carmen; according to rumor she retired prematurely because of newspaper criticism.

Geraldine Farrar as Carmen.

Emma Calvé as Carmen.

Enrico Caruso as Don José, a role he first performed at Salerno in 1896.

Lawrence Tibbett as Escamillo.

Three recent interpreters of Carmen. (*From left to right:*) Victoria De Los Angeles (*courtesy Angel Records*), Maria Callas (*courtesy Angel Records*), Leontyne Price (*courtesy RCA Victor Records*).

Don José has attracted many of the finest tenors. In the early period Italo Campanini excelled; he was followed by Jean de Reszke. The finest Don José of all, apparently, was Caruso, who evoked the tragic elements in Don José better than his rivals.

The opera *Carmen* has long been a favorite among singers because it has been one of the few works in the standard repertory which allow dramatic, realistic acting—and also permit the singers to assault one another. The stories of brawls and fracases in performances of *Carmen* are many. Calvé, who played her role roughly at times, once struck the baritone Antonio Scotti a little too vigorously; Scotti responded with a right to her solar plexus that floored her. Scotti may have won by a knockout, but the performance had to be halted for an hour until Calvé recovered her breath. Caruso and Farrar notoriously wrestled all over the stage. Clara Kellogg once broke her collarbone in her struggles. Ravelli, the tenor with the 1885 Mapleson production in New York, swore he would kill Minnie Hauk, and Mapleson had to post a bond for him before the performances could continue. It turned out years later that Ravelli was offended because Hauk would pretend that José had twisted her wrist during one of their quarrels; he felt that this cast aspersions upon his gentility. On another occasion Calvé was performing *Carmen* before the Sultan of Turkey, in what must have been a semi-private performance, when the Sultan suddenly leaped up and fled, convinced that Calvé was going to stab him.

Not all singers and not all managements, however, have agreed with this interpretation, for a counter-interpretation has seen Carmen as basically a very decent, sweet, devoted Spanish girl, capable of great love and commendable for her praise of freedom: it is her misfortune that she grew up in a bad environment. It is hard to say how sincere this interpretation has always been, since one suspects that it is calculated to reassure an audience that might otherwise be prudish and unsympathetic to the play. One thread of this interpretation is that Bizet's *Carmen* has been confused with Mérimée's, and that while Mérimée's Gypsy is a Gypsy wanton, Bizet's is not. This seems to push distinctions too far.

Because of its strong plot *Carmen* has lent itself well to pastiches, reworkings and parodies. It has been turned into a movie several times; the most famous was DeMille's film starring Farrar. In typical Hollywood style, it attempts to "improve" the original: the picture begins with Lillas Pastia approaching Don José in the mountains, trying to bribe him with a handful of gold; it ends with José committing suicide over Carmen's body. Another famous motion picture based upon *Carmen* was *Gypsy Love*, starring Pola Negri.

The most famous pastiche of *Carmen* is, of course, *Carmen Jones*, by Oscar Hammerstein II, with new orchestration (from Bizet) by Robert Russell Bennett; it appeared in 1945·and was quite successful. Other pastiches include *Carmencita and the Soldier*, produced in the 1920's by the Moscow Art Theatre, also translated into English and published in America. As recently as 1962 a Yiddish *Carmen* was given in New York; Miriam (Carmen) had been rescued from the Nazis by the Gypsies, and Escamillo became a border guard in the Negev.

Although it is not generally known, Charles Chaplin made two parody motion pictures of *Carmen*, basing his humor upon the DeMille picture. Chaplin played Don Hosiery; Ben Turpin played El Remendado; John Rand played Escamillo; and Edna Purviance played Carmen. These pictures are considered to be among Chaplin's few failures. Apparently Chaplin was basically undecided whether to play straight or for humor, and Edna Purviance could neither parody nor be tragic. Chaplin is said to have died marvelously at the end.

Two stills from the cigarette factory sequence in the Cecil B. DeMille film version of *Carmen*, 1915, starring Geraldine Farrar.

Still from Charlie Chaplin's 1916 film parody of *Carmen*.

THE MUSIC OF BIZET

I. General Characteristics

Bizet's music is a very strange fusion of modernist and traditional elements, in which the modernist feeling was eventually winning out at the time of his death. To a listener of our own generation, unfortunately, this dynamic struggle within Bizet's music is not too obvious, since we are living several generations after the older "rules" were destroyed. But for Bizet's contemporaries, his music must often have been painful in its seeming arbitrariness.

This mixture of new and old can be found in many aspects of his musical practice. In tonality, or the problem of maintaining an established key, or shifting only to closely related keys, Bizet was very much a modernist. It is reported that the academicians at the première of *Carmen* murmured in horror at modulations that broke the rules. Similarly, Bizet often created chords and combinations of chords that were simply ungrammatical to the conservatives of 1875; that these chords were psychologically sound was ignored. Bizet's orchestration, always one of his strong points, even in his earliest work, was usually highly individual and unexpected, except for the many occasions when he succumbed to the methods of Meyerbeer and Gounod. But in his best work, like *Carmen*, he is sparse, economical, vigorous and original. He seems to have been one of the few composers who have had a special predilection for the wind instruments.

In his melody, however, Bizet was often traditional, and not always beyond criticism, for he sometimes made great concessions to the public or to his singers. *La Jolie Fille de Perth* was rightly criticized, as Bizet himself admitted, because of the unjustifiable vocal ornament which he inserted for the soprano; this backfired in another respect, too, since Nilsson, who was intended to sing the role, did not accept it, and the singer who did accept could not sing the ornament. And in *Carmen* Bizet definitely pandered to the singers in the matters of the "Toreador Song" and the "Habanera." In this, perhaps, we should not blame

Bizet too much, for he has had company. Mozart wrote music that deliberately played up the technical specialties of his prima donnas, and also rewrote music for singers who could not perform his original work.

Where form was concerned, Bizet was in no sense an innovator or experimentalist. Unlike Wagner, he was perfectly content to accept the basic ideas of the *opéra comique*, or other forms, and perhaps stretch them somewhat for his own purposes. In 1875 he was still writing arias as set pieces, and there is no record that he ever protested against them.

During his lifetime Bizet was often called a Wagnerian, but this was an accusation that often meant little more than that the critic did not like the music. Bizet admired much in Wagner's work, but he never imitated it, since Wagner's way of doing things was not his own. Their basic philosophies of relations between music and drama, orchestra and voice, composer and audience, were radically different. Whereas Wagner usually developed his music in a symphonic way, Bizet usually made use of varied restatement within a single "number." After a theme had been presented, Bizet would continue the music by repeating the theme with different orchestration, different dynamics, different harmonies, and occasionally changes of key. Bizet was remarkably skilled in this technique.

The difference between Wagner and Bizet can be seen in their use of musical guideposts, or, in Wagnerian terminology, leitmotifs. For Wagner, in his mature work, the leitmotif or leading theme was the very structure of music; for Bizet, as can be seen in *Carmen*, the leitmotif is simply a characterizing device that is used to indicate the presence of a person or to comment editorially. Dramatically Bizet's leitmotifs are important to the opera; musically, for the most part, they are much less important.

Bizet's strongest point, apart from his technical skills in harmony and orchestration, is his truly remarkable dramatic and coloristic ability. It is sometimes almost incomprehensible how his music, by means of a few notes upon unexpected instruments, can evoke whole landscapes, create characters, indicate mood and even communicate more specific matters. In his youth Bizet occasionally used this remarkable gift to amuse his friends with his *tour de force*, the musical newspaper. He would place a newspaper upon his music rack and extemporize, creating such an incredible synesthesia that his listeners knew well what he was saying. In this area of color and dramatics Bizet has seldom if ever been excelled.

II. NON-OPERATIC MUSIC

Bizet once told his friend Saint-Saëns that the only kind of music that had any real meaning to him was operatic music. This statement holds basically true for his whole life, but he did produce other music as well.

Bizet wrote three significant symphonic works: the juvenile Symphony in *C* of 1855, the *Roma* Symphony and the *Patrie* overture. The first of these, the juvenile Symphony, has been highly praised for its precocity. It is academic, but quite pleasant, and the reader who searches can find in it foreshadowings of the mature Bizet. It is still alive, with several recordings on the American market.

The other symphonic pieces are less esteemed. The *Roma* Symphony, the exact history of which is obscure, was started in Bizet's Prix de Rome days in Italy and was revised, enlarged and redirected several times until it became a somewhat puzzling combination of formal symphony and program music. It has been called confused, pretentious and dull. Bizet's *Patrie* overture, evoked by the Franco-Prussian War, is now seldom performed.

Bizet wrote quite a few songs, mostly in his youth. Most of them, surprisingly enough, are trivial and without much musical interest beyond an occasional flash of local color or characterization. Bizet himself apparently did not take them too seriously. In addition to solo songs, he also wrote a few vocal duets with piano, some sacred music (in which he was admittedly ill at ease) and several cantatas, at which he did not excel.

Despite his prowess as a pianist, Bizet did not write very much piano music, and the little that he did write has almost universally been held in low esteem, with the possible exception of *Jeux d'enfants*; but even this work, a collection of twelve short pieces for four hands, is best liked in the later orchestral version of five pieces made by Bizet in 1871. Bizet's piano music has been called orchestral rather than pianistic, sounding more like a transcription than true piano music. Perhaps this is because Bizet spent so many years preparing just such transcriptions.

All in all, apart from his operatic work Georges Bizet would be considered a very minor composer, but he finds a remarkable parallel here in Richard Wagner, who also was completely obsessed with the operatic dream.

A full listing of Bizet's operas and other works for the stage will be found in the table on pages 58 and 59.

BIZET'S OPERAS AND STAGE WORKS

This table includes only operas that Bizet is definitely known to have worked upon. Works which were completed and survive in full are followed by an asterisk.

TITLE	WRITTEN	FIRST PERFORMED	FIRST PUBLISHED	COMMENTS
1. La Maison du docteur	Before 1856?	None?	—	MS vocal score in Paris Conservatoire.
2. Le Docteur Miracle*	1856 or 1857	1857	—	MS at Paris Conservatoire.
3. Don Procopio*	1858–9	1906 in revised version; 1958 in original form.	1905 (revised)	Full score at Conservatoire.
4. La Guzla de l'Émir	1861–2	—	—	Lost.
5. Les Pêcheurs de perles*	1862–3	1863	1863	First publication differs from later editions.
6. Ivan IV (Ivan le Terrible)*	1865	1946, with adaptations and new libretto.	1951	MS at Conservatoire, last act incomplete.
7. La Jolie Fille de Perth*	1866	1867	1868	First publication differs from later editions.
8. Malbrough s'en va-t-en guerre, first act	1867	1867	—	Lost. Questionable if Bizet finished Act One himself.
9. La coupe du roi de Thulé	1868	—	—	Fragments, only, survive in MS in the Conservatoire and a private collection.

10. Noë	1868–9	1885	1885 (vocal score)	Unfinished opera by F. Halévy, completed by Bizet.
11. Grisélidis	1870–1	—	—	Sketches only, in private collection.
12. Clarissa Harlowe	1870–1	—	—	Sketches only, in Conservatoire.
13. Djamileh*	1871	1872	1872 (vocal score)	—
14. Sol-si-ré-pif-pan	1872?	1872?	—	Lost. Somewhat questionable whether the 1872 production of this name was really by Bizet.
15. L'Arlésienne, incidental music*	1872	1872	1872	—
16. Don Rodrigue	1873	—	—	Fragments only, in Conservatoire.
17. Carmen*	1873–4	1875	1875 (vocal score)	First publication differs from later editions.

MUSICAL ANALYSIS OF "CARMEN"

Overture

Carmen begins with a loud brassy overture, which in instrumental color, rhythmical patterns and melody prefigures the excitement and violence of the opera which is to follow. In its gaiety mingled with sombreness and its vividness the overture also suggests the wild savagery of Andalusia.

The first theme which Bizet uses in the overture is an *allegro giocoso*, which is later used in the crowd scene of Act Four to convey a sense of background for the bullfight:

Suddenly and dramatically the overture shifts key from *A* to *F*—a shift which greatly incensed the academicians of Bizet's day—and the melody that is later associated with the toreador Escamillo is played softly by the violins, violas and cellos, to the accompaniment of staccato chords by the trumpets and trombones:

This section is repeated with full orchestra, and then the music shifts back to the first theme, again in the key of *A*. Soon this recapitulation ends and there is a moment of silence.

This section is repeated with full orchestra, and then the music shifts back to the first theme, again in the key of *A*. Soon this recapitulation ends and there is a moment of silence.

The overture recommences in a new key, *C* minor, which conveys a strong emotional contrast to the bright music of the earlier section: a tremolo of violins, gradually rising in pitch, provides the background for a short motive played by the reeds, trumpets and stringed instruments, with punctuation by the tympani. This is the so-called fate motive (in a briefer, more rapid form it is later used as a musical symbol for Carmen):

This motive is repeated several times, with chromatic alternations, until a sudden dissonant chord interrupts it and ends the overture. This violent ending presumably prefigures the ending of the opera and symbolizes death.

ACT ONE

Act One begins with a few bars of curtain-raising music, much in the general French tradition. A male chorus and a baritone (Morales) exchange comments, while flutes and clarinets play motives in parallel, which the violins echo. The music is light and airy, brief in phrase. There is a shift in key, and a descending violin figure suggesting a mincing or tripping young woman announces Micaëla's appearance upon the stage. Micaëla and Morales exchange words to brisk witty turns of music, with the chorus joining in on occasion. As the music takes on suggestions of farce, Morales and the chorus try to capture Micaëla, but she escapes to the accompaniment of rapid light runs by the flute, reeds and violins. Morales reflects musically, with mock regret, and then returns to his original comments upon the passers-by. The scene ends with a flourish by the chorus. Throughout this first section the music has been light and insinuating, deft and graceful, far more French, especially Parisian, than Spanish.

After a brief pause a trumpet call is heard in the distance, and repeated closer by. Two piccolos then play a weird minor music with many grace notes and unexpected intervals, intermingled with trumpet calls. This is the music of the guard:

After the piccolos have carried the melody several times, the orchestra gradually enters in full; the reeds and strings alternately carry the melody, while trumpet calls sound. Eventually, when the motive has been lifted to full strength and development, a chorus of gamins joins in. Many effects for color appear in the music—such as a triangle—and the melody undergoes several ingenious modulations; the children sing with marked musical stress upon unexpected places, producing a very peculiar effect. This guard theme is repeated several times; it builds up to a statement by the full orchestra and then halts.

In a brief recitative Morales and Don José converse for a moment, after which trumpets sound, the children's chorus resumes its marching song, and the music gradually fades away. Another recitative follows as Zuñiga and Don José discuss the factory girls and Micaëla.

The factory bell rings loudly and mob noises introduce a horde of young men. An *allegretto*, suggestive of ballet movements, briefly anticipates the chorus, which then sings a simple melody fragmented into segments of two measures. The female chorus then enters, and divided into two sections, sings the "Cigarette Song"; this is really a rising scale, with occasional dips to lower notes, suggesting a cyclical, repeated motion. As the two parts of the chorus sing in simple counterpoint, the musical phrases seem to rise like spirals of smoke into the air.

After more crowd noises the male chorus asks where Carmen is. She enters; the violins announce her entrance with a vehement motive derived from the fate motive of the overture. It is appropriate at this point to observe how cleverly Bizet has characterized his *personae*: Morales with suave, ironic, witty music; Micaëla with music suggestive of rapid motion and youth; Carmen with impetuosity and ungoverned passion.

Carmen and the male chorus converse. The chorus asks Carmen when she will love them; Carmen replies laughingly in a quasi-recitative with many changes of key. After a few introductory measures have established a tango-like bass figure in the cellos, Carmen begins the well-known "Habanera," which Bizet adapted from a song by Yradier:

L'amour   est un oi-seau re -bel-le Que nul   ne   peut ap-pri-voi-ser,

To the bass figure Carmen sings the beautiful line of the "Habanera," supported sometimes by the violins. She pauses at the end of each long phrase, and the chorus repeats her melody while Carmen intones

The beginning of the "Habanera" from Bizet's manuscript score of *Carmen*. (*Department of Music, Bibliothèque Nationale, Paris; photo courtesy Bibliothèque Nationale*)

The beginning of the "Toreador Song" from Bizet's manuscript score of *Carmen.*
(*Department of Music, Bibliothèque Nationale, Paris; photo courtesy Bibliothèque
Nationale*)

"*amour*" in contrast. Carmen and the chorus repeat the figure several times with varying orchestration and dynamics until the "Habanera" finally ends in a burst of mocking laughter.

With feverish short phrases the male chorus again proposes to Carmen, but she, to the background of the Carmen–fate motive in violins and violas, approaches Don José and throws her flower to him. After a moment of silence the female chorus briefly mocks José, laughs, and streams off the stage as the factory bell rings. The orchestra continues with the Carmen motive and fragments of the "Cigarette Song."

José, alone on the stage, sings a recitative about his reactions to Carmen, while the orchestra plays first the Carmen–fate motive, then a very sweetly orchestrated phrase from the "Habanera," with flutes, clarinets, bassoons and horns.

Micaëla enters to rapid pattering music, like that of her first entrance; she and José sing first individually, then finally in true duet. The two personalities are indicated by their music: José's short in phrase, narrow in range, and sometimes harsh in harmony and intervals; Micaëla's more flowing, more conventional in melody and harmony. As Micaëla talks of José's mother, the music achieves a lush, smothering orchestration with harp arpeggios, evoking an atmosphere that is almost religious in its suggestions of sanctity and incredible goodness. José sings in ecstasy about his memories of the past, while Micaëla comments with innocent enthusiasm about José's rapture.* The orchestra closes this section and Don José, in recitative, reads his mother's letter after Micaëla has left. While the orchestra plays themes from his mother's music and the Carmen motive, José reads, denounces Carmen as a witch, and again rhapsodizes about the past. There is a sudden interruption.

A burst of mob music from the orchestra is accompanied by shouts; workers stream in, with a whirling musical figure that suggests milling crowds. Staccato chords, two female choruses singing strophe and antistrophe to one another, sudden shifts of key, and heavy syncopation all convey the wild turmoil as the women surround Zuñiga and alternately blame Carmen for the fracas in the factory and exonerate her. As the music grows more and more frantic, Zuñiga sends José into the factory, and as the mob scene ends, José and Carmen come on the stage.

In recitative José reports what has happened, and Zuñiga interrogates Carmen. Carmen will not answer civilly, and replies with "tra-la-las" and fragments of a ballad. The orchestration becomes fuller, and

* In performance this duet is often cut, usually the latter part.

when Carmen ends, violins repeat her cadenza-like melody. Everyone leaves the stage except Carmen and José; Carmen thereupon tells José in recitative to release her.

After a brief orchestral section, in which a solo flute anticipates the melody, Carmen begins the long melodic line of the "Seguidilla," while the orchestra plays a rhythmic bass; pizzicato violins and cellos provide syncopated staccato chords:

Près des rem-parts de Sé   vil -   -le,

Chez_ mon a - mi _ Lil-las   Pas tia ____

Bizet designated this piece of music a Seguidilla, which is, properly speaking, a dance form, usually of Gypsy origin. Authorities upon Spanish music consider Bizet's dance to be only suggestive of a true Seguidilla.

After a recitative interruption by Don José, Carmen repeats the Seguidilla with other variations in texture, one of which is so light and bewitching that it overcomes José's resolution. When he asks her if she will really become his mistress, she responds in a very sensuous, bouncy stanza, with full lush orchestration.

Zuñiga returns and Carmen and José start to leave the stage, with Carmen singing "*amour*" from the "Habanera" derisively to Zuñiga. Flutes modulate upon the "Habanera," there are repetitions of the crowd music and argument music, there is much shouting and running around as Carmen breaks away, and an exciting orchestral passage closes the act.

Act Two

The second act begins with a brief Entr'acte which is an orchestral anticipation of the unaccompanied song which Don José will later sing. Bassoons, against a pizzicato background of all the strings, and snare drums, introduce the melody, which is repeated several times as flutes, clarinets and other instruments join in.

A brief instrumental prelude to Carmen's "Gypsy Song" is played by flutes, harps, violas and cellos, and then Carmen sings her dancing song:

In the course of each stanza, the oboe echoes her, and she and Frasquita and Mercedes sing a "tra-la-la" refrain. With each stanza the music grows wilder and faster and more frenzied, until it becomes a veritable bacchanale, what with semi-oriental cadences in the background, thumping drums, triangles and cymbals, and the thud of naked feet. As Carmen and the other Gypsies stop singing, the orchestra bursts forth into a bedlam of sound, abandoning itself to a raging ecstasy, suddenly to end in a trilling dissonant chord, with a very brief resolution.

The soldiers in the inn and the Gypsy girl talk in recitative, until an unaccompanied male chorus outside the inn sings *viva*'s like trumpet calls. As the procession for Escamillo is announced, the orchestra supplements the chorus, and the Gypsies and soldiers join the singing. To a lively march-like piece of instrumental music the bullfighter enters the inn.

Escamillo now sings his toast to the soldiers and girls, first the arrogant, barbaric music of the bullring, and then the famous refrain known as the "Song of the Toreador":

Bizet marked this music to be sung "*avec fatuité*" (conceitedly); it is pompous and brassy, with many crashing chords; the chorus assists occasionally. During the last repetition the women join in a complex musical figure, introducing the concept of *l'amour*. Chorus, orchestra and singers finish with a flourish.

After a brief recitative in which Escamillo and Carmen converse, the pompous bullring music begins again and dies away in the distance as the procession moves away, vanishing in softened chromatic harmonizations of the melody.

After another recitative, when El Remendado and El Dancaïro enter, the great Quintet begins with Carmen, Frasquita, Mercedes and the two men. An extremely light and ebullient piece of music with strong comic elements, it is a marvel of complexity in both overlapping and interlocking figures and ensembles. Half-whispered at times, it is almost a patter song in its clever syncopation and rhythmic ingenuity. In the second part of the Quintet the orchestra takes the melody for a time, while the singers in unison and very close harmony add new material. Many variations are provided for the two basic themes.

After a recitative in which the Gypsies and Carmen converse, José's voice sounds from the distance singing an unaccompanied ballad. Although this music sounds like an authentic ballad of folkloristic provenience, it seems to have been composed by Bizet without special reference to Spanish sources. The voice comes closer and closer, and José enters after the others, except Carmen, have left.

Carmen and José converse in quasi-recitative, after which Carmen sings a greeting song in which she offers to dance; her music is surprisingly dainty and formal at this point, indicating ironic courtesy.

Carmen now dances for Don José, singing "la-la-la" to herself, to keep time; her only accompaniment is the string section which joins in at the end of phrases with pizzicato chords. If the production is fortunate enough to have a singer who can play castanets, she often uses them as she dances, though technically Gypsy dancing does not use castanets. As Carmen dances, gradually building up passion, distant bugles are heard, forming, after a short time, a very interesting counterpoint to her song—one of the most attractive musical moments in the opera:

José interrupts her, telling her it is roll call, but Carmen, perhaps pretending to misunderstand, simply continues her counterpoint to the bugles, now deliberately shaping her dance and music to the rhythm of the bugles. José interrupts her again. Carmen, in a torrent of rage which is paralleled by the orchestra, abandons herself to abuse and recrimination, imitating bugle calls and mocking José. José replies in a pathetic, bleating aria, while Carmen continues to mock him with crescendos of rage. Carmen and José sing a discordant duet as the music becomes more and more violent.

After the English horn and tremolo violins present the fate motive, José sings the "Flower Song":

La fleur que tu m'avais je - té - e, Dans

ma pri-son— m'é-tait res - té - e,

Typically French, perhaps the work of a superior Meyerbeer, this is a set piece all too reminiscent of Hollywood musical scores. José finally finishes to the accompaniment of harp arpeggios and very sweet harmonies.

Carmen and José join in a duet. Just as José is leaving, a knock is heard on the door and Zuñiga enters to sinister music. To light, suave, sarcastic music, he scolds Carmen. When he strikes José there is a loud dissonant chord.

The music becomes mockingly serene as Carmen now informs Zuñiga that he must be held captive and the other Gypsies follow in a masterful assumption of ironic courtesy, almost a fugue in complexity. The act ends with an ensemble in which previous themes—those of the Quintet, the chords which Bizet used while Carmen talked of freedom and other ideas are all worked together.

Act Three

The third act begins with an Entr'acte which Bizet had probably originally written for *L'Arlésienne*, but did not use. Critics have often pointed out that this music, with its suggestions of open countryside, smiling verdure and rustic tranquility, does not suit *Carmen* very well, but Bizet included it, and it is usually played.

In this intermezzo a flute sounds a clear simple melody, accompanied by a harp; as the music becomes more complex other instruments enter; a solo clarinet and strings. The full orchestra eventually takes part, with modulations and variations of the theme, which is presented by the bassoon and English horn. All then clears away back to flutes and harps and a few other instruments.

The sinister "Smugglers' March" begins with hollow chords which are a marvel of structure; the flute carries the melody while the violas and cellos play a pizzicato bass line. As the dissonances increase, the music becomes more complex, conveying the image of hordes of people creeping around in the dark. Eventually the male chorus enters. Woodwinds and violins take the melody and for a time the men sing the accompaniment. The five Gypsy characters and Don José then enter with a fresh theme in a very dissonant harmony after which the entire group goes back to the main theme of the "Smugglers' March."

El Dancaïro, in recitative, tells the Gypsies to halt for a time, and then the "Smugglers' March" breaks out again briefly.

Carmen and José converse. As José talks about his mother, the saccharine sequences from his conversation with Micaëla appear again; as he and Carmen argue, the fate motive appears in the orchestral background. Carmen and Don José part company and the "Card Song" begins.

The two Gypsy girls Frasquita and Mercedes deal out cards and read their fortunes while singing a very light, very graceful duet, semi-humorous in tone, showing that they know their predictions are all nonsense:

Contrasted to this delicate music is Carmen's entry with discordant figures, sombreness and slow melody. Carmen sees her fate in the cards and takes it seriously. Textures contrast greatly in this trio as Carmen sings her lament against the tinkling patter of the other two Gypsies:

El Dancaïro returns and describes the city guard in recitative. The three girls thereupon break into a very light, leaping dance music as they prance off to seduce the guards. All but José leave the stage.

Micaëla enters with light, tripping music, as in the first act. After some recitative, she sings her big aria, "Micaëla's Prayer." The harmony here is very lush, with horns and harps and strings, and the melody is typically French:

Je dis,— que rien ne m'é-pou - van - te Je— dis,— hé - las!

Don José shoots at Escamillo, who then enters. They converse and then sing a duet together as they prepare to fight. Don José's music, as usual, is gnarled; Escamillo's carries suggestions of pomposity and self-satisfaction. While Escamillo sings ironically, Don José murmurs "Carmen" in the background. The two men fight, with sharp violin strokes indicating blows.

The Gypsies interrupt the fight; Escamillo maintains his usual aplomb, and with combined amorousness and self-esteem asks Carmen to attend the next bullfight; following this, the cellos and clarinets play the Toreador motive softly and sweetly.

Micaëla is caught lurking in the rocks, and Carmen and José quarrel again, with angry music, while Micaëla, as she sings about José's mother, is given the usual lush harmony and orchestration. While Carmen and the chorus urge José to leave, José refuses in a passage of descending flurries of notes. After further exchange, he tells Carmen he is leaving, while the orchestra first plays the fate motive in woodwinds and horns, and then shifts to the Toreador theme, as Escamillo is heard in the distance. Music taken from the opening chorus of the act ends the scene.

ACT FOUR

The Entr'acte begins with the music of the bull arena, as heavy brass figures are followed by a thrumming pizzicato of stringed instruments. In the background brushed cymbals create a rhythmic Spanish pattern; however, some conductors, like Toscanini, substitute castanets for the cymbals. An oboe introduces a sweetly tragic theme, while dance rhythms persist in the rest of the orchestra.

After the Entr'acte ends, there are two musical possibilities within the production of the opera *Carmen*. The producer can use the so-called ballet version, in which a ballet occupies the first part of the last act. In this form of *Carmen*, dance music may be borrowed from *La Jolie Fille de Perth*, and a chorus from *L'Arlésienne*. If the producer prefers to stage *Carmen* as Bizet wrote it, the procession music is used. The procession music is described here.

As the curtain rises, the orchestra shifts into heavy syncopation, while male and female choruses shout street cries, somewhat like a round. The procession then begins, with bullfight music, trumpet calls and choral figures. As each *cuadrilla* enters, the chorus of men, women and children comments, cheers and insults. Escamillo, the *espada*, enters last. (It has been pointed out that Bizet and his librettists violated the ceremonial order of the *cuadrilla*, and that the *espadas*, who were two, not just one, should enter first. Dramatic reasons were probably behind this departure from actual practice.)

Escamillo enters to the very brassy accompaniment of his "Toreador Song" theme. When the grand march ends, Escamillo and Carmen sing a brief duet, "*Si tu m'aimes*." The light, fluttery music of the Gypsies announces Frasquita and Mercedes, who warn Carmen that José is present in the crowd.

The march of the *cuadrilla* begins again and the crowd streams into the arena with shouts and cries, leaving Carmen and José alone outside. They first greet one another in semi-recitative, then gradually, as the music grows more and more animated, sing a true duet. Notes of hysteria enter José's music, and sinister minor chords signal the approaching end. After José tells Carmen that he still loves her and Carmen triumphantly sings that she will never yield, the offstage chorus sings a portion of the *cuadrilla* march.

Carmen and José continue their dispute while rising storms in the orchestra are followed by further backstage music; the fate motive is sounded strongly. The chorus sings a fragment of the "Toreador Song," with wailing cellos added. As José stabs Carmen the fate motive breaks in again during Don José's emotion-fraught closing statement, which reaches its climax after its opening note has been repeated ten times. The opera ends with an orchestral echo of Don José's last notes, and one final reiterated chord.

SPANISH MUSIC AND
GEORGES BIZET

Most listeners consider *Carmen* to be the great exemplar of Spanish music, and find that Bizet's work evokes the Spain that they have created mentally, but musicologists (and Spaniards) agree that *Carmen* is primarily French music and owes relatively little directly to Spanish music.

In all probability Georges Bizet knew very little about Spanish music, either classical or popular. He had never been in Spain and Spanish music does not seem to have been played much in Paris during his productive period. Indeed, the only evidence that Bizet ever made any special effort to examine Spanish music is a library slip for the Paris Conservatoire, written just before the composition of *Carmen*; on this slip Bizet asked for information about collections of Spanish songs. It has also been suggested that Bizet's friend Sarasate, the Spanish violinist, may have recommended musical models, and that Bizet's presence in the Rossini circle, which had Spanish connections, may have provided background.

While Bizet copied dance rhythms in many places, wrote the "Seguidilla" in imitation of Spanish forms, and imitated the flamenco guitar style in the "Gypsy Song," at present we can identify only a few direct influences in his work. First is a song called "El Arreglito," written by the Spanish-American composer Sebastián Yradier (who also wrote "La Paloma"). Somewhere Bizet seems to have heard this music, for he incorporated it bodily in his opera, with only minor changes, as the "Habanera." He apparently considered it a popular song without definite authorship. When Yradier's publisher protested at its use, Bizet acknowledged his debt to Yradier in a footnote in the score. It should be noted, however, that this song is Latin American in style rather than Spanish.

A quotation from Yradier's melody and refrain will show exactly what Bizet did to alter it:

As might be expected, there is a difference of opinion about Bizet's
changes. Critics working from a background in Northern European
music agree that Bizet improved it; critics like Gilbert Chase who look
at *Carmen* from a Spanish point of view can demonstrate that Bizet
spoiled it. The listener can decide for himself.

The second identifiable piece of music that Bizet used is Carmen's
defiance ballad in the first act. Istel, a German musicologist, has
discovered that this is a very close rendering of a mocking song once
sung in Ciudad P.al in Spain about the strange coiffures affected by
the ladies—large enough to carry forty chairs, benches, etc. Where
Bizet came upon this music is unknown, perhaps from Sarasate.

Bizet's most important Spanish source, however, seems to have been
a *polo* (rapid, highly syncopated music, based on a dance form, sung
with elaborate coloratura on certain syllables) written by the famous
tenor and composer Manuel García. García is also famous not only as
the father of the great singers Malibran and Pauline Viardot and the
voice teacher Manuel García the younger, but as the man who
introduced Italian opera into America. García, who was an associate
of Rossini's, and a famous man in his own right, died in Paris; it
would seem almost inconceivable that Bizet would not be aware of
him and consult his work.

Bizet adapted a *polo* by García, the song "Cuerpo bueno, alma
divina," to create the music for the Entr'acte to Act Four, and possibly
used other parts of the *polo* for the fate–Carmen theme. Other influences
of tonality and cadence from García's *polo* occur elsewhere in *Carmen*,
so that, as Gilbert Chase has pointed out, Manuel García deserves to
be called "the grandfather of *Carmen*."

THE TEXT

There are two essentially different versions of *Carmen*: the grand opera and the *opéra comique*.

The grand opera version of *Carmen* is the one that we all know, the *Carmen* that is performed everywhere, with one exception. The term grand opera, however, in this technical sense does not mean that the opera is different in staging, general outlook or performance; it simply means that there are no spoken parts in the opera. Instead there are recitatives in certain places, where the actors recite their lines in a conventional declamatory style, halfway between speech and song, to a sparse, often conventionalized instrumental background.

Georges Bizet himself was not responsible for the grand opera version of Carmen, and did not even live long enough to hear it. His friend Guiraud prepared it, abridging the original spoken dialogue and turning it into recitative, to a musical accompaniment based upon Bizet's themes. This is the usual version of *Carmen*.

The *Carmen* that Georges Bizet and his associates Halévy and Meilhac staged in 1875, however, was not a grand opera. Instead, it was technically an *opéra comique* or comic opera. This does not mean that it was intended to be humorous; it simply means that it conformed to certain conventions of the French stage, the most important of which were complete cessation of the music at times and the presence of spoken passages.

Two important *opéra comique* versions of *Carmen* must be mentioned. In the 1875 presentation, there were long sections of spoken dialogue and monologue between the musical numbers. There were also two musical numbers (with vocal parts) which were later dropped by Bizet some time in 1875, after the first few performances. These were Morales's pantomime in Act One and part of the duel between Don José and Escamillo in Act Three.

The second *opéra comique* version of *Carmen*, a greatly abridged form of the original 1875 work, is now performed only at the Opéra-Comique in Paris; there it is the established text. This is the only place in the world where Guiraud's recitatives are not used, and even here Micaëla's recitative when she comes upon the stage in Act Three has been retained.

The use of speech instead of recitative makes this Opéra-Comique *Carmen* closer to Bizet's original intention than the grand opera, and it does not suffer from the addition of another man's music. But it is too limited in performance to be used as a basis for this book. It is presented at only one house in Paris, and, as far as can be determined, it has been put upon the world market in only one record set, which has been out of print in the United States for many years.

There have been other major revisions of *Carmen*, but it is very unlikely that they are performed any more. In the revival of 1883 a bowdlerized version was given, but this *Carmen*, fortunately, has disappeared from the stage. There also used to be a Vienna version, in which Guiraud's recitatives were combined with fragments of the older spoken text, since Jauner, the director of the Vienna opera, felt that Guiraud's material was too scanty. This Viennese text was used for the *Carmen* that was given in Brussels in 1876 and (in an Italian translation) was the *Carmen* that first spread over Europe. It was later driven off the stage by Guiraud's version. In 1900 it was finally retired in Vienna by Gustav Mahler, who adopted the modern grand opera.

The following table summarizes the important versions of *Carmen*.

I. *Opéra comique.*
   A. The 1875 version as first staged.
   B. The 1875 version with certain cuts, as staged later in the same season.
   C. The established text currently used at the Opéra-Comique in Paris. The spoken passages have been greatly abridged from the 1875 versions.

II. Grand opera.
   A. Guiraud's adaptation. All spoken passages have been omitted and sections of recitative have been added by Guiraud. This is the standard version (with some fluidity of text on small points) that is almost universally performed.
   B. The Vienna text. A mixture of Guiraud's recitatives with some spoken material. This text is apparently dead.

The first part of Act Four was also changed by Guiraud. Bizet and his librettists wrote a street scene in which hordes of peddlers and concessionaires swarm among the onlookers. This did not please the Vienna management, and in addition to his other changes, Guiraud was commissioned to prepare a ballet. Guiraud combined the "Bohemian Dance" from *La Jolie Fille de Perth* and a chorus from *L'Arlésienne*. The resulting ballet sequence was almostly universally used in Europe and America well into the twentieth century, instead of Bizet's own crowd scene. Here again the gap between printed texts and actual performance opens, for most printed texts of the nineteenth century gave the street scene.

At present Bizet's street music seems to be preferred, especially on record sets, where it is more effective than the purely ballet music, and a ballet is only occasionally given. Where the ballet is performed, in most instances, nowadays, it is performed to Bizet's street scene music, but with a new set of words. It is uncertain exactly where these words arose, but they were in existence by the last part of the nineteenth century. They are given along with the street scene words in the basic libretto.*

*   *   *

In this volume Guiraud's grand opera has been used as the basic text, following Schirmer's vocal and piano score on specific points. It is true that there is great variation in small details between various live performances and recordings, as the reader can hear for himself: words may be added, omitted, or changed, according to the singing traditions of the vocal group or house that happens to be performing. But these differences are almost always trivial, and Schirmer's remains as close to a standard text as is generally available in America.

In addition to the Schirmer text of Guiraud's grand opera *Carmen*, we have included at the end of this book an apparatus for comparing the grand opera with the other two most important texts, the 1875 full *opéra comique* and the abridged *opéra comique* currently staged in Paris.

This material serves two purposes. First, Guiraud's pruning, it is generally conceded, was much too drastic in omitting material that provided background, explained motivations, or developed character. Many of the puzzling situations and seeming illogicalities in the grand opera (such as the unexplained appearance of Micaëla in Act Three) were adequately explained in the libretto as Halévy and Meilhac originally wrote it. The reader who examines this collateral text will

---

* The words for the ballet scene are given on the first three left-hand pages of Act Four, the words for the crowd scene on the first three right-hand pages.

find his understanding of the opera deepened. In addition, within the past few years, there has been a revival of interest in the full 1875 text and a tendency to return to it (in varying degree). Germany and England have led in this development, and besides local performances London and Essen have seen the original *Carmen* staged. In all probability this trend will continue, even though it is unlikely that the grand opera version of *Carmen* will soon be dethroned.

CARMEN

Opera in Four Acts
Music by Georges Bizet
Libretto by Henri Meilhac
and
Ludovic Halévy

Set design for Act 1 by Nicola Benois. *(Courtesy Teatro di San Carlo, Naples)*

ACT ONE

Scene One

A square in Seville, around 1820. On the right side of the stage is a door leading to the tobacco factory. At the back of the stage is a bridge crossing the entire stage; the bridge is sturdy, so that actors can walk upon it. At the right, near the door to the tobacco factory, is a spiral stairway leading to the bridge. At the left is the guardhouse, which rises two or three stories, with balconies. In front of the guardhouse stands a rack, against which the soldiers have leaned their lances and pennants.

As the curtain rises about fifteen soldiers (dragoons of the regiment of Alcalá) are seen grouped in front of the guardhouse. Some are seated, smoking; others are leaning over the balustrades of the balcony. The square is lively with people, who pass back and forth, meet, greet one another, and so on.

TENORS, BASSES: Sur la place, chacun passe, chacun vient, chacun va; drôles de gens que ces gens-là! Drôles de gens que ces gens-là!

BASSES: Drôles de gens!

TENORS: Drôles de gens!

TENORS, BASSES: Drôles de gens que ces gens-là!

BASSES: Drôles de gens! Drôles de gens!

TENORS, BASSES: Drôles de gens!

BASSES: Drôles de gens!

TENORS, BASSES: In the square everyone goes by, everyone is coming, everyone is going; what odd people these people are! What odd people these people are!

BASSES: Odd people!

TENORS: Odd people!

TENORS, BASSES: What odd people these people are!

BASSES: Odd people! Odd people!

TENORS, BASSES: Odd people!

BASSES: Odd people!

TENORS, BASSES: Drôles de gens!

MORALÈS: À la porte du corps de garde, pour tuer le temps, on fume, on jase, l'on regarde passer les passants. Sur la place, chacun passe, chacun vient, chacun va.

TENORS, BASSES: Sur la place, chacun passe, chacun vient, chacun va; drôles de gens que ces gens-là! Drôles de gens que ces gens-là!

BASSES: Drôles de gens!

TENORS: Drôles de gens!

TENORS, BASSES: Drôles de gens que ces gens-là!

MORALÈS: Drôles de gens!

BASSES: Drôles de gens!

TENORS, BASSES: Drôles de gens!

{ MORALÈS: Drôles de gens!

BASSES: Drôles de gens!

MORALÈS, TENORS, BASSES: Drôles de gens!

TENORS, BASSES: Odd people!

MORALES: At the guardhouse door, to kill the time, you smoke, you chat, you watch the passers-by. In the square everyone goes by, everyone is coming, everyone is going.

TENORS, BASSES: In the square everyone goes by, everyone is coming, everyone is going; what odd people these people are! What odd people these people are!

BASSES: Odd people!

TENORS: Odd people!

TENORS, BASSES: What odd people these people are!

MORALES: Odd people!

BASSES: Odd people!

TENORS, BASSES: Odd people!

MORALES: Odd people!

BASSES! Odd people!

MORALES, TENORS, BASSES: Odd people!

Micaëla enters; she is wearing a blue skirt, and has long braids. She seems timid and hesitant, and is obviously uncertain about addressing the soldiers.

MORALÈS: Regardez donc cette petite qui semble vouloir nous parler. Voyez, voyez! elle tourne, elle hésite.

TENORS, BASSES: À son secours il faut aller!

MORALÈS (*to Micaëla*): Que cherchez-vous, la belle?

MICAËLA: Moi, je cherche un brigadier.

MORALES: Look at that girl who seems to want to talk to us. Look, look! She's turning, she is hesitant.

TENORS, BASSES: We have to go and help her!

MORALES (*to Micaëla*): Are you looking for something, Miss?

MICAËLA: I'm looking for a corporal.

MORALÈS: Je suis là, voilà!

MICAËLA: Mon brigadier à moi s'appelle Don José. Le connaissez-vous?

MORALÈS: Don José! Nous le connaissons tous.

MICAËLA: Vraiment! est-il avec vous, je vous prie?

MORALÈS: Il n'est pas brigadier dans notre compagnie.

MICAËLA (*disappointed*): Alors, il n'est pas là?

MORALÈS: Non, ma charmante, non, ma charmante, il n'est pas là; mais tout à l'heure il y sera, oui, tout à l'heure il y sera, il y sera quand la garde montante remplacera la garde descendante.

MORALÈS, TENORS, BASSES: Il y sera quand la garde montante remplacera la garde descendante.

MORALÈS: Mais en attendant qu'il vienne, voulez-vous, la belle enfant, voulez-vous prendre la peine d'entrer chez nous un instant?

MICAËLA: Chez vous?

MORALÈS, TENORS, BASSES: Chez nous!

MICAËLA: Chez vous?

MORALÈS, TENORS, BASSES: Chez nous!

MICAËLA: Non pas, non pas, grand merci, messieurs les soldats.

MORALES: I'm one. There!

MICAËLA: The corporal I mean is called Don José. Do you know him?

MORALES: Don José? We all know him.

MICAËLA: Really! Is he with you?

MORALES: He's not a corporal in our company.

MICAËLA (*disappointed*): Then he isn't here?

MORALES: No, my charming girl, no, my charming girl, he isn't here; but he will be here any minute, yes, he will be here any minute, he will be here when the new guard relieves the old guard.

MORALES, TENORS, BASSES: He will be here when the new guard relieves the old guard.

MORALES: But while you're waiting for him to come, would you care to come in with us for a little while, my pretty child?

MICAËLA: In there with you?

MORALES, TENORS, BASSES: In here!

MICAËLA: In there with you?

MORALES, TENORS, BASSES: In here!

MICAËLA: Oh, no; oh, no; thank you very much, sirs.

MORALÈS: Entrez sans crainte, mignonne, je vous promets qu'on aura pour votre chère personne tous les égards qu'il faudra.

MORALES: You needn't be afraid to come in, sweetheart; I promise you that you'll be treated with all due respect.

MICAËLA: Je n'en doute pas, cependant, je reviendrai, je reviendrai, c'est plus prudent. Je reviendrai quand la garde montante remplacera la garde descendante.

MICAËLA: I don't doubt it at all, but I'll return, I'll return. It's more prudent. I'll come back when the new guard relieves the old guard.

Je reviendrai quand la garde montante remplacera la garde descendante.

I'll come back when the new guard relieves the old guard.

MORALÈS, TENORS, BASSES: Il faut rester car la garde montante va remplacer la garde descendante.

MORALES, TENORS, BASSES: You should stay, for the new guard is about to relieve the old guard.

MORALÈS: Vous resterez—

MORALES: You'll stay—

MICAËLA: Non pas, non pas!

MICAËLA: Oh, no; oh, no!

MORALÈS, TENORS, BASSES: Vous resterez—

MORALES, TENORS, BASSES: You'll stay—

Soldiers crowd around Micaëla.

MICAËLA: Non pas, non pas! Non, non! non! non! non!

MICAËLA: Oh, no; oh, no! No, no, no, no, no!

MORALÈS, TENORS, BASSES: Vous resterez, vous resterez, oui, vous resterez, vous resterez!

MORALES, TENORS, BASSES: You'll stay, you'll stay, yes, you'll stay, you'll stay!

Soldiers pretend to have Micaëla surrounded.

MICAËLA: Au revoir, messieurs les soldats!

MICAËLA: Au revoir, sirs!

Micaëla escapes and runs off the stage.

MORALÈS: L'oiseau s'envole, on s'en console, reprenons notre passetemps et regardons passer les gens.

MORALES: The bird's flown, we have to console ourselves; let's resume our pastime and watch the people passing by.

TENORS, BASSES: Sur la place, chacun passe, chacun vient, chacun va; drôles de gens que ces gens-là! Drôles de gens que ces gens-là!

BASSES: Drôles de gens!

TENORS: Drôles de gens!

{ TENORS, BASSES: Drôles de gens que ces gens-là!

MORALÈS: Drôles de gens!

BASSES: Drôles de gens!

{ TENORS, BASSES: Drôles de gens!

MORALÈS: Drôles de gens!

BASSES: Drôles de gens!

MORALÈS, TENORS, BASSES: Drôles de gens!

TENORS, BASSES: In the square everyone goes by, everyone is coming, everyone is going; what odd people these people are! what odd people these people are!

BASSES: Odd people!

TENORS: Odd people!

TENORS, BASSES: What odd people these people are!

MORALES: Odd people!

BASSES: Odd people!

TENORS, BASSES: Odd people!

MORALES: Odd people!

BASSES: Odd people!

MORALES, TENORS, BASSES: Odd people!

Scene Two

In the far distance is heard a military march, with bugles and fifes. It is the new guard coming to relieve the old guard. The soldiers on post come out of the guardhouse, pick up their lances, and fall in in front of the guardhouse. In the square people gather in groups to watch the changing of the guard. The music comes nearer and nearer, and finally the new guard enters the stage from the left. Two bugles and two fifes comes first, then a band of street boys who march with exaggeratedly long strides to match the soldiers. Behind the children march Lieutenant Zuñiga and Corporal Don José, then the dragoons with their lances.

CHORUS OF BOYS: Avec la garde montante, nous arrivons, nous voilà! Sonne, trompette éclatante! Ta ra ta ta ta ra ta ta. Nous marchons la tête haute

CHORUS OF BOYS: We've come with the new guard, we're coming, here we are! Sound out, blaring bugle! Ta ra ta ta ta ra ta ta. We're marching

comme de petits soldats, marquant sans faire de faute, une,
deux, marquant le pas. Les
épaules en arrière, et la poitrine
en dehors, les bras de cette
manière, tombant tout le long
du corps. Avec la garde montante, nous arrivons, nous voilà!
Sonne, trompette éclatante, ta
ra ta ta ta ra ta ta, ta ra ta ta
ra ta ta, ta ra ta ta ra ta ta ta,
ta ra ta ta ra ta ta ra ta ta ra ta
ta ra ta ta ra ta ta ta; ta ra ta
ta ra ta ta, ta ra ta ta ra ta ta
ta, ta ra ta ta ra ta ta ra ta ta
ra ta ta ra ta ta ra ta ta ta. Nous
marchons la tête haute comme
de petits soldats, marquant sans
faire de faute, une, deux, marquant le pas, les épaules en
arrière et la poitrine en dehors,
les bras de cette manière,
tombant tout le long du corps,
nous arrivons! Nous voilà! Ta
ra ta ta ra ta ta ra ta ta ta ta,
ta ra ta ta.

with our heads high like little
soldiers, keeping step without
a mistake, one, two, keeping
step. Shoulders back, chest out,
arms like this, aligned with our
bodies. We are coming with the
new guard, here we are! Sound
out, blaring bugle, ta ra ta ta ta
ra ta ta, ta ra ta ta ra ta ta, ta ra
ta ta ra ta ta ta, ta ra ta ta ra ta
ta ra ta ta ra ta ta ra ta ta ra
ta ta ta; ta ra ta ta ra ta ta, ta
ra ta ta ra ta ta, ta ra ta ta
ra ta ta ra ta ta ra ta ta ra ta
ta ra ta ta. We are marching
with our heads high like little
soldiers, keeping step without a
mistake, one, two, keeping
step; shoulders back, chest out,
arms like this, aligned with our
bodies, we are coming! Here
we are! Ta ra ta ta ra ta ta ra
ta ta ta ta, ta ra ta ta.

*The new guard is drawn up on the right, facing the old guard.
While the children are still singing, the officers salute one another
with their swords and speak to one another in low voices. The
sentinels are changed.*

MORALÈS (*to Don José*): Une jeune
fille charmante vient de nous
demander si tu n'étais pas là!
Jupe bleue et natte tombante.
DON JOSÉ: Ce doit être Micaëla.

MORALES (*to Don José*): A charming girl just asked us if you
weren't here! Blue skirt and
long braids.
DON JOSÉ: That must be Micaëla.

*Bugles sound. The old guard parades before the new guard. The
street urchins take their place behind the bugles and fifes and the
old guard marches off the stage to the left.*

Set design for Act 1 by Wakhevitch. (*Courtesy Royal Opera House, Covent Garden, London; photo by Derek Allen*)

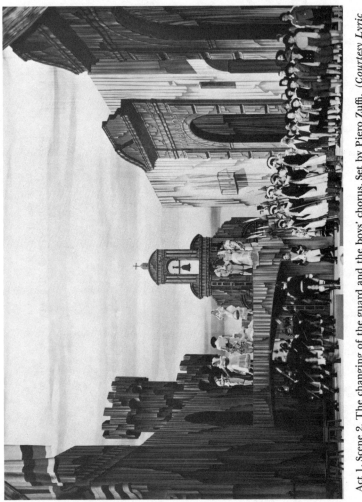

Act 1, Scene 2. The changing of the guard and the boys' chorus. Set by Piero Zuffi. *(Courtesy Lyric Opera of Chicago)*

CHORUS OF BOYS: Et la garde descendante rentre chez elle et s'en va. Sonne, trompette éclatante! Ta ra ta ta ta ra ta ta. Nous marchons la tête haute comme de petits soldats, marquant sans faire de faute, une, deux, marquant le pas. Ta ra ta ta ra ta ta, ta ra ta ta ra ta ta ta, ta ra ta ta ra ta ta ra ta ta ra ta ta ra ta ta ra ta ta, ta ra ta ta ra ta ta ta ra ta ta ra ta ta, ta ra ta ta ra ta ta ra ta ta ra ta ta ra ta ta ra ta ta ta.

CHORUS OF BOYS: And the guard going off duty is returning to its quarters and is going away. Sound, blaring trumpet! Ta ra ta ta ta ra ta ta. We are marching with heads high like little soldiers, keeping step without a mistake, one, two, keeping step. Ta ra ta ta ra ta ta, ta ra ta ta ra ta ta ta, ta ra ta ta ra ta ta ra ta ta ra ta ta ra ta ta, ta ra ta ta ra ta ta ta ra ta ta ra ta ta ra ta ta, ta ra ta ta ra ta ta ra ta ta ra ta ta ta.

The march music fades into the distance and disappears.

ZUÑIGA (*to Don José*): C'est bien là, n'est-ce pas, dans ce grand bâtiment que travaillent les cigarières?

DON JOSÉ: C'est là, mon officier, et bien certainement on ne vit nulle part, filles aussi légères.

ZUÑIGA: Mais au moins sont-elles jolies?

DON JOSÉ: Mon officier, je n'en sais rien, et m'occupe assez peu de ces galanteries.

ZUÑIGA: Ce qui t'occupe, ami, je le sais bien, une jeune fille charmante qu'on appelle Micaëla. Jupe bleue et natte tombante. Tu ne réponds rien à cela?

DON JOSÉ: Je réponds que c'est vrai, je réponds que je l'aime! Quant aux ouvrières d'ici,

ZUÑIGA (*to Don José*): It's right over there, isn't it, in that big building, that the cigarette girls work?

DON JOSÉ: That's where it is, sir, and I'm sure you never saw such irresponsible girls anywhere.

ZUÑIGA: But at least they're goodlooking?

DON JOSÉ: Sir, I don't know anything about it; I spend very little time playing around.

ZUÑIGA: I know very well what you spend your time on, my friend, a nice girl named Micaëla. Blue skirt and long braids. You don't answer anything to that?

DON JOSÉ: I answer that it's true, I answer that I love her! About the girls that work here, about

quant à leur beauté, les voici!
Et vous pouvez juger vous-
même!

their beauty—here they are.
And you can judge for yourself.

*Don José sits down on a bench outside the guardhouse and sets to
work with a piece of wire, making himself a lanyard for his
priming pin. The factory bell sounds, indicating that the
working girls should finish their lunch and start back to the factory.
Young men gather in the square to watch and talk to the girls. The
girls enter a little later.*

TENORS: La cloche a sonné; nous,
des ouvrières, nous venons ici
guetter le retour; et nous vous
suivrons, brunes cigarières, en
vous murmurant des propos
d'amour! En vous murmurant
des propos d'amour! des propos
d'amour! des propos d'amour!

TENORS: The bell has rung; we
have come here to wait until
the working girls come back;
and we'll follow you, dark
cigarette girls, murmuring
offers of love to you, murmuring offers of love to you, offers
of love, offers of love!

*The factory girls start to come upon the scene, crossing the bridge
and descending the stairway onto the stage. They are all smoking
cigarettes, and carry themselves boldly.*

BASSES (SOLDIERS): Voyez-les!
regards impudents, mine coquette! Fumant toutes, du bout
des dents, la cigarette.

BASSES (SOLDIERS): Look at them!
Bold looks, flirting ways! All
of them smoking, cigarettes
between their teeth.

FIRST SOPRANOS: Dans l'air nous
suivons des yeux la fumée, la
fumée qui vers les cieux monte,
monte parfumée; cela monte
gentiment à la tête, à la tête,
tout doucement, cela vous met
l'âme en fête!

FIRST SOPRANOS: We follow the
smoke through the air with our
eyes, the smoke that rises to the
heavens, rises perfumed; it goes
to your head very nicely, to
your head, and sweetly, it sets
your spirits to rejoicing!

SECOND SOPRANOS: Dans l'air
nous suivons des yeux la fumée,
la fumée qui vers les cieux
monte, monte parfumée; cela
monte gentiment à la tête, à la
tête, tout doucement, cela vous
met l'âme en fête!

SECOND SOPRANOS: We follow the
smoke through the air with our
eyes, the smoke that rises to
the heavens, rises perfumed; it
goes to your head very nicely,
to your head, and sweetly, it
sets your spirits to rejoicing!

FIRST SOPRANOS: Le doux parler, le doux parler des amants ...

SECOND SOPRANOS: C'est fumée!

FIRST SOPRANOS: Leur transports, leurs transports et leurs serments ...

SECOND SOPRANOS: C'est fumée!

FIRST SOPRANOS: Le doux parler des amants ...

SECOND SOPRANOS: C'est fumée!

FIRST SOPRANOS: Leurs transports et leurs serments ...

SECOND SOPRANOS: C'est fumée!

FIRST AND SECOND SOPRANOS: Oui, c'est fumée, c'est fumée!

SECOND SOPRANOS: Dans l'air nous suivons des yeux, dans l'air nous suivons des yeux—

FIRST SOPRANOS: Dans l'air nous suivons des yeux, des yeux—

la fumée!

SECOND SOPRANOS: La fumée!

FIRST SOPRANOS: La fumée!

SECOND SOPRANOS: La fumée! Ah!

FIRST SOPRANOS: Dans l'air—

FIRST AND SECOND SOPRANOS: —nous suivons la fumée qui monte en tournant, en tournant vers les cieux! La fumée, la fumée!

SOLDIERS: Mais nous ne voyons pas la Carmencita!

FIRST SOPRANOS: The sweet conversation, the sweet conversation of lovers ...

SECOND SOPRANOS: It's smoke!

FIRST SOPRANOS: Their ecstasies, their ecstasies, and their vows...

SECOND SOPRANOS: It's smoke!

FIRST SOPRANOS: The sweet conversation of lovers ...

SECOND SOPRANOS: It's smoke!

FIRST SOPRANOS: Their ecstasies and their vows ...

SECOND SOPRANOS: It's smoke!

FIRST AND SECOND SOPRANOS: Yes, it's smoke, it's smoke!

SECOND SOPRANOS: We follow through the air with our eyes, we follow through the air with our eyes—

FIRST SOPRANOS: We follow through the air with our eyes, with our eyes— the smoke!

SECOND SOPRANOS: The smoke!

FIRST SOPRANOS: The smoke!

SECOND SOPRANOS: The smoke! ah!

FIRST SOPRANOS: Through the air!

FIRST AND SECOND SOPRANOS: —we follow the smoke that rises in swirls, in swirls to the skies! The smoke! the smoke!

SOLDIERS: But we don't see Carmencita!

TENORS (WORKERS): La voilà!
BASSES (SOLDIERS): La voilà!
SOPRANOS, TENORS: La voilà, voilà la Carmencita!

TENORS (WORKERS): There she is!
BASSES (SOLDIERS): There she is!
SOPRANOS, TENORS: There she is! There's Carmencita!

Carmen enters, costumed as in Mérimée's work. She has a bouquet of cassia-flowers as a corsage, and carries a sprig of cassia-flowers in the corner of her mouth. Three or four young men come in with her, following her, moving around her, talking to her; she flirts with them. Don José lifts his head from his work, looks at Carmen, and then calmly resumes his work.

TENORS (WORKERS): Carmen! sur tes pas nous nous pressons tous! Carmen, sois gentille, au moins réponds-nous, et dis-nous quel jour tu nous aimeras! Carmen, dis-nous quel jour tu nous aimeras!

CARMEN (*looking at the workers*): Quand je vous aimerai? ma foi, je ne sais pas! Peut-être jamais! peut-être demain! Mais pas aujourd'hui, c'est certain.

L'amour est un oiseau rebelle que nul ne peut apprivoiser, et c'est bien en vain qu'on l'appelle, s'il lui convient de refuser. Rien n'y fait, menace ou prière, l'un parle bien, l'autre se tait; et c'est l'autre que je préfère. Il n'a rien dit; mais il me plaît.

SOPRANOS, TENORS (WORKERS): L'amour est un oiseau rebelle que nul ne peut apprivoiser, et c'est bien en vain qu'on l'appelle s'il lui convient de refuser!

TENORS (WORKERS): Carmen! we all crowd along after you! Carmen, be kind, at least answer us, and tell us what day you'll love us! Carmen, tell us what day you'll love us!

CARMEN (*looking at the workers*): When will I love you? Oh, I don't know! Perhaps never. Perhaps tomorrow. But not today, that's for sure.

Love is a stubborn and contrary bird that no one can tame, and it's a waste of time to call him if it suits him to say no. There's nothing you can do, threats or pleas. One talks well, the other keeps quiet; and it's the other that I prefer. He hasn't said anything, but he pleases me.

SOPRANOS, TENORS (WORKERS): Love is a stubborn and contrary bird that no one can tame, and it's a waste of time to call him if it suits him to say no.

Act 1, Scene 2. The cigarette factory girls and their admirers. *(Courtesy Bolshoi Theater, Moscow)*

Act 1, Scene 2. The factory girls in the square. Set and costumes by Georges Wakhevitch. *(Courtesy Teatro alla Scala, Milan; photo by E. Piccagliani)*

Act 1, Scene 2. Don José (Arturo Sergi) quells the confusion in the factory while Carmen (Regina Sarfaty) watches him wryly. Set by Dominik Hartmann. *(Courtesy Städtische Bühnen, Frankfurt am Main; photo by Günter Englert)*

CARMEN: L'amour! L'amour! L'amour! L'amour!

L'amour est enfant de Bohême, il n'a jamais, jamais connu de loi. Si tu ne m'aimes pas, je t'aime; si je t'aime, prends garde à toi!

SOPRANOS, TENORS (WORKERS): Prends garde à toi!

CARMEN: Si tu ne m'aimes pas, si tu ne m'aimes pas, je t'aime!

SOPRANOS, TENORS (WORKERS): Prends garde à toi!

CARMEN: Mais si je t'aime, si je t'aime, prends garde à toi!

SOPRANOS: L'amour est enfant de Bohême, il n'a jamais, jamais connu de loi. Si tu ne m'aimes pas, je t'aime; si je t'aime, prends garde à toi! Prends garde à toi!

TENORS: L'amour est enfant de Bohême! Prends garde à toi!

CARMEN: Si tu ne m'aimes pas, si tu ne m'aimes pas, je t'aime!

SOPRANOS, TENORS: Prends garde à toi!

CARMEN: Mais si je t'aime, si je t'aime, prends garde à toi!

SOPRANOS, TENORS: —à toi!

CARMEN: L'oiseau que tu croyais surprendre battit de l'aile et s'envola; l'amour est loin, tu peux l'attendre; tu ne l'attends plus, il est là! Tout autour de

CARMEN: Love! Love! Love! Love!

Love is a child of Egypt; he has never, never recognized any law. If you don't love me, I love you! If I love you, watch out for yourself!

SOPRANOS, TENORS (WORKERS): Watch out for yourself!

CARMEN: If you don't love me, if you don't love me, I love you!

SOPRANOS, TENORS (WORKERS): Watch out for yourself!

CARMEN: But if I love you, if I love you, watch out for yourself!

SOPRANOS: Love is a child of Egypt; he has never, never recognized any law. If you don't love me, I love you. If I love you, watch out for yourself, watch out for yourself!

TENORS: Love is a child of Egypt! Watch out for yourself!

CARMEN: If you don't love me, if you don't love me, I love you!

SOPRANOS, TENORS: Watch out for yourself!

CARMEN: But if I love you, if I love you, watch out for yourself!

SOPRANOS, TENORS: —for yourself!

CARMEN: The bird you thought you would take by surprise beat his wings and flew away; when love is far away—you can wait for him; if you don't wait

toi vite, vite, il vient, s'en va,
puis il revient; tu crois le tenir,
il t'évite; tu crois l'éviter, il te
tient!

SOPRANOS: Tout autour de toi
vite, vite, il vient, s'en va, puis
il revient; tu crois le tenir, il
t'évite; tu crois l'éviter, il te
tient!

CARMEN: L'amour! L'amour!
L'amour! L'amour!
L'amour est enfant de Bohême,
il n'a jamais, jamais connu de
loi. Si tu ne m'aimes pas, je
t'aime; si je t'aime, prends
garde à toi!

SOPRANOS, TENORS: Prends garde
à toi!

CARMEN: Si tu ne m'aimes pas,
si tu ne m'aimes pas, je t'aime!

SOPRANOS, TENORS: Prends garde
à toi!

CARMEN: Mais si je t'aime, si je
t'aime, prends garde à toi!

SOPRANOS: L'amour est enfant de
Bohême, il n'a jamais, jamais
connu de loi. Si tu ne m'aimes
pas, je t'aime; si je t'aime,
prends garde à toi! Prends
garde à toi!

TENORS: L'amour est enfant de
Bohême! Prends garde à toi!

CARMEN: Si tu ne m'aimes pas, si
tu ne m'aimes pas, je t'aime.

any longer—he's here! All
around you, fast, fast, he comes,
he goes away, then he comes
back. You think you have him,
he escapes. You think you'll
get away, he has you!

SOPRANOS: All around you, fast,
fast, he comes, he goes away,
then he comes back. You
think you have him, he escapes. You think you'll get
away, he has you!

CARMEN: Love! Love! Love!
Love!
Love is a child of Egypt; he
has never, never recognized
any law. If you don't love me,
I love you; if I love you, watch
out for yourself!

SOPRANOS, TENORS: Watch out
for yourself!

CARMEN: If you don't love me,
if you don't love me, I love you!

SOPRANOS, TENORS: Watch out
for yourself!

CARMEN: But if I love you, if I
love you, watch out for yourself!

SOPRANOS: Love is a child of
Egypt; he has never, never
recognized any law. If you
don't love me, I love you; if I
love you, watch out for yourself! Watch out for yourself!

TENORS: Love is a child of
Egypt! Watch out for yourself!

CARMEN: If you don't love me,
if you don't love me, I love you.

SOPRANOS, TENORS: Prends garde à toi!

SOPRANOS, TENORS: Watch out for yourself!

CARMEN: Mais si je t'aime, si je t'aime, prends garde à toi!

CARMEN: But if I love you, if I love you, watch out for yourself!

SOPRANOS, TENORS: —à toi!

SOPRANOS, TENORS: —for yourself!

TENORS (*to Carmen*): Carmen! sur tes pas nous nous pressons tous! Carmen, sois gentille, au moins réponds-nous! réponds-nous! Ô Carmen! sois gentille, au moins réponds-nous!

TENORS (*to Carmen*): Carmen! We all crowd along after you! Carmen! Be nice, at least answer us, answer us! Oh, Carmen! Be nice, at least answer us!

The men surround Carmen. She examines them one by one, then breaks out of the circle they have formed around her, and walks over to where Don José is sitting. She takes a cassia-flower from her corsage and throws it like a dart at Don José. It strikes him on the chest, and he leaps to his feet. There is a general burst of laughter as the flower falls to the ground in front of him. The factory bell sounds, calling the workers back to their jobs. Carmen is among the first to go, running into the factory. Lieutenant Zuñiga, who has been exchanging badinage with a couple of the girls, enters the guardhouse, followed by the other soldiers. As the workers leave the stage, the women sing.

SOPRANOS: L'amour est enfant de Bohême, il n'a jamais, jamais connu de loi; si tu ne m'aimes pas, je t'aime! si je t'aime, prends garde à toi!

SOPRANOS: Love is a child of Egypt; he has never, never recognized any law; if you don't love me, I love you! if I love you, watch out for yourself!

Don José is now alone upon the stage. He picks up the flower that Carmen had darted at him.

DON JOSÉ: Quels regards! quelle effronterie! Cette fleur-là m'a fait l'effet d'une balle qui m'arrivait!

DON JOSÉ: The way she looked at me ... What boldness! That flower had the effect of a bullet hitting me.

He smells the flower.

Le parfum est fort et la fleur est jolie! Et la femme— S'il est vraiment des sorcières, c'en est une certainement.

It has a strong perfume, and the flower is pretty! And the woman— If there really are witches, she's certainly one.

Micaëla enters; when Don José sees her, he quickly hides the cassia-flower in his tunic.

MICAËLA: José!

DON JOSÉ: Micaëla!

MICAËLA: Me voici!

DON JOSÉ: Quelle joie!

MICAËLA: C'est votre mère qui m'envoie!

DON JOSÉ: Parle-moi de ma mère! Parle-moi de ma mère!

MICAËLA: J'apporte de sa part, fidèle messagère, cette lettre—

DON JOSÉ: Une lettre!

MICAËLA: Et puis un peu d'argent pour ajouter à votre traitement. Et puis—

DON JOSÉ: Et puis?

MICAËLA: Et puis—vraiment je n'ose! Et puis, et puis encore une autre chose qui vaut mieux que l'argent, et qui pour un bon fils aura sans doute plus de prix!

DON JOSÉ: Cette autre chose, quelle est-elle? Parle donc!

MICAËLA: Oui, je parlerai. Ce que l'on m'a donné, je vous le donnerai. Votre mère avec moi sortait de la chapelle, et c'est alors qu'en m'embrassant: Tu vas, m'a-t-elle dit, t'en aller à

MICAËLA: José!

DON JOSÉ: Micaëla!

MICAËLA: I'm here!

DON JOSÉ: What a pleasure!

MICAËLA: Your mother sent me!

DON JOSÉ: Tell me about my mother. Tell me about my mother.

MICAËLA: I'm bringing this letter from her like a faithful messenger—

DON JOSE: A letter!

MICAËLA: And also a little money to add to your pay. And also—

DON JOSÉ: And also?

MICAËLA: And also—really, I don't dare! And also, something else that's more valuable than money, and will be worth more to a good son, no doubt.

DON JOSÉ: This something else, what is it? Tell me!

MICAËLA: Yes, I will tell you. I'll give you what I've been given. Your mother was coming out of the chapel with me, and then, embracing me, she said, "You are going to leave for the city;

la ville: la route n'est pas longue, une fois à Séville, tu chercheras mon fils, mon José, mon enfant! Tu chercheras mon fils, mon José, mon enfant! Et tu lui diras que sa mère songe nuit et jour à l'absent, qu'elle regrette et qu'elle espère, qu'elle pardonne, et qu'elle attend. Tout cela, n'est-ce pas, mignonne, de ma part, tu le lui diras; et ce baiser que je te donne, de ma part tu le lui rendras.

DON JOSÉ: Un baiser de ma mère!

MICAËLA: Un baiser pour son fils!

DON JOSÉ: Un baiser de ma mère!

MICAËLA: Un baiser pour son fils! José, je vous le rends comme je l'ai promis!

Micaëla shyly gives Don José a maternal kiss. There is a moment of silence.

DON JOSÉ: Ma mère, je la vois! Oui, je revois mon village! Ô souvenirs d'autrefois, doux souvenirs du pays!

MICAËLA: Sa mère, il la revoit! Il revoit son village! Ô souvenirs d'autrefois! Souvenirs du pays! Vous remplissez son cœur de force et de courage— Ô souvenirs chéris! Sa mère, il la revoit, il revoit son village!

it's not a long way. Once you are in Seville, you will look up my son, my José, my child. You will look up my son, my José, my child. And you will tell him that his mother dreams about her absent son night and day, that she is regretful and that she is hopeful, that she forgives him and that she is waiting for him. You'll tell him all that for me, won't you, dear, and this kiss that I'm giving you you'll give to him for me."

DON JOSÉ: A kiss from my mother!

MICAËLA: A kiss for her son!

DON JOSÉ: A kiss from my mother!

MICAËLA: A kiss for her son! José, I give it to you as I promised.

DON JOSÉ: I see my mother. Yes, I see my village again! O memories of the past, sweet memories of my country!

MICAËLA: He sees his mother again! He sees his village again! O memories of the past! Memories of his country. You fill his heart with strength and courage— O dear memories! He sees his mother again, he sees his village again!

DON JOSÉ: Doux souvenirs du pays! Ô souvenirs chéris! Ô souvenirs! Ô souvenirs chéris— vous remplissez mon cœur de force et de courage— Ô souvenirs chéris! Ma mère, je la vois, je revois mon village.

DON JOSÉ (*looking at the factory*): Qui sait de quel démon j'allais être la proie! Même de loin ma mère me défend, et ce baiser qu'elle m'envoie, ce baiser qu'elle m'envoie écarte le péril et sauve son enfant!

MICAËLA: Quel démon, quel péril! je ne comprends pas bien. Que veut dire cela?

DON JOSÉ: Rien! Rien! Parlons de toi, la messagère; tu vas retourner au pays?

MICAËLA: Oui, ce soir même; demain je verrai votre mère!

DON JOSÉ: Tu la verras! Eh bien! tu lui diras: Que son fils l'aime et la vénère et qu'il se repent aujourd'hui; il veut que là-bas sa mère soit contente de lui! Tout cela, n'est-ce pas, mignonne, de ma part, tu le lui diras! Et ce baiser que je te donne, de ma part, tu le lui rendras!

DON JOSÉ: Sweet memories of my country! O dear memories! O memories! O dear memories— you fill my heart with strength and courage— O dear memories! I see my mother, I see my village again!

DON JOSÉ (*looking at the factory*): Who knows what devil I was going to fall victim to! Even from afar my mother protects me, and that kiss she sends me, that kiss she sends me removes the danger and saves her child.

MICAËLA: What devil? What danger? I don't understand. What does that mean?

DON JOSÉ: Nothing! Nothing! Let's speak about you, the messenger. You're going back to our home country?

MICAËLA: Yes, this very night. Tomorrow I'll see your mother!

DON JOSÉ: You will see her? Good! You will tell her: "That her son loves her and respects her, and that today he is sorry; he wants his mother to be satisfied with him back there." You'll tell her all that for me, won't you, dear, and this kiss that I give you, you'll give to her for me!

He embraces and kisses her.

MICAËLA: Oui, je vous le promets, de la part de son fils, José, je le rendrai, comme je l'ai promis.

DON JOSÉ: Ma mère, je la vois!

MICAËLA: Yes, I promise you, I shall give it to her for her son, José, as I have promised.

DON JOSÉ: I see my mother!

Oui, je revois mon village! Ô souvenirs d'autrefois, doux souvenirs du pays!

MICAËLA: Sa mère, il la revoit! Il revoit son village. Ô souvenirs d'autre fois! Souvenirs du pays! vous remplissez son cœur de force et de courage! Ô souvenirs chéris! Sa mère, il la revoit, il revoit son village! Il te revoit, ô mon village! Doux souvenirs, souvenirs du pays! Vous remplessez son cœur de courage, ô souvenirs, ô souvenirs chéris.

DON JOSÉ: Doux souvenirs du pays! Ô souvenirs chéris! Ô souvenirs! Ô souvenirs chéris, vous remplissez mon cœur de force et de courage! Ô souvenirs chéris! Ma mère, je la vois, je revois mon village! Je te revois, ô mon village! Doux souvenirs, souvenirs du pays! Vous remplissez mon cœur de courage, ô souvenirs, ô souvenirs chéris.

JOSÉ: Je revois mon village! Ô souvenirs chéris!

MICAËLA: Ô souvenirs chéris, il revoit son village ...

JOSÉ: Vous me rendez tout mon courage, ô souvenirs du pays!

MICAËLA: Vous lui rendez tout son courage, ô souvenirs du pays!

Yes, I see my village again! O memories of the past, sweet memories of my country.

MICAËLA: He sees his mother again! He sees his village again! O memories of the past! Memories of his country! You fill his heart with strength and courage. O dear memories! He sees his mother again, he sees his village again! He sees you again, O my village! Sweet memories, memories of his country! You fill his heart with courage, O memories, O dear memories.

DON JOSÉ: Sweet memories of my country! O dear memories! O memories! O dear memories, you fill my heart with strength and courage! O dear memories! I see my mother, I see my village again! I see you again, O my village! Sweet memories, memories of my country! You fill my heart with courage, O memories, O dear memories.

JOSÉ: I see my village again! O dear memories!

MICAËLA: O dear memories, he sees his village again ...

JOSÉ: You restore all my courage, O memories of my country!

MICAËLA: You restore all his courage, O memories of his country!

Micaëla hands Don José the letter; he kisses it.

DON JOSÉ: Reste là maintenant, pendant que je lirai.

DON JOSÉ: Wait here now, while I read it.

MICAËLA: Non pas, lisez d'abord, et puis—je reviendrai!

MICAËLA: No, read it first, and then—I'll come back.

DON JOSÉ: Pourquoi t'en aller?

DON JOSÉ: Why are you going away?

MICAËLA: C'est plus sage, cela me convient davantage. Lisez! puis je reviendrai.

MICAËLA: It is more proper; it is more fitting for me. Read it, then I'll come back.

DON JOSÉ: Tu reviendras?

DON JOSÉ: You'll come back?

MICAËLA: Je reviendrai!

MICAËLA: I'll come back!

Don José reads the letter, while Micaëla leaves the stage.

DON JOSÉ: Ne crains rien, ma mère, ton fils t'obéira, fera ce que tu lui dis; j'aime Micaëla, je la prendrai pour femme, quant à tes fleurs, sorcière infâme! ...

DON JOSÉ: No fear, mother, your son will obey you. He will do what you tell him. I love Micaëla, I'll make her my wife. So much for your flowers, you dirty witch ...

He reaches into his jacket for the flowers which he had thrust there, when suddenly an uproar breaks out. Shrieks are heard from the factory, and Zuñiga runs out of the guardhouse, followed by several soldiers.

ZUÑIGA: Que se passe-t-il donc là-bas?

ZUÑIGA: What's going on there?

Excited factory girls rush onto the stage.

FIRST SOPRANOS: Au secours! au secours! n'entendez-vous pas?

FIRST SOPRANOS: Help! Help! Don't you hear it?

SECOND SOPRANOS: Au secours! au secours! messieurs les soldats!

SECOND SOPRANOS: Help! Help! You soldiers!

FIRST SOPRANOS: C'est la Carmencita!

FIRST SOPRANOS: It's Carmencita!

SECOND SOPRANOS: Non, non, ce n'est pas elle!

SECOND SOPRANOS: No, no, it's not Carmencita!

FIRST SOPRANOS: C'est la Carmencita!

FIRST SOPRANOS: It's Carmencita!

SECOND SOPRANOS: Non, non, ce n'est pas elle! pas du tout!

SECOND SOPRANOS: No, no, it isn't, not at all!

FIRST SOPRANOS: C'est elle! si fait, si fait, c'est elle! Elle a porté les premiers coups!

FIRST SOPRANOS: It is! It's true, it's true. It is! She hit first.

SECOND SOPRANOS: Ne les écoutez pas!

SECOND SOPRANOS: Don't listen to them!

FIRST SOPRANOS: Ne les écoutez pas!

FIRST SOPRANOS: Don't listen to them!

The girls mill excitedly around Zuñiga, each group trying to get his attention.

SECOND SOPRANOS: Écoutez-nous, monsieur!   Écoutez-nous! écoutez-nous!   écoutez-nous! écoutez-nous!   écoutez-nous! monsieur, monsieur, écoutez-nous!

SECOND SOPRANOS: Listen to us, señor. Listen to us! Listen to us! Listen to us! Listen to us! Listen to us, señor, señor! Listen to us!

FIRST SOPRANOS: Monsieur! écoutez-nous!   écoutez-nous! écoutez-nous!   écoutez-nous! écoutez-nous!   écoutez-nous, monsieur, monsieur, écoutez-nous!

FIRST SOPRANOS: Señor! Listen to us! Listen to us! Listen to us! Listen to us! Listen to us! Listen to us, señor, señor! Listen to us!

SECOND SOPRANOS: La Manuelita disait, et répétait à voix haute qu'elle achèterait sans faute un âne qui lui plaisait.

SECOND SOPRANOS: Manuelita kept saying over and over in a loud voice that she was definitely going to buy a donkey she liked.

FIRST SOPRANOS: Alors la Carmencita railleuse à son ordinaire, dit, "Un âne pour quoi faire? Un balai te suffira."

FIRST SOPRANOS: Then Carmen said in her usual sarcastic way, "A donkey! Why bother! A broom is good enough for you."

SECOND SOPRANOS: Manuelita riposta et dit à sa camarade, "Pour certaine promenade mon âne te servira!"

SECOND SOPRANOS: Manuelita came back at her and said, "I know of a trip where my donkey will serve you."

FIRST SOPRANOS: "Et ce jour-là tu pourras à bon droit faire la

FIRST SOPRANOS: "And on that day you'll have a right to be

fière, deux laquais suivront derrière t'émouchant à tour de bras."

proud; two footmen will walk behind you and beat the flies off you with all their might."*

FIRST, SECOND SOPRANOS: Là-dessus, toutes les deux se sont prises aux cheveux, toutes les deux, toutes les deux, se sont prises aux cheveux!

FIRST, SECOND SOPRANOS: And at that the pair of them grabbed each other by the hair, the pair of them, the pair of them grabbed each other by the hair!

ZUÑIGA (*shouting in rage and disgust*): Au diable tout ce bavardage! Au diable tout ce bavardage! Prenez, José, deux hommes avec vous, et voyez là-dedans qui cause ce tapage!

ZUÑIGA (*shouting in rage and disgust*): To hell with all this gabble! To hell with all this gabble! José! Take two men with you and see who's making that racket in there!

José points to two soldiers, who follow him at a run into the factory.

FIRST SOPRANO: C'est la Carmencita!

FIRST SOPRANOS: It's Carmencita!

SECOND SOPRANOS: Non, non, ce n'est pas elle!

SECOND SOPRANOS: No, no, it's not!

FIRST SOPRANOS: C'est la Carmencita!

FIRST SOPRANOS: It's Carmencita!

SECOND SOPRANOS: Non, non, ce n'est pas elle!

SECOND SOPRANOS: No, no, it's not!

FIRST SOPRANOS: Si fait, si fait, c'est elle!

FIRST SOPRANOS: It's true, it's true, it is Carmencita!

SECOND SOPRANOS: Pas du tout!

SECOND SOPRANOS: Not at all!

FIRST SOPRANOS: Elle a porté les premiers coups!

FIRST SOPRANOS: She hit first!

ZUÑIGA: Holà! Éloignez-moi toutes ces femmes-là!

ZUÑIGA: Hey! Get these women away from me!

He bursts away from them.

FIRST SOPRANOS: Monsieur!

FIRST SOPRANOS: Señor!

SECOND SOPRANOS: Monsieur!

SECOND SOPRANOS: Señor!

FIRST SOPRANOS: Monsieur!

FIRST SOPRANOS: Señor!

*That is, she will be whipped out of town as a whore.

SECOND SOPRANOS: Monsieur!   SECOND SOPRANOS: Señor!

*The girls surround Zuñiga again, pulling him back and
forth between the two factions.*

FIRST, SECOND SOPRANOS: Ne les écoutez pas! Monsieur, écoutez-nous, écoutez-nous, écoutez-nous, écoutez-nous, écoutez-nous, écoutez-nous, monsieur, monsieur, écoutez-nous!

FIRST, SECOND SOPRANOS: Don't listen to them! Señor! Listen to us! Listen to us! Listen to us! Listen to us! Listen to us! Listen to us! Señor, Señor! Listen to us!

The woman again besiege Zuñiga.

FIRST SOPRANOS: C'est la Carmencita qui porta les premiers coups!

FIRST SOPRANOS: It's Carmencita who hit first!

SECOND SOPRANOS: C'est la Manuelita qui porta les premiers coups!

SECOND SOPRANOS: It's Manuelita who hit first!

FIRST SOPRANOS: La Carmencita!

FIRST SOPRANOS: Carmencita!

SECOND SOPRANOS: La Manuelita!

SECOND SOPRANOS: Manuelita!

FIRST SOPRANOS: La Carmencita!

FIRST SOPRANOS: Carmencita!

SECOND SOPRANOS: La Manuelita!

SECOND SOPRANOS: Manuelita!

FIRST SOPRANOS: Si! Si! Si! Si! Si! Si! Si! Elle a porté les premiers coups! Elle a porté les premiers coups! C'est la Carmencita! C'est la Carmencita! C'est la Carmencita! Carmencita!

FIRST SOPRANOS: Yes! Yes! Yes! Yes! Yes! Yes! Yes! She hit first! She hit first! It's Carmencita! It's Carmencita! It's Carmencita! Carmencita!

SECOND SOPRANOS: Non! Non! Non! Non! Non! Non! Elle a porté les premiers coups! Elle a porté les premiers coups! C'est la Manuelita! C'est la Manuelita! Manuelita! Manuelita!

SECOND SOPRANOS: No! No! No! No! No! No! She hit first! She hit first! It's Manuelita! It's Manuelita! Manuelita! Manuelita!

*The soldiers push the women away while Don José enters
with Carmen, followed by the two dragoons.*

DON JOSÉ: Mon officier, c'était une querelle; des injures d'abord, puis à la fin des coups; une femme blessée.

ZUÑIGA: Et par qui?

DON JOSÉ (indicating Carmen): Mais par elle.

ZUÑIGA (to Carmen): Vous entendez; que nous répondrez-vous?

CARMEN (insolently): Trá la la la la la la la. Coupe-moi, brûle-moi, je ne te dirai rien. Tra la la la la la la. Je brave tout, le feu, le fer et le ciel même.

ZUÑIGA: Fais-nous grâce de tes chansons, et puisque l'on t'a dit de répondre, réponds!

CARMEN (with an insolent smirk): Tra la la la la la la. Mon secret, je le garde et je le garde bien! Tra la la la la la la. J'en aime un autre, et meurs en disant que je l'aime.

ZUÑIGA: Puisque tu le prends sur ce ton, tu chanteras ton air aux murs de la prison.

SOPRANOS: En prison! En prison!

DON JOSÉ: Sir, it was a quarrel that began with insults and ended with blows. One woman hurt.

ZUÑIGA: And by whom?

DON JOSÉ (indicating Carmen): By this one.

ZUÑIGA (to Carmen): You hear—what do you have to say to us?

CARMEN (insolently): "Tra la la la la la la la. Cut me, burn me, I'll tell you not a thing. Tra la la la la la la la. I defy everything, fire, steel and heaven itself."

ZUÑIGA: That's enough of your songs. When someone tells you to answer, answer!

CARMEN (with an insolent smirk): "Tra la la la la la la la. My secret I guard and I guard it well! Tra la la la la la la la. My love is another, and I die saying that I love him."

ZUÑIGA: Since you take that line, you'll sing your tune to the walls of the prison.

SOPRANOS: Prison! Prison!

Carmen leaps viciously at the girls, but José seizes her and drags her back. The soldiers thereupon drive the women back, and completely out of the square.

ZUÑIGA (to Carmen): La peste! Décidément vous avez la main leste.

CARMEN: Tra la la la la la la la la la la la la la la la la la la la la la la la la la la la la la la la la la la la la la la la la la.

ZUÑIGA (to Carmen): Damn it! You're really fast with your hands.

CARMEN: Tra la la la la la la la la la la la la la la la la la la la la la la la la la la la la la la la la la la la la la la la la la.

Act 1, Scene 2. Carmen (Joyce Blackham) is interrogated by Zuñiga (Lawrence Folley) while Don José (Jon Andrew) stands by. (*Courtesy Sadler's Wells Opera, London; photo by Donald Southern*)

Act 1, Scene 2. Don José (Richard Martell) is sorely tempted to release Carmen (Regina Resnik) and let her escape. *(Courtesy San Francisco Opera; photo by Carolyn Mason Jones)*

ZUÑIGA: C'est dommage, c'est grand dommage, car elle est gentille vraiment, mais il faut bien la rendre sage. Attachez ces deux jolis bras.

ZUÑIGA: It's too bad; it's a real shame, because she's really goodlooking. But she has to be taught a lesson. Tie up those two pretty arms.

A soldier brings a piece of rope. Carmen smilingly holds out her arms to Don José, who ties her wrists together in front of her. The lieutenant, followed by the soldiers, returns to the guardhouse. Don José and Carmen are alone upon the stage. Don José in some embarrassment, does not look at her.

CARMEN: Où me conduirez-vous?

CARMEN: Where will you take me?

DON JOSÉ: À la prison et je n'y puis rien faire.

DON JOSÉ: To prison, and there's nothing I can do about it!

CARMEN: Vraiment tu n'y peux rien faire.

CARMEN: You really can't do anything about it!

DON JOSÉ: Non, rien! j'obéis à mes chefs.

DON JOSÉ: No, nothing! I'm obeying my superiors.

CARMEN: Eh bien, moi, je sais bien qu'en dépit de tes chefs eux-mêmes tu feras tout ce que je veux, et cela, parce que tu m'aimes.

CARMEN: Oh well, as for me—I know very well you'll do everything I want in spite of your superiors; that's because you love me.

DON JOSÉ: Moi t'aimer!

DON JOSÉ: I—love you!

CARMEN: Oui, José! La fleur dont je t'ai fait présent, tu sais, la fleur de la sorcière, tu peux la jeter maintenant, le charme opère!

CARMEN: Yes, José. You know the flower I gave you, the witch's flower; you can throw it away now, the charm is working.

DON JOSÉ: Ne me parle plus, tu m'entends? Ne parle plus, je le défends.

DON JOSÉ: Don't say anything more to me, do you hear? Don't say anything more. I forbid it.

CARMEN: Près des remparts de Séville, chez mon ami Lillas Pastia j'irai danser la séguedille

CARMEN: Near the ramparts of Seville, at my friend Lillas Pastia's, I'll go to dance the

et boire du manzanilla. J'irai chez mon ami Lillas Pastia. Oui, mais toute seule on s'ennuie, et les vrais plaisirs sont à deux; donc, pour me tenir compagnie, j'emmènerai mon amoureux! Mon amoureux, il est au diable, Je l'ai mis à la porte hier! Mon pauvre cœur très consolable, mon cœur est libre comme l'air! J'ai des galants à la douzaine, mais ils ne sont pas a mon gré. Voici la fin de la semaine: Qui veut m'aimer? Je l'aimerai! Qui veut mon âme? Elle est à prendre! Vous arrivez au bon moment! Je n'ai guère le temps d'attendre, car avec mon nouvel amant,— Près des remparts de Séville, chez mon ami Lillas Pastia j'irai danser la séguedille et boire du manzanilla. Oui, j'irai chez mon ami Lillas Pastia!

DON JOSÉ (*wildly*): Tais-toi! je t'avais dit de ne pas me parler!

CARMEN: Je ne te parle pas, je chante pour moi-même, je chante pour moi-même! Et je pense! il n'est pas défendu de penser! Je pense à certain officier, je pense à certain officier qui m'aime et qu'à mon tour, oui, qu'à mon tour je pourrais bien aimer!

DON JOSÉ (*obviously disturbed*): Carmen!

*A sherry.

seguidilla and drink manzanilla.* I'll go to my friend Lillas Pastia's. Yes, but it's boring all alone, and the real pleasures are for two; so I'll bring along my lover to keep me company. My lover, he's gone to the devil, I showed him the door yesterday! My poor heart is very consolable, my heart is free as the air! I've got would-be lovers by the dozen, but they don't suit me. Now it's the weekend: Who wants to love me? I'll love him! Who wants my heart? It's for the taking! You have come in the nick of time! I don't have much time to wait, because with my new lover— Near the ramparts of Seville, at my friend Lillas Pastia's, I'll go to dance the seguidilla and drink manzanilla. Yes, I'll go to my friend Lillas Pastia's!

DON JOSÉ (*wildly*): Quiet! I've told you not to talk to me!

CARMEN: I'm not talking to you, I'm singing to myself! I'm singing to myself! And I'm thinking. There's no law against thinking. I'm thinking of a certain officer, I'm thinking of a certain officer, who loves me, and on my side, yes, on my side, I really could love him!

DON JOSÉ (*obviously disturbed*): Carmen!

CARMEN: Mon officier n'est pas un capitaine; pas même un lieutenant, il n'est que brigadier; mais c'est assez pour une Bohémienne, et je daigne m'en contenter!

CARMEN: My officer is not a captain, not even a lieutenant, he's only a corporal; but that's enough for a Gypsy girl, and I feel quite satisfied!

DON JOSÉ: Carmen, je suis comme un homme ivre, si je cède, si je me livre, ta promesse tu la tiendras, ah! si je t'aime, Carmen, Carmen, tu m'aimeras?

DON JOSÉ: Carmen, I'm like a drunken man; If I surrender, if I give in, will you keep your promise? And if I love you, Carmen, Carmen, will you love me?

CARMEN: Oui ...

CARMEN: Yes ...

Don José loosens the rope around her wrists.

DON JOSÉ: Chez Lillas Pastia—

DON JOSÉ: At Lillas Pastia's—

CARMEN: Nous danserons ...

CARMEN: We'll dance ...

DON JOSÉ: —tu le promets!

DON JOSÉ: —you promise?

CARMEN: ... la séguedille ...

CARMEN: ... the seguidilla ...

DON JOSÉ: Carmen, —

DON JOSÉ: Carmen—

CARMEN: ... en buvant du manzanilla.

CARMEN: ... drinking manzanilla.

DON JOSÉ: —tu le promets!

DON JOSÉ: —you promise?

CARMEN: Ah! Pres des remparts de Séville, chez mon ami Lillas Pastia, nous danserons la séguedille et boirons du manzanilla: Tra la la la la la la la la la, tra la la la la la la la la la la.

CARMEN: Ah! Near the ramparts of Seville, at my friend Lillas Pastia's, we'll dance the seguidilla and drink manzanilla; tra la la la la la la la la la la, tra la la la la la la la la la la la.

Zuñiga emerges from the guardhouse. Carmen conceals the fact that her wrists are not secured.

ZUÑIGA (*to Don José*): Voici l'ordre; partez. Et faites bonne garde.

ZUÑIGA (*to Don José*): Here's the order; be off. And guard her well.

CARMEN (*softly to Don José*): En chemin je te pousserai, je te

CARMEN (*softly to Don José*): On the way I'll push you, I'll

pousserai aussi fort que je le pourrai. Laisse-toi renverser. La reste me regarde. (*Boisterously to Zuñiga:*) L'amour est enfant de Bohême, il n'a jamais, jamais connu de loi; si tu ne m'aimes pas, je t'aimes; si je t'aime, prends garde à toi! Si tu ne m'aimes pas, si tu ne m'aimes pas, je t'aime! mais si je t'aime, si je t'aime, prends garde à toi!

push you as hard as I can. Let yourself fall. I'll take care of the rest. (*Boisterously to Zuñiga:*) Love is a child of Egypt; He has never, never recognized any law; if you don't love me, I love you; if I love you, watch out for yourself! If you don't love me, if you don't love me, I love you! But if I love you, if I love you, watch out for yourself!

She marches off gaily with Don José. When they reach the bridge, she turns suddenly and gives José a shove; he topples over and Carmen darts away.

Act Two

Set design for Act 2 by Nicola Benois. *(Courtesy Teatro di San Carlo, Naples)*

ACT TWO

Scene One

After a brief prelude the curtain arises upon Lillas Pastia's tavern. There are tables to the right and left. Present are Carmen, Mercedes and Frasquita (Gypsies), Morales, Lt. Zuñiga and other soldiers. They have just finished eating, and the table is in disarray. The officers and Gypsies are smoking cigarettes. Two Gypsy men play guitars in a corner of the tavern and two Gypsy women dance in the middle of the scene. Carmen is seated watching the Gypsies dance; the Lieutenant is talking to her in a low voice, but she is not paying any attention to him. Suddenly she gets up and starts to sing.

CARMEN: Les tringles des sistres tintaient avec un éclat métallique, et sur cette étrange musique les Zingarellas se levaient. Tambours de Basque allaient leur train, et les guitarres forcenées grinçaient sous des mains obstinées, même chanson, même refrain, même chanson, même refrain!

CARMEN: The jingles of the rattles whirred with a metallic ring, and to that weird music the Gypsy girls were getting up to dance. Tambourines were following their lead, and the frenzied guitars, under remorselessly insistent hands, kept screaming out the same song, the same refrain, same song, same refrain.

The Gypsies dance while Carmen sings.

CARMEN: Tra la la la, tra la la la, tra la la la, tra la la la la la la la.

CARMEN: Tra la la la, tra la la la, tra la la la, tra la la la la la la la.

CARMEN, FRASQUITA, MERCÉDÈS: Tra la la la, tra la la la, tra la la la, tra la la la la la la la.

CARMEN, FRASQUITA, MERCEDES: Tra la la la, tra la la la, tra la la la, tra la la la la la la la.

CARMEN: Les anneaux de cuivre

CARMEN: Rings of copper and of

et d'argent reluisaient sur les peaux bistrées; d'orange et de rouge zébrées, les étoffes flottaient au vent. La danse au chant se mariait, la danse au chant se mariait, d'abord indécise et timide, plus vive ensuite et plus rapide. Cela montait, montait, montait, montait! Tra la la la, tra la la la, tra la la la, tra la la la la la la la.

CARMEN, FRASQUITA, MERCÉDÈS: Tra la la la, tra la la la, tra la la la, tra la la la la la la la.

CARMEN: Les Bohémiens à tour de bras de leurs instruments faisaient rage, et cet éblouissant tapage ensorcelait les Zingaras. Sous le rythme de la chanson, sous le rythme de la chanson, ardentes, folles, enfiévrées, elles se laissaient, enivrées, emporter par le tourbillon! Tra la la la, tra la la la, tra la la la, tra la la la la la la la.

CARMEN, FRASQUITA, MERCÉDÈS: Tra la la la, tra la la la, tra la la la, tra la la la la la la la, tra la la la, tra la la la, tra la la la, tra la la la, tra la la la.

silver glitter on their swarthy skin; clothing, zebra-striped with orange and red, floats in the air. The dance is wed to the song, the dance is wed to the song. At first hesitant and shy, soon livelier and faster, it rises, rises, rises, rises. Tra la la la, tra la la la, tra la la la, tra la la la la la la la.

CARMEN, FRASQUITA, MERCEDES: Tra la la la, tra la la la, tra la la la, tra la la la la la la la.

CARMEN: With all their power the Gypsies drive their instruments to frenzy, and this blinding, bewildering uproar, seizes, as if by magic, the Gypsy girls. To the rhythm of the song, to the rhythm of the song, hotly, madly, deliriously, they let themselves, drunken, be carried away by the whirlwind! Tra la la la, tra la la la, tra la la la, tra la la la la la la la.

CARMEN, FRASQUITA, MERCEDES: Tra la la la, tra la la la, tra la la la, tra la la la la la la la, tra la la la, tra la la la, tra la la la, tra la la la, tra la la la.

The dance becomes very rapid and very violent. Carmen joins, and with the last notes of the orchestra flings herself out of breath upon a bench. After the dance Pastia whispers to Frasquita, who approaches the officers.

FRASQUITA: Messieurs, Pastia me dit ...
ZUÑIGA: Que nous veut-il encor, maître Pastia?

FRASQUITA Gentlemen, Pastia says ...
ZUÑIGA: What more does Pastia want from us?

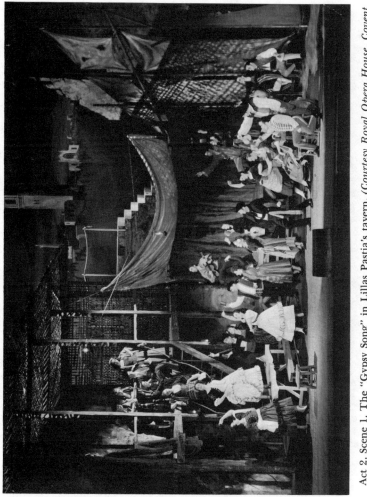

Act 2, Scene 1. The "Gypsy Song" in Lillas Pastia's tavern. *(Courtesy Royal Opera House, Covent Garden, London)*

Act 2, Scene 1. The "Gypsy Song." Set by Dominik Hartmann. (Courtesy Städtische Bühnen, Frankfurt am Main; photo by Günter Englert)

FRASQUITA: Il dit que le corré-gidor veut que l'on ferme l'auberge.

ZUÑIGA: Eh bien, nous partirons. Vous viendrez avec nous?

Pastia signals the girls to refuse.

FRASQUITA: Non pas! nous, nous restons.

ZUÑIGA: Et toi, Carmen? Tu ne viens pas? Écoute! Deux mots dits tout bas: Tu m'en veux.

CARMEN: Vous en vouloir! Pourquoi?

ZUÑIGA: Ce soldat l'autre jour emprisonné pour toi ...

CARMEN: Qu'a-t-on fait de ce malheureux?

ZUÑIGA: Maintenant il est libre!

CARMEN: Il est libre! tant mieux. Bonsoir, messieurs nos amoureux.

CARMEN, FRASQUITA, MERCÉDÈS: Bonsoir, messieurs nos amoureux!

Noise, chorus from back stage.

BASSES (*offstage*): Vivat! vivat le toréro!

TENORS, BASSES (*offstage*): Vivat! vivat le toréro!

BASSES (*offstage*): Vivat! vivat Escamillo!

TENORS, BASSES (*off stage*): Vivat! Vivat Escamillo! Vivat! Vivat! Vivat!

FRASQUITA: He says that the corregidor wants the inn closed.

ZUÑIGA: Very well, we'll leave. You'll come with us?

FRASQUITA: Oh no. We're staying here.

ZUÑIGA: And you, Carmen? Aren't you coming? Listen! A couple of words in your ear: You have a grudge against me.

CARMEN: A grudge against you? Why?

ZUÑIGA: That soldier they locked up the other day because of you ...

CARMEN: What have they done with the poor fellow?

ZUÑIGA: He's free now.

CARMEN: He's free! So much the better. Good night, sweethearts.

CARMEN, FRASQUITA, MERCEDES: Good night, sweethearts.

BASSES (*offstage*): Viva! Viva the torero!

TENORS, BASSES (*off stage*): Viva! Viva the torero!

BASSES (*offstage*): Viva! Viva Escamillo!

TENORS, BASSES (*offstage*): Viva! Viva Escamillo! Viva! Viva! Viva!

Zuñiga goes to the window.

ZUÑIGA: Une promenade aux flambeaux! C'est le vainqueur des courses de Grenade. (*Leaning out the window and calling to Escamillo:*) Voulez-vous avec nous boire, mon camarade? À vos succès anciens, à vos succès nouveaux.

ZUÑIGA: A torchlight parade! It's the winner in the Granada corridas. (*Leaning out the window and calling to Escamillo:*) Will you drink with us, my friend? To your past triumphs, to your future triumphs.

Escamillo and some of his followers enter with a flourish. Escamillo makes a sweeping bow to the company.

ZUÑIGA, TENORS, BASSES: Vivat! vivat le toréro!

CARMEN, FRASQUITA, MERCÉDÈS, MORALÈS, ZUÑIGA, TENORS, BASSES: Vivat! vivat le toréro!

ZUÑIGA, BASSES: Vivat! vivat Escamillo!

CARMEN, FRASQUITA, MERCÉDÈS, MORALÈS, ZUÑIGA, TENORS, BASSES: Vivat! vivat Escamillo! Vivat! Vivat! Vivat! Vivat!

ZUÑIGA, TENORS, BASSES: Viva! Viva! the torero!

CARMEN, FRASQUITA, MERCEDES, MORALES, ZUÑIGA, TENORS, BASSES: Viva! Viva the torero!

ZUÑIGA, BASSES: Viva! viva Escamillo!

CARMEN, FRASQUITA, MERCEDES, MORALES, ZUÑIGA, TENORS, BASSES: Viva! Viva Escamillo! Viva! Viva! Viva! Viva!

They drink together.

ESCAMILLO: Votre toast, je peux vous le rendre, señors, señors—car avec les soldats, oui, les toréros peuvent s'entendre; pour plaisirs, pour plaisirs, ils ont les combats! Le cirque est plein, c'est jour de fête! Le cirque est plein du haut en bas; les spectateurs, perdant la tête, les spectateurs s'interpellent à grand fracas! Apostrophes, cris et tapage, poussés jusques à la fureur! Car c'est la fête du courage! C'est la fête des gens

ESCAMILLO: Your toast I can return, señores, señores—because soldiers and bullfighters can understand one another; their pleasure, their pleasure lies in combat! The arena is full, it's a holiday! The arena is full from top to bottom. The fans, losing their heads, the fans are thrown into a mad uproar; cheers and catcalls, shouting and a wild din, screaming like mad! Because it's the festival of courage, it's

de cœur! Allons! en garde!
Allons! allons! ah!—Toréador,
en garde! Toréador! Toréador!
et songe bien, oui, songe en
combattant qu'un œil noir te
regarde et que l'amour t'attend,
Toréador, l'amour, l'amour
t'attend!

CARMEN, FRASQUITA, MERCÉDÈS,
MORALÈS, ZUÑIGA, TENORS,
BASSES: Toréador, en garde!
Toréador! Toréador!

CARMEN: En combattant songe
qu'un œil noir te regarde et que
l'amour, l'amour, l'amour
t'attend!

MORALÈS, ZUÑIGA: En combattant, oui, songe que l'amour,
l'amour, l'amour t'attend!

ESCAMILLO: Et songe bien, oui,
songe en combattant, qu'un
œil noir te regarde et que
l'amour t'attend, Toréador!
L'amour, l'amour t'attend!

TENORS: En combattant, oui,
songe que l'amour t'attend!

BASSES: Et songe bien, oui, songe
en combattant, qu'un œil noir
te regarde et que l'amour
t'attend, oui, l'amour t'attend!

FRASQUITA, MERCÉDÈS: Et songe
bien, oui, songe en combattant,
qu'un œil noir te regarde et que
l'amour t'attend, Toréador,
l'amour, l'amour t'attend!

the festival for men of heart!
Let's go! Look out! Let's go!
Let's go! ah—Toreador, look
out! Toreador! Toreador! And
dream, while you're fighting,
dream that dark eyes are
watching you and that love is
waiting for you, Toreador, love,
love is waiting for you!

CARMEN, FRASQUITA, MERCEDES,
MORALES, ZUÑIGA, TENORS,
BASSES: Toreador, look out!
Toreador! Toreador!

CARMEN: Dream while fighting
that dark eyes are watching
you and that love, love, love is
waiting for you!

MORALES, ZUÑIGA: Yes, dream
while fighting that love, love,
love is waiting for you!

ESCAMILLO: And dream, yes,
dream while fighting that dark
eyes are watching you and that
love is waiting for you, toreador! Love, love, is waiting for
you!

TENORS: Yes, dream while fighting that love is waiting for you!

BASSES: And dream, yes, dream
while fighting that dark eyes
are watching you and that love
is waiting for you, yes, love is
waiting for you!

FRASQUITA, MERCEDES: And
dream, yes, dream while fighting that dark eyes are watching
you and that love is waiting
for you, toreador, love, love is
waiting for you!

Carmen refills Escamillo's glass.

ESCAMILLO: Tout d'un coup, on fait silence, on fait silence … Ah! que se passe-t-il? Plus de cris, c'est l'instant! Plus de cris, c'est l'instant! Le taureau s'élance en bondissant hors du toril! Il s'élance! il entre, il frappe! un cheval roule, entraînant un picador. Ah! bravo! Toro! hurle la foule! Le taureau va, il vient, il vient et frappe encor! En secouant ses banderilles, plein de fureur, il court! le cirque est plein de sang! On se sauve, on franchit les grilles! c'est ton tour maintenant! Allons! en garde! allons! allons! ah!—Toréador, en garde! Toréador! Toréador! et songe bien, oui, songe en combattant, qu'un œil noir te regarde, et que l'amour t'attend, Toréador, l'amour, l'amour t'attend!

CARMEN, FRASQUITA, MERCÉDÈS, MORALÈS, ZUÑIGA, TENORS, BASSES: Toréador, en garde, Toréador! Toréador!

CARMEN: En combattant songe qu'un œil noir te regarde et que l'amour, l'amour, l'amour t'attend!

MORALÈS, ZUÑIGA: En combattant, oui, songe que l'amour, l'amour, l'amour t'attend!

ESCAMILLO: Et songe bien, oui, songe en combattant, qu'un œil noir te regarde et que

ESCAMILLO: All at once, there's silence, there's silence … Ah! What's happening? No more shouts, it's the moment! No more shouts, it's the moment! The bull leaps and bounds out of the toril! He leaps, he's in, he strikes, a horse goes down, dragging a picador. "Ah! Bravo! Toro!" howls the mob! The bull runs away, runs back, runs back and strikes again! Shaking his banderillas, full of fury, he runs around. The ring is full of blood! They escape, they leap the barrier! Now it's your turn! Let's go! Look out! Let's go! Let's go! Ah! Toreador, look out! Toreador! Toreador! And dream, yes, dream while fighting that dark eyes are watching you, and that love is waiting for you, toreador, love, love is waiting for you!

CARMEN, FRASQUITA, MERCEDES, MORALES, ZUÑIGA, TENORS, BASSES: Toreador, look out, toreador! Toreador!

CARMEN: And dream while fighting that dark eyes are watching you, and that love, love, love is waiting for you!

MORALES, ZUÑIGA: Yes, dream while fighting that love, love, love is waiting for you!

ESCAMILLO: And dream, yes, dream while fighting that dark eyes are watching you and that

Act 2, Scene 1. The "Toreador Song." *(Courtesy Bolshoi Theater, Moscow)*

Act 2, Scene 1. The "Toreador Song" in a modern-dress production. (*Courtesy National Theatre, Prague*)

l'amour t'attend, Toréador, l'amour, l'amour t'attend!

TENORS: En combattant, oui, songe, que l'amour t'attend!

BASSES: Et songe bien, oui, songe en combattant, qu'un œil noir te regarde et que l'amour t'attend, oui, l'amour t'attend!

FRASQUITA, MERCÉDÈS: ———Et songe bien, oui, songe en combattant, qu'un œil noir te regarde et que l'amour t'attend, Toréador, l'amour, l'amour t'attend!

MERCÉDÈS: L'amour!

ESCAMILLO: L'amour!

FRASQUITA: L'amour!

ESCAMILLO: L'amour!

CARMEN: L'amour!

ESCAMILLO: L'amour!

ALL: Toréador! Toréador! L'amour t'attend!

ESCAMILLO (*to Carmen*): La belle, un mot: comment t'appelle-t-on? Dans mon premier danger je veux dire ton nom.

CARMEN: Carmen! Carmencita! Cela revient au même.

ESCAMILLO: Si l'on te disait que l'on t'aime ...

CARMEN: Je répondrais qu'il ne faut pas aimer.

ESCAMILLO: Cette réponse n'est pas tendre. Je me contenterai d'espérer et d'attendre.

love is waiting for you, toreador, love, love is waiting for you!

TENORS, Yes, dream while fighting that love is waiting for you!

BASSES: And dream, yes, dream while fighting that dark eyes are watching you and that love is waiting for you, yes love is waiting for you!

FRASQUITA, MERCEDES: ———And dream, yes, dream while fighting that dark eyes are watching you and that love is waiting for you, toreador, love, love is waiting for you!

MERCEDES: Love!

ESCAMILLO Love!

FRASQUITA: Love!

ESCAMILLO: Love!

CARMEN: Love!

ESCAMILLO: Love!

ALL: Toreador! Toreador! Love is waiting for you!

ESCAMILLO (*to Carmen*): Señorita, a word: what's your name? The first time I'm in danger I want to say your name.

CARMEN: Carmen! Carmencita! It all comes to the same thing.

ESCAMILLO: If someone told you he loves you ...

CARMEN: I'd answer that he shouldn't love me.

ESCAMILLO: That's not a tender answer. I'll satisfy myself with hoping and waiting.

CARMEN: Il est permis d'attendre, il est doux d'espérer.

CARMEN: Waiting is allowed, hoping is sweet.

ZUÑIGA: Puisque tu ne viens pas, Carmen, je reviendrai.

ZUÑIGA: Since you're not coming, Carmen, I'll come back.

CARMEN: Et vous aurez grand tort!

CARMEN: You'll be making a big mistake!

ZUÑIGA: Bah! je me risquerai!

ZUÑIGA: Bah! I'll take my chances.

All the soldiers leave. Escamillo and his followers leave. Carmen, Frasquita, Mercedes, Pastia and other Gypsies remain. Pastia goes to the window and beckons to someone outside. El Dancaïro and El Remendado enter. Pastia closes the shutters and locks the doors.

Scene Two

FRASQUITA: Eh bien, vite, quelles nouvelles?

FRASQUITA: Quick, what's the news?

LE DANCAÏRE: Pas trop mauvaises les nouvelles, et nous pouvons encor faire quelques beaux coups. Mais nous avons besoin de vous ...

EL DANCAÏRO: The news isn't too bad, and we can still make some good hauls. But we need you ...

CARMEN, FRASQUITA, MERCÉDÈS: Besoin de nous?

CARMEN, FRASQUITA, MERCEDES: Need us?

LE DANCAÏRE: Oui, nous avons besoin de vous.

EL DANCAÏRO: Yes, we need you.

LE REMENDADO: Nous avons en tête une affaire ...

EL REMENDADO: We have some business in mind ...

MERCÉDÈS: Est-elle bonne, dites-nous?

MERCEDES: Tell us, is it good?

FRASQUITA: Est-elle bonne, dites-nous?

FRASQUITA: Tell us, is it good?

LE DANCAÏRE: Elle est admirable, ma chère; mais nous avons besoin de vois!

LE REMENDADO: Oui, nous avons besoin de vous!

CARMEN: De nous?

LE DANCAÏRE: De vous!

FRASQUITA: De nous?

LE REMENDADO! De vous!

MERCÉDÈS: De nous?

LE REMENDADO, LE DANCAÏRE: De vous!

CARMEN, FRASQUITA, MERCÉDÈS: De nous? Quoi?

LE REMENDADO, LE DANCAÏRE: Oui, nous avons besoin de vous!

CARMEN, FRASQUITA, MERCÉDÈS: Quoi! Vous avez besoin de nous?

CARMEN: De nous?

LE DANCAÏRE: De vous!

FRASQUITA: De nous?

LE REMENDADO: De vous!

MERCÉDÈS: De nous?

LE DANCAÏRE: De vous!

CARMEN, FRASQUITA, MERCÉDÈS: De nous?

LE REMENDADO, LE DANCAÏRE: De vous!

CARMEN, FRASQUITA, MERCÉDÈS: Quoi! Vous avez besoin de nous?

LE DANCAÏRE, LE REMENDADO: Oui, nous avons besoin de vous!

LE DANCAÏRE, LE REMENDADO: Car nous l'avouons humble-

EL DANCAÏRO: It's wonderful, dear, but we need you!

EL REMENDADO: Yes, we need you!

CARMEN: Us?

EL DANCAÏRO: You!

FRASQUITA: Us?

EL REMENDADO: You!

MERCEDES: Us?

EL REMENDADO, EL DANCAÏRO: You!

CARMEN, FRASQUITA, MERCEDES: Us? What?

EL REMENDADO, EL DANCAÏRO: Yes, we need you!

CARMEN, FRASQUITA, MERCEDES: What? You need us?

CARMEN: Us?

EL DANCAÏRO: You.

FRASQUITA: Us?

EL REMENDADO: You!

MERCEDES: Us?

EL DANCAÏRO: You!

CARMEN, FRASQUITA, MERCEDES: Us?

EL REMENDADO, EL DANCAÏRO: You!

CARMEN, FRASQUITA, MERCEDES: What! You need us?

EL DANCAÏRO, EL REMENDADO: Yes, we need you!

EL DANCAÏRO, EL REMENDADO: Because we confess humbly and

ment et fort respectueusement, oui, nous l'avouons humblement: quand il s'agit de tromperie, de duperie, de volerie, il est toujours bon, sur ma foi, d'avoir les femmes avec soi. Et sans elles, mes toutes belles, on ne fait jamais rien de bien!

CARMEN, FRASQUITA, MERCÉDÈS: Quoi! sans nous jamais rien de bien, sans nous, quoi! jamais rien de bien?

LE REMENDADO, LE DANCAÏRE: N'êtes-vous pas de cet avis?

CARMEN, FRASQUITA, MERCÉDÈS: Si fait, je suis de cet avis.

LE DANCAÏRE, LE REMENDADO: N'êtes-vous pas de cet avis?

CARMEN, MERCÉDÈS, FRASQUITA: Si fait, je suis de cet avis.

CARMEN, MERCÉDÈS, FRASQUITA: Si fait, vraiment, je suis de cet avis.

LE REMENDADO, LE DANCAÏRE: Vraiment, n'êtes-vous pas de cet avis?

FRASQUITA, LE REMENDADO, LE DANCAÏRE: Quand il s'agit de volerie—

CARMEN, MERCÉDÈS: Quand il s'agit de tromperie, de duperie, de volerie—

CARMEN, LE REMENDADO, LE DANCAÏRE, MERCÉDÈS, FRASQUITA: Il est toujours bon, sur ma foi, d'avoir les femmes avec soi. Et sans elles, les toutes

very respectfully, yes, we confess humbly: When it comes to cheating, swindling, thieving, it's always good, by God! to to have women along. And without them, my beauties, nothing turns out right.

CARMEN, FRASQUITA, MERCEDES: What! Without us nothing turns out right, without us, what? nothing turns out right?

EL REMENDADO, EL DANCAÏRO: Don't you think so, too?

CARMEN, FRASQUITA, MERCEDES: True, I think so.

EL DANCAÏRO, EL REMENDADO: Don't you think so, too?

CARMEN, MERCEDES, FRASQUITA: True, I think so.

CARMEN, MERCEDES, FRASQUITA: True, I really think so.

EL REMENDADO, EL DANCAÏRO: Really, don't you think so?

FRASQUITA, EL REMENDADO, EL DANCAÏRO: When it comes to thieving—

CARMEN, MERCEDES: When it comes to cheating, swindling, thieving—

CARMEN, EL REMENDADO, EL DANCAÏRO, MERCEDES, FRASQUITA: It's always good, by God, to have women along. And without them, the

belles, on ne fait jamais rien de bien! Et sans elles, les toutes belles, on ne fait jamais rien de bien! Oui, quand il s'agit de tromperie, de duperie, de volerie, il est toujours bon, sur ma foi, d'avoir les femmes avec soi!

FRASQUITA: Oui, sur ma foi—

CARMEN, MERCÉDÈS, LE DANCAÏRE, LE REMENDADO: Sur ma foi, sur ma foi—

FRASQUITA: Oui, sur ma foi, il faut avoir—

CARMEN, MERCÉDÈS, LE DANCAÏRE, LE REMENDADO: Il est toujours, toujours bon d'avoir—

CARMEN, MERCÉDÈS, LE DANCAÏRE, LE REMENDADO, FRASQUITA: —les femmes avec soi!

LE DANCAÏRE: C'est dit, alors; vous partirez?

FRASQUITA: Quand vous voudrez.

MERCÉDÈS: Quand vous voudrez.

LE DANCAÏRE: Mais tout de suite.

CARMEN: Ah! Permettez, permettez! S'il vous plaît de partir—partez! Mais je ne suis pas du voyage. Je ne pars pas, je ne pars pas.

LE DANCAÏRE, LE REMENDADO: Carmen, mon amour, tu viendras, et tu n'auras pas le courage—

CARMEN: Je ne pars pas, je ne pars pas, je ne pars pas, je ne pars pas!

beauties, nothing turns out right. And without them, the beauties, nothing turns out right. Yes, when it comes to cheating, swindling, thieving, it's always good, by God, to have women along.

FRASQUITA: Yes, by God—

CARMEN, MERCEDES, EL DANCAÏRO, EL REMENDADO: By God, by God—

FRASQUITA: Yes, by God, you have to have—

CARMEN, MERCEDES, EL DANCAÏRO, EL REMENDADO: It's always, always good to have—

CARMEN, MERCEDES, EL DANCAÏRO, EL REMENDADO, FRASQUITA: —women along.

EL DANCAÏRO: That's it, then; you will come?

FRASQUITA: Whenever you want.

MERCEDES: Whenever you want.

EL DANCAÏRO: Right away.

CARMEN: Ah! Excuse me, excuse me. If you want to go, go ahead. But I'm not one of the party. I'm not leaving, I'm not leaving.

EL DANCAÏRO, EL REMENDADO: Carmen, dear, you'll come, and you won't have the heart—

CARMEN: I'm not leaving, I'm not leaving, I'm not leaving, I'm not leaving!

LE DANCAÏRE, LE REMENDADO:
—de nous laisser dans l'em-
barras.

FRASQUITA, MERCÉDÈS: Ah! ma
Carmen, tu viendras—

CARMEN: Je ne pars pas, je ne
pars pas, je ne pars pas, je ne
pars pas!

LE DANCAÏRE: Mais, au moins, la
raison, Carmen, tu la diras!

MERCÉDÈS: La raison—

LE REMENDADO, MERCÉDÈS: La
raison—

FRASQUITA, LE REMENDADO,
MERCÉDÈS: La raison—

FRASQUITA, MERCÉDÈS, LE DAN-
CAÏRE, LE REMENDADO: La
raison!

CARMEN: Je la dirai certainement.

LE DANCAÏRE: Voyons!

LE REMENDADO: Voyons!

FRASQUITA: Voyons!

MERCÉDÈS: Voyons!

CARMEN: La raison, c'est qu'en
ce moment—

LE REMENDADO, LE DANCAÏRE:
Eh bien?

FRASQUITA, MERCÉDÈS: Eh bien?

CARMEN: Je suis amoureuse!

LE DANCAÏRE: Qu'a-t-elle dit?

LE DANCAÏRE, LE REMENDADO:
Qu'a-t-elle dit?

FRASQUITA, MERCÉDÈS: Elle dit
qu'elle est amoureuse!

LE DANCAÏRE, LE REMENDADO:
Amoureuse!

EL DANCAÏRO, EL REMENDADO:
—to leave us in the lurch.

FRASQUITA, MERCEDES: Ah! Carmen, you'll come—

CARMEN: I'm not leaving, I'm
not leaving, I'm not leaving,
I'm not leaving!

EL DANCAÏRO: But at least you'll
tell us the reason, Carmen.

MERCEDES: The reason—

EL REMENDADO, MERCEDES: The
reason—

FRASQUITA, EL REMENDADO,
MERCEDES: The reason—

FRASQUITA, MERCEDES, EL DAN-
CAÏRO, EL REMENDADO: The
reason!

CARMEN: Of course I'll tell you.

EL DANCAÏRO: All right!

EL REMENDADO: All right!

FRASQUITA: All right!

MERCEDES: All right!

CARMEN: The reason is that right
now—

EL REMENDADO, EL DANCAÏRO:
Well?

FRASQUITA, MERCEDES: Well?

CARMEN: I'm in love!

EL DANCAÏRO: What'd she say?

EL DANCAÏRO, EL REMENDADO:
What'd she say?

FRASQUITA, MERCEDES: She says
she's in love!

EL DANCAÏRO, EL REMENDADO:
In love!

FRASQUITA, MERCÉDÈS, LE DANCAÏRE, LE REMENDADO: Amoureuse!

CARMEN: Oui, amoureuse!

LE DANCAÏRE: Voyons, Carmen, sois sérieuse!

CARMEN: Amoureuse à perdre l'esprit!

LE REMENDADO, LE DANCAÏRE: La chose, certes, nous étonne. Mais ce n'est pas le premier jour où vous aurez su, ma mignonne, faire marcher de front le devoir, le devoir et l'amour, faire marcher le devoir et l'amour.

CARMEN: Mes amis, je serais fort aise de partir avec vous ce soir; mais cette fois, ne vous déplaise, il faudra que l'amour passe avant le devoir; ce soir l'amour passe avant le devoir!

LE DANCAÏRE: Ce n'est pas là ton dernier mot?

CARMEN: Absolument!

LE REMENDADO: Il faut que tu te laisses attendrir!

FRASQUITA, MERCÉDÈS, LE REMENDADO, LE DANCAÏRE: Il faut venir, Carmen, il faut venir!

LE REMENDADO, LE DANCAÏRE: Pour notre affaire ...

FRASQUITA, MERCÉDÈS: Pour notre affaire ...

LE REMENDADO, LE DANCAÏRE: ... c'est nécessaire;

FRASQUITA, MERCEDES, EL DANCAÏRO, EL REMENDADO: In love!

CARMEN: Yes, in love!

EL DANCAÏRO: Come on, Carmen, be serious!

CARMEN: In love enough to lose my mind!

EL REMENDADO, EL DANCAÏRO: This really surprises us, but this isn't the first day, darling, that you've known how to make duty, duty, and love go hand in hand, make duty and love go hand in hand.

CARMEN: My friends, I would be very glad to leave with you tonight, but this time, if you don't mind, love will have to come before duty; tonight love will have to come before duty.

EL DANCAÏRO: That's not your last word?

CARMEN: Absolutely!

EL REMENDADO: You've got to let us change your mind!

FRASQUITA, MERCEDES, EL REMENDADO, EL DANCAÏRO: You have to come, Carmen, you have to come!

EL REMENDADO, EL DANCAÏRO: For our job ...

FRASQUITA, MERCEDES: For our job ...

EL REMENDADO, EL DANCAÏRO: ... it's necessary;

FRASQUITA, MERCÉDÈS: ... c'est nécessaire;

LE REMENDADO, LE DANCAÏRE: ... car entre nous—

FRASQUITA, MERCÉDÈS: ... car entre nous—

CARMEN: Quant à cela, je l'admets avec vous:

CARMEN, FRASQUITA, MERCÉDÈS, LE DANCAÏRE, LE REMENDADO: Quant il s'agit de tromperie, de duperie, de volerie, il est toujours bon, sur ma foi, d'avoir les femmes avec soi; et sans elles, les toutes belles, on ne fait jamais rien de bien! Et sans elles, les toutes belles, on ne fait jamais rien de bien! Oui, quand il s'agit de tromperie, de duperie, de volerie, il est toujours bon, sur ma foi, d'avoir les femmes avec soi!

FRASQUITA: Oui, sur ma foi!

CARMEN, MERCÉDÈS, LE REMENDADO, LE DANCAÏRE: Sur ma foi!

CARMEN, MERCÉDÈS, LE REMENDADO, LE DANCAÏRE: ... sur ma foi, il est toujours, toujours bon d'avoir—

FRASQUITA: Oui, sur ma foi, il faut avoir—

CARMEN, MERCÉDÈS, FRASQUITA, LE REMENDADO, LE DANCAÏRE: les femmes avec soi, toujours les femmes avec soi!

LE DANCAÏRE: Mais qui donc attends-tu?

FRASQUITA, MERCEDES: ... it's necessary;

EL REMENDADO, EL DANCAÏRO: ... for between us—

FRASQUITA, MERCEDES: ... for between us—

CARMEN: As for that, I admit it, too.

CARMEN, FRASQUITA, MERCEDES, EL DANCAÏRO, EL REMENDADO: When it comes to cheating, swindling, thieving, it's always good, by God, to have women along. And without them, the beauties, nothing turns out right! And without them, the beauties, nothing turns out right! Yes, when it comes to cheating, swindling, thieving, it is always good, by God, to have women along!

FRASQUITA: Yes, by God!

CARMEN, MERCEDES, EL REMENDADO, EL DANCAÏRO: By God!

CARMEN, MERCEDES, EL REMENDADO, EL DANCAÏRO: By God, it is always, always good to have—

FRASQUITA: Yes, by God, you must have—

CARMEN, MERCEDES, FRASQUITA, EL REMENDADO, EL DANCAÏRO: Women along, always have women along!

EL DANCAÏRO: Who is it you're waiting for?

CARMEN: Presque rien, un soldat qui l'autre jour pour me rendre service s'est fait mettre en prison.

LE REMENDADO: Le fait est délicat!

LE DANCAÏRE: Il se peut qu'après tout ton soldat réfléchisse. Es-tu bien sûre qu'il viendra?

Don José's voice is heard from a distance.

DON JOSÉ: Halte-là! Qui va là? Dragon d'Alcala!

CARMEN: Écoutez!

DON JOSÉ: Où t'en vas-tu par là, dragon d'Alcala?

Carmen runs over to the window, opens one of the shutters, and peers out.

CARMEN: Le voilà.

Don José's voice keeps coming closer.

DON JOSÉ: Moi, je m'en vais faire mordre la poussière à mon adversaire. S'il en est ainsi, passez, mon ami. Affaire d'honneur, affaire de cœur, pour nous tous est là, dragons d'Alcala.

By now the others have joined Carmen at the window, looking out at Don José.

FRASQUITA: C'est un beau dragon.

MERCÉDÈS: Un très beau dragon.

LE DANCAÏRE: Qui serait pour nous un fier compagnon.

CARMEN: It's not much—a soldier who let himself be put in jail the other day to do me a favor.

EL REMENDADO: That's a ticklish matter.

EL DANCAÏRO: It's possible your soldier will change his mind after all. Are you very sure he'll come?

DON JOSÉ: "Halt! Who goes there?" "Dragoon from Alcalá!"

CARMEN: Listen!

DON JOSÉ: "Where are you going there, dragoon from Alcalá?"

CARMEN: There he is!

DON JOSÉ: "I'm going to make my enemy bite the dust." "If that's the case, pass, my friend. Affair of honor, affair of heart, for us that's everything, dragoons of Alcalá."

FRASQUITA: That's a good-looking dragoon.

MERCEDES: A very goodlooking dragoon.

EL DANCAÏRO: Who'd be a bold companion for us.

LE REMENDADO: Dis-lui de nous suivre.

CARMEN: Il refusera.

EL REMENDADO: Mais, essaye, au moins.

CARMEN: Soit! on essayera.

EL REMENDADO: Tell him to come along with us.

CARMEN: He'll refuse.

EL REMENDADO: But try at least.

CARMEN: All right! I'll try.

All leave by an inside door except Carmen. Don José's
voice comes closer and closer.

DON JOSÉ: Halte-là! Qui va là? Dragon d'Alcala! Où t'en vas-tu par là, dragon d'Alcala? Exact et fidèle, je vais ou m'appelle l'amour de ma belle! S'il en est ainsi, passez, mon ami. Affaire d'honneur, affaire de cœur, pour nous tout est là, dragons d'Alcala!

DON JOSÉ: "Halt! Who goes there?" "Dragoon from Alcalá." "Where are you going there, dragoon from Alcalá?" "Straight and true, I'm going where love of my fair one calls me." "If that's the case, pass, my friend. Affair of honor, affair of heart, for us that's everything, dragoons of Alcalá!"

Carmen unbars the door and Don José enters.

Scene Three

CARMEN: Enfin c'est toi!

DON JOSÉ: Carmen!

CARMEN: Et tu sors de prison?

DON JOSÉ: J'y suis resté deux mois.

CARMEN: Tu t'en plains?

DON JOSÉ: Ma foi non! Et si c'était pour toi, j'y voudrais être encore.

CARMEN: It's you at last!

DON JOSÉ: Carmen!

CARMEN: And you're out of prison!

DON JOSÉ: I've been there for two months.*

CARMEN: Are you complaining about it?

DON JOSÉ: My God, no! If it was for you, I'd be willing to be there still.

*This seems to be an error. It should be one month.

CARMEN: Tu m'aimes donc?

DON JOSÉ: Moi, je t'adore.

CARMEN: Vos officiers sont venus tout-à-l'heure; ils nous ont fait danser.

DON JOSÉ: Comment, toi!

CARMEN: Que je meure si tu n'es pas jaloux.

DON JOSÉ: Eh, oui—je suis jaloux.

CARMEN: Tout doux, monsieur, tout doux. Je vais danser en votre honneur, et vous verrez, seigneur, comment je sais moi-même accompagner ma danse. Mettez-vous là, Don José; je commence.

CARMEN: Then you love me?

DON JOSÉ: I adore you.

CARMEN: Your officers were here just a little while ago. They had us dance.

DON JOSÉ: What, you?

CARMEN: I'll die if you're not jealous!

DON JOSÉ: Oh yes—I'm jealous.

CARMEN: Calm down, señor, calm down. I'm going to dance in your honour, and you'll see, señor, how I can accompany my dance myself. Sit down there, Don José. I'm starting.

Carmen leads José to a bench in the corner, where he sits. She picks up her castanets, and singing "la, la, la" as she dances, accompanies herself with them. Don José devours her with his eyes. In the far distance Army bugles are heard blowing a call. Don José tries to listen, but the noise of Carmen's castanets prevents him from hearing. Don José gets up, takes Carmen in his arms, thereby forcing her to stop.

DON JOSÉ: Attends un peu, Carmen, rien qu'un moment arrête.

CARMEN: Et pourquoi, s'il te plaît?

DON JOSÉ: Il me semble là-bas— Oui, ce sont nos clairons qui sonnent la retraite; ne les entends-tu pas?

CARMEN: Bravo! Bravo! j'avais beau faire; il est mélancolique de danser sans orchestre. Et vive la musique qui nous tombe du ciel!

DON JOSÉ: Wait a minute, Carmen. Stop for just a minute.

CARMEN: And why, if you please?

DON JOSÉ: I thought down there— Yes, those are our bugles sounding retreat. Don't you hear them?

CARMEN: Bravo! Bravo! I tried, but it gets me down to dance without an orchestra. Hurray for this music from the sky!

Carmen continues her singing, now clicking her castanets in time with the bugles. She starts to dance again, while Don José watches her. The bugles approach, come nearer and nearer, pass beneath the window of the tavern, then gradually become fainter. Don José makes another effort to break away from Carmen's attraction. Again he takes her in his arms and obliges her to stop dancing.

DON JOSÉ: Tu ne m'as pas compris ... Carmen, c'est la retraite. Il faut que, moi, je rentre au quartier pour l'appel.

DON JOSÉ: You didn't understand me ... Carmen, it's retreat. I have to go back to quarters for roll call.

The sound of the bugles is no longer heard. Carmen watches as Don José puts on his cartridge pouch and saber belt again.

CARMEN: Au quartier! pour l'appel! Ah! j'étais vraiment trop bête! Ah! j'étais vraiment trop bête! Je me mettais en quatre et je faisais des frais, oui, je faisais des frais pour amuser monsieur. Je chantais! je dansais! Je crois, Dieu me pardonne, qu'un peu plus je l'aimais! Ta ra ta ta—c'est le clairon qui sonne! Ta ra ta ta— il part—il est parti! Va-t'en donc, canari! Tiens!

CARMEN: To quarters! For roll call! Ah! I was really too stupid! Ah! I was really too stupid! I went the limit and I really knocked myself out, yes, I knocked myself out to amuse the señor. I sang! I danced! I think, God forgive me, that I was about to fall in love with him! Ta ra ta ta—it's the bugle! Ta ra ta ta— he's going! He's gone! So get out, canary! Here!

In a fury Carmen throws Don José's shako at him.

Prends ton shako, ton sabre, ta giberne, et va-t'en, mon garçon, va-t'en! retourne à ta caserne!

Take your shako, your saber, your cartridge pouch, and get out, sonny, get out! Go back to your barracks!

DON JOSÉ: C'est mal à toi, Carmen, de te moquer de moi! Je souffre de partir, car jamais, jamais femme, jamais femme avant toi, non, non, jamais, jamais femme avant toi, aussi

DON JOSÉ: It's not right of you, Carmen, to make fun of me! It hurts me to leave, because no woman has ever, no woman before you has ever—no, no, never—no woman—no woman

Act 2, Scene 2. The Quintet. El Dancaïro, El Remendado, Frasquita and Mercedes persuade Carmen (Marijana Radev) to join them. *(Courtesy Croatian National Theatre, Zagreb)*

Act 2, Scene 3. Don José (Richard Martell) sings the "Flower Song" to Carmen (Regina Resnik). *(Courtesy San Francisco Opera; photo by Carolyn Mason Jones)*

Act 2, Scene 3. Carmen (Joyce Blackham) urges Don José (Jon Andrew) to desert. *(Courtesy Sadler's Wells Opera, London; photo by Donald Southern)*

Act 2, Scene 4. The Gypsies capture Zuñiga (Lawrence Folley) while Carmen (Joyce Blackham) mocks him and Don José (Jon Andrew) sits in the background. *(Courtesy Sadler's Wells Opera, London; photo by Donald Southern)*

profondément n'avait troublé mon âme!

CARMEN: Ta ra ta ta—mon Dieu! C'est la retraite! Ta ra ta ta— je vais être en retard! Ô mon Dieu! ô mon Dieu! c'est la retraite! Je vais être en retard! Il perd la tête. Il court! Et voilà son amour.

DON JOSÉ: Ainsi, tu ne crois pas à mon amour!

CARMEN: Mais non!

DON JOSÉ: Eh bien! tu m'entendras!

CARMEN: Je ne veux rien entendre!

DON JOSÉ: Tu m'entendras!

CARMEN: Tu vas te faire attendre!

DON JOSÉ: Tu m'entendras!

CARMEN: Tu vas te faire attendre—

DON JOSÉ: Oui—tu m'entendras!

CARMEN: Non! non! non! non!

DON JOSÉ: Je le veux, Carmen, tu m'entendras.

before you has troubled me so deeply!

CARMEN: Ta ra ta ta—My Lord! It's retreat! Ta ra ta ta—I'm going to be late. O Lord, Lord! It's retreat! I'm going to be late. He's losing his head. He's running! And there's his love!

DON JOSÉ: So you don't believe in my love?

CARMEN: Of course not!

DON JOSÉ: All right, you'll listen to me!

CARMEN: I don't want to listen to anything!

DON JOSÉ: You'll listen to me!

CARMEN: You're going to keep them waiting!

DON JOSÉ: You'll listen to me!

CARMEN: You're going to keep them waiting—

DON JOSÉ: Yes, you'll listen to me!

CARMEN: No, no, no, no!

DON JOSÉ: Carmen, you've got to listen to me!

With his left hand Don José seizes Carmen violently by the arm, while with his right hand he searches in his uniform blouse, until he finds the cassia-flower which Carmen had tossed at him one month earlier.

DON JOSÉ: La fleur que tu m'avais jetée, dans ma prison m'était restée, flétrie et sèche, cette fleur gardait toujours sa douce odeur; et pendant des heures entières, sur mes yeux fermant

DON JOSÉ: The flower that you threw at me stayed with me in prison. Faded and dry, this flower always kept its sweet smell, and for whole hours, I held it to my eyes, lids closed;

mes paupières, de cette odeur je m'enivrais, et dans la nuit je te voyais! Je me prenais à te maudire, à te détester, à me dire: Pourquoi faut-il que le destin l'ait mise là sur mon chemin! Puis je m'accusais de blasphème, et je ne sentais en moi-même, je ne sentais qu'un seul désir, un seul désir, un seul espoir: te revoir, ô Carmen, oui, te revoir! Car tu n'avais eu qu'à paraître, qu'à jeter un regard sur moi, pour t'emparer de tout mon être, ô ma Carmen! Et j'étais une chose à toi! Carmen, je t'aime!

CARMEN: Non, tu ne m'aimes pas!

DON JOSÉ: Que dis-tu?

CARMEN: Non! tu ne m'aimes pas! Non! car si tu m'aimais, là-bas, là-bas, tu me suivrais!

DON JOSÉ: Carmen!

CARMEN: Oui! Là-bas, là-bas dans la montagne, ...

DON JOSÉ: Carmen!

CARMEN: ... là-bas, là-bas tu me suivrais! Sur ton cheval tu me prendrais, et comme un brave à travers la campagne, en croupe tu m'emporterais! Là-bas, là-bas dans la montagne, ...

DON JOSÉ: Carmen!

CARMEN: ... là-bas, là-bas tu me suivrais, tu me suivrais—si tu m'aimais! Tu n'y dépendrais de

I got drunk with that smell, and at night I would see you! I began to curse you, to hate you, to say to myself: "Why did fate have to put her there in my way?" Then I would accuse myself of blasphemy, and I would feel within myself, I would feel only a single desire, a single desire, a single hope: to see you again, Carmen, yes, to see you again! Because all you had to do was come along and throw a glance at me, to take possession of all of me, O my Carmen. And I was yours! Carmen, I love you!

CARMEN: No, you don't love me!

DON JOSÉ: What are you saying?

CARMEN: No! You don't love me! No! Because if you loved me, you would go with me out there, out there.

DON JOSÉ: Carmen!

CARMEN: Yes! Out there, out there, in the mountains, ...

DON JOSÉ: Carmen!

CARMEN: ... out there, out there you'd go with me! You'd take me up on your horse, and like a real man you'd carry me away across the countryside behind you. Out there, out there in the mountains, ...

DON JOSÉ: Carmen!

CARMEN: ... you'd go with me out there, out there, you'd go with me—if you loved me!

personne; point d'officier à qui tu doives obéir, et point de retraite qui sonne pour dire à l'amoureux qu'il est temps de partir! Le ciel ouvert, la vie errante; pour pays l'univers; et pour loi, sa volonté! Et surtout la chose enivrante: la liberté! la liberté!

DON JOSÉ: Mon Dieu!

CARMEN: Là-bas, là-bas, dans la montagne.

DON JOSÉ: Carmen!

CARMEN: Là-bas, là-bas si tu m'aimais—

DON JOSÉ: Tais toi!

CARMEN: Là-bas, là-bas, tu me suivrais! Sur ton cheval tu me prendrais!

DON JOSÉ: Ah! Carmen, hélas, tais-toi, …

DON JOSÉ: … tais-toi, mon Dieu!

CARMEN: Sur ton cheval tu me prendrais et comme un brave …

CARMEN: … à travers la campagne, oui tu m'emporterais, si tu m'aimais—

DON JOSÉ: Hélas! hélas! pitié, Carmen, pitié! Ô mon Dieu! hélas!

CARMEN: Oui, n'est-ce pas, là-bas, là-bas, tu me suivras, tu me suivras!

CARMEN: Là-bas, là-bas tu me suivras, tu m'aimes et tu me

There you wouldn't be under anyone's thumb; no officer you've got to obey, no retreat sounding to tell a lover it's time to leave! The open sky, life on the road; the world for your country; and for law, what you want to do! And most of all, what makes you alive—freedom! Freedom!

DON JOSÉ: God!

CARMEN: Out there, out there in the mountains.

DON JOSÉ: Carmen!

CARMEN: Out there, out there, if you loved me—

DON JOSÉ: Shut up!

CARMEN: Out there, out there, you'd go with me! You'd take me up on your horse!

DON JOSÉ: Ah! Carmen, my God, shut up!

DON JOSÉ: Shut up, my God!

CARMEN: You'd take me up on your horse and like a real man …

CARMEN: … you'd take me away across the countryside, yes, you'd take me away, if you loved me—

DON JOSÉ: My God, my God, have a heart, Carmen, have a heart! My God, my God!

CARMEN: Yes, why not? Out there, out there you will take me, you will take me!

CARMEN: Out there, out there you will take me, you love me and

suivras! Là-bas, ...

CARMEN: ... là-bas, emporte-moi!

DON JOSÉ: Ah! tais-toi! tais-toi!

you will take me! Out there—

CARMEN: ... out there, take me away!

DON JOSÉ: Ah! Shut up, shut up!

Carmen throws her arms around Don José, who pulls away.

DON JOSÉ: Non! Je ne veux plus t'écouter. Quitter mon drapeau —déserter— C'est la honte— c'est l'infamie. Je n'en veux pas!

CARMEN: Eh bien! Pars!

DON JOSÉ: Carmen, je t'en prie!

CARMEN: Non! Je ne t'aime plus!

DON JOSÉ: Écoute!

CARMEN: Va! je te hais!

DON JOSÉ: Carmen!

CARMEN: Adieu, mais adieu pour jamais!

DON JOSÉ: Eh bien! soit ... adieu! Adieu pour jamais!

CARMEN: Va-t'en!

DON JOSÉ: Carmen! adieu! adieu pour jamais!

CARMEN: Adieu!

DON JOSÉ: No! I don't want to listen to you any more. To leave my flag, to desert—that would be a disgrace, infamy. I don't want any of it.

CARMEN: All right! Get out!

DON JOSÉ: Carmen, I beg you!

CARMEN: No! I don't love you any more!

DON JOSÉ: Listen!

CARMEN: Out! I hate you!

DON JOSÉ: Carmen!

CARMEN: Goodbye. But good-bye for ever!

DON JOSÉ: All right. If that's the way it is ... Goodbye! Good-bye for ever!

CARMEN: Get out!

DON JOSÉ: Carmen! Goodbye! Goodbye forever!

CARMEN: Goodbye!

Don José almost runs to the door, but at the moment he reaches it, there is a knock, and Zuñiga's voice is heard from outside.

Scene Four

ZUÑIGA: Holà! Carmen! holà! holà!

DON JOSÉ: Qui frappe? Qui vient là?

ZUÑIGA: Hey in there, Carmen! Hey, hey in there!

DON JOSÉ: Who's that knocking? Who's coming?

CARMEN: Tais-toi, tais-toi!

CARMEN: Shut up! Shut up!

Zuñiga kicks the door open, and enters.

ZUÑIGA: J'ouvre moi-même—et j'entre ...

ZUÑIGA: I'm opening it myself and coming in ...

He is surprised at seeing Don José, and turns to Carmen.

Ah! fi! ah! fi! la belle! Le choix n'est pas heureux! C'est se mésallier de prendre le soldat quand on a l'officier ... (*Contemptuously to Don José:*) Allons, décampe!

Bad! Bad! Goodlooking— you've got poor taste! It's a bad match to take an enlisted man when you have an officer ... (*Contemptuously to Don José:*) Go on, get out!

DON JOSÉ: Non!

DON JOSÉ: No!

ZUÑIGA: Si fait! tu partiras!

ZUÑIGA: Yes! You'll leave!

DON JOSÉ: Je ne partirai pas.

DON JOSÉ: I won't leave!

ZUÑIGA (*striking Don José*): Drôle!

ZUÑIGA (*striking Don José*): Idiot!

DON JOSÉ: Tonnerre! il va pleuvoir des coups!

DON JOSÉ: God damn it! I'll take off your head!

Don José draws his saber. Carmen leaps between them as the Lieutenant has his saber half out of its scabbard.

CARMEN: Au diable le jaloux! À moi! À moi!

CARMEN: Damn the jealous fool! Hey! Hey! Romanis!

The Gypsies, hearing Carmen's call, rush into the room. Carmen indicates the Lieutenant with a gesture, and the Gypsies rush upon him and disarm him.

CARMEN: Bel officier, bel officier, l'amour vous joue en ce moment un assez vilain tour! Vous arrivez fort mal! Vous arrivez fort mal! hélas! et nous sommes forcés, ne voulant être dénoncés, de vous garder au moins pendant une heure.

CARMEN: Pretty officer, pretty officer, right now love is playing a very dirty trick on you! You've come at a bad time, and since we don't want to be turned in, we're forced to keep you for at least an hour.

LE REMENDADO AND LE DANCAÏRE (*covering Zuñiga with pistols and addressing him with mock courtesy*): Mon cher monsieur! mon cher monsieur! mon cher monsieur!

EL REMENDADO, EL DANCAÏRO (*covering Zuñiga with pistols and addressing him with mock courtesy*): My dear sir, my dear sir, my dear sir, my dear sir! If you

mon cher monsieur, nous allons, s'il vous plaît, quitter cette demeure. Vous viendrez avec nous? Vous viendrez avec nous? Vous viendrez avec nous? Vous viendrez avec nous?

CARMEN: C'est une promenade!

LE DANCAÏRE, LE REMENDADO: Consentez-vous?

LE DANCAÏRE, LE REMENDADO, OTHER MEN: Répondez, camarade!

ZUÑIGA (*with similar mock courtesy*): Certainement, d'autant plus que votre argument est un de ceux auxquels on ne résiste guère! Mais, gare à vous! gare à vous plus tard!

LE DANCAÏRE: La guerre, c'est la guerre! En attendant, mon officier, passez devant sans vous faire prier!

LE REMENDADO, OTHER MEN: Passez devant sans vous faire prier!

CARMEN (*to Don José*): Es-tu des nôtres maintenant?

DON JOSÉ (*with resignation*): Il le faut bien!

CARMEN: Ah! le mot n'est pas galant! mais, qu'importe! va— tu t'y feras quand tu verras comme c'est beau, la vie errante, pour pays l'univers; et pour loi, sa volonté! Et surtout, la chose enivrante: la liberté, la liberté!

please, we are going to leave these premises! Will you come with us? Will you come with us? Will you come with us? Will you come with us?

CARMEN: For a walk!

EL DANCAÏRO, EL REMENDADO: Do you consent?

EL DANCAÏRO, EL REMENDADO, OTHER MEN: Answer, comrade!

ZUÑIGA (*with similar mock courtesy*): Why certainly, especially since your argument is one of those that can hardly be resisted. But, watch out, watch out later!

EL DANCAÏRO: That's life! And meanwhile, Señor Officer, let us not have to beg you to go ahead of us!

EL REMENDADO, OTHER MEN: Let us not have to beg you to go ahead of us!

CARMEN (*to Don José*): Are you one of us now?

DON JOSÉ (*with resignation*): I have to be!

CARMEN: Ah! That's not very complimentary! But what's the difference? Come—you'll get used to it when you see how fine life on the road is, with the world for your country; and for law, what you want to do! And most of all what makes you alive: freedom! Freedom!

CARMEN, FRASQUITA, MERCÉDÈS, FIRST SOPRANOS, SECOND SOPRANOS: Suis-nous à travers la campagne, viens avec nous dans la montagne, suis-nous et tu t'y feras, tu t'y feras quand tu verras, là-bas—

LE REMENDADO, LE DANCAÏRE, TENORS, BASSES: Ami, suis-nous dans la campagne, viens avec nous à la montagne, tu t'y feras, tu t'y feras quand tu verras, là-bas, là-bas—

CARMEN, FRASQUITA, MERCÉDÈS, FIRST SOPRANOS, TENORS: —comme c'est beau, la vie errante; pour pays l'univers; et pour loi, sa volonté! et surtout, la chose enivrante: la liberté!

LE REMENDADO, LE DANCAÏRE, SECOND SOPRANOS, BASSES: —comme c'est beau, la vie errante; pour pays l'univers; et surtout, la chose enivrante: Oui!

ALL EXCEPT DON JOSÉ: —la liberté!

DON JOSÉ: Ah!

SOPRANOS, TENORS, BASSES: Le ciel ouvert, la vie errante ...

CARMEN, DON JOSÉ, FRASQUITA, MERCÉDÈS, LE REMENDADO, LE DANCAÏRE: La vie errante ...

SOPRANOS, TENORS, BASSES: ... le ciel ouvert, la vie errante ...

CARMEN, FRASQUITA, MERCEDES, FIRST SOPRANOS, SECOND SOPRANOS: Come with us across the countryside, come with us into the mountains, come with us and you'll get used to it, you'll get used to it, when you see, out there—

EL REMENDADO, EL DANCAÏRO, TENORS, BASSES: Pal, come with us in the countryside, come with us to the mountains, you'll get used to it, you'll get used to it, when you see, out there, out there—

CARMEN, FRASQUITA, MERCEDES, FIRST SOPRANOS, TENORS: —how fine it is, life on the road, with the world for your country; and for law, what you want to do; and most of all, what makes you alive: freedom!

EL REMENDADO, EL DANCAÏRO, SECOND SOPRANOS, BASSES: —how fine it is, life on the road, with the world for your country; and most of all, what makes you alive: freedom!

ALL EXCEPT DON JOSÉ: Freedom!

DON JOSÉ: Ah!

SOPRANOS, TENORS, BASSES: The open sky, life on the road ...

CARMEN, DON JOSÉ, FRASQUITA, MERCEDES, EL REMENDADO, EL DANCAÏRO: Life on the road ...

SOPRANOS, TENORS, BASSES: ... the open sky, life on the road ...

CARMEN, DON JOSÉ, FRASQUITA, MERCÉDÈS, LE REMENDADO, LE DANCAÏRE: Le ciel ouvert ...

ALL: ... pour pays, tout l'univers, pour pays tout l'univers; pour loi, sa volonté—

CARMEN, DON JOSÉ, FRASQUITA, MERCÉDÈS, FIRST SOPRANOS, TENORS: Oui, pour pays, tout l'univers, tout l'univers; pour loi, sa volonté, et surtout—

LE REMENDADO, LE DANCAÏRE, SECOND SOPRANOS: Oui, surtout, surtout, oui, surtout—

BASSES: Oui, surtout, surtout—

ALL BUT BASSES: —la chose enivrante: la liberté! la liberté!

BASSES: Oui, la liberté! la liberté!

CARMEN, DON JOSÉ, FRASQUITA, MERCEDES, EL REMENDADO, EL DANCAÏRO: The open sky ...

ALL: ... the whole world for your country, the whole world for your country; for law, what you want to do—

CARMEN, DON JOSÉ, FRASQUITA, MERCEDES, FIRST SOPRANOS, TENORS: Yes, for your country the whole world, the whole world; for law, what you want to do; and most of all—

EL REMENDADO, EL DANCAÏRO, SECOND SOPRANOS: Yes, most of all, most of all, yes, most of all—

BASSES: Yes, most of all, most of all—

ALL BUT BASSES: —what makes you alive: freedom! Freedom!

BASSES: Yes, freedom! Freedom!

Act Three

Set design for Act 3 by Nicola Benois. (*Courtesy Teatro di San Carlo, Naples*)

ACT THREE

Scene One

The curtain rises upon a picturesque and savage scene; gigantic rock formations descend from the sides and rear of the stage. It is a dark night and the stage is completely empty. A musical prelude. After a few moments a smuggler appears high among the rocks, then another, then two others, then about twenty others, here and there, clambering among the rocks. The men are carrying large bales upon their backs. Present are Carmen, Don José, El Dancaïro, El Remendado, Frasquita, Mercedes, and others.

MEN: Écoute, écoute, compagnon, écoute! La fortune est là-bas, là-bas; mais prends garde pendant la route, prends garde de faire un faux pas! Prends garde de faire un faux pas! Prends garde de faire un faux pas! Écoute, compagnon, écoute, écoute! La fortune est là-bas, là-bas! Prends garde, prends garde, pendant la route, prends garde de faire un faux pas!

MEN: Listen, listen, pal, listen. A fortune is down there, down there. But watch out along the way, watch out and don't make a false step! Watch out and don't make a false step! Watch out and don't make a false step! Watch out and don't make a false step! Listen, pal, listen, listen, a fortune is down there, down there! Watch out, watch out, along the way, watch out and don't make a false step!

CARMEN, DON JOSÉ, FRASQUITA, MERCÉDÈS, LE REMENDADO, LE DANCAÏRE: Notre métier, notre métier est bon; mais pour le faire il faut avoir, avoir une âme forte! Et le péril, le péril est

CARMEN, DON JOSÉ, FRASQUITA, MERCEDES, EL REMENDADO, EL DANCAÏRO: Our trade, our trade is good, but to carry it on, you have to have courage! And danger, danger

en haut, il est en bas, il est en haut, il est partout, qu'importe! Nous allons devant nous sans souci du torrent, sans souci du torrent, sans souci de l'orage! Sans souci du soldat, qui là-bas nous attend, qui là-bas nous attend, et nous guette au passage, sans souci nous allons en avant!

is above, it's below, it's above, it's everywhere—what's the difference? We keep on going without worrying about the mountain floods, without worrying about the mountain floods, without worrying about the storm! Without worrying about the soldier who is lying in wait for us down there, who is lying in wait for us down there, who is hiding, waiting for us along the way; without worrying, we keep going forward!

SOPRANOS, FIRST BASSES: Ami, là-bas est la fortune, écoute, écoute, compagnon, prends garde pendant la route, prends garde de faire un faux pas!

SOPRANOS, FIRST BASSES: Pal, down there is a fortune, listen, listen, pal, watch out along the way, watch out and don't make a false step!

CARMEN, DON JOSÉ, FRASQUITA, MERCÉDÈS, LE REMENDADO, LE DANCAÏRE: Écoute, écoute, compagnon, écoute! La fortune est là-bas, là-bas; mais prends garde, pendant la route, prends garde de faire un faux pas!

CARMEN, DON JOSÉ, FRASQUITA, MERCEDES, EL REMENDADO, EL DANCAÏRO: Listen, listen, pal, listen! A fortune is down there, down there; but watch out along the way; watch out and don't make a false step!

TENORS: Oui, la fortune est là-bas—écoute, écoute, écoute!

TENORS: Yes, a fortune is down there—listen, listen, listen!

SECOND BASSES: Oui, la fortune est là-bas, prends garde de faire un faux pas!

SECOND BASSES: Yes, a fortune is down there, watch out and don't make a false step!

ALL: Prends garde de faire un faux pas! Prends garde de faire un faux pas!

ALL: Watch out and don't make a false step! Watch out and don't make a false step!

CARMEN, FRASQUITA, MERCÉDÈS, SOPRANOS: Écoute, compagnon, écoute, écoute, la fortune est là-bas, là-bas; prends garde, prends garde, pendant la route,

CARMEN, FRASQUITA, MERCEDES, SOPRANOS: Listen, pal, listen, listen. A fortune is down there, down there; watch out, watch out along the way, watch out

prends garde de faire un faux pas!

DON JOSÉ, LE REMENDADO, LE DANCAÏRE, TENORS, BASSES: Compagnon, écoute, compagnon, écoute, la fortune est là-bas; mais prends garde, oui, prends garde, pendant la route, de faire un faux pas!

ALL: Prends garde! Prends garde! Prends garde! Prends garde!

LE DANCAÏRE: Reposons-nous une heure ici, mes camarades. Nous, nous allons nous assurer que le chemin est libre et que sans algarades la contrebande peut passer.

El Dancaïro and El Remendado leave.

CARMEN (*to Don José*): Que regardes-tu donc?

DON JOSÉ: Je me dis que là-bas il existe une bonne et brave vieille femme qui me croit honnête homme. Elle se trompe, hélas!

CARMEN: Qui donc est cette femme?

DON JOSÉ: Ah! Carmen, sur mon âme, ne raille pas—car c'est ma mère.

CARMEN: Eh, bien—va la retrouver tout de suite. Notre métier, vois-tu, ne te vaut rien et tu ferais fort bien de partir au plus vite.

and don't make a false step!

DON JOSÉ, EL REMENDADO, EL DANCAÏRO, TENORS, BASSES: Pal, listen, pal, listen, a fortune is down there; but watch out, yes, watch out along the way, and don't make a false step!

ALL: Watch out! Watch out! Watch out! Watch out!

EL DANCAÏRO: Let's rest here an hour, pals. We are going on to make sure that the road is free and that the contraband can get through without trouble.

CARMEN (*to Don José*): What are you looking at?

DON JOSÉ: I'm telling myself that down there there lives a good and worthy old woman who believes I'm an honest man. She's wrong.

CARMEN: And who is this woman?

DON JOSÉ: Ah! Carmen, by my soul, don't make fun—because it's my mother.

CARMEN: Very well—go back to her again, right away. Our trade, you see, doesn't agree with you, and you'd do very well to go away as fast as you can.

DON JOSÉ: Partir, nous séparer?

CARMEN: Sans doute!

DON JOSÉ: Nous séparer, Carmen— Écoute, si tu redis ce mot—

CARMEN: Tu me tuerais, peut-être. Quel regard—tu ne réponds rien— Que m'importe? Après tout, le destin est le maître!

DON JOSÉ: Go away? Separate from each other?

CARMEN Of course!

DON JOSÉ: Separate from each other, Carmen— Listen, if you say that word again ...

CARMEN: You'd kill me, I suppose. What a look—you don't have any answer— What's the difference? After all, fate rules.

Scene Two

Mercedes and Frasquita have dealt out a pack of cards. They shuffle the cards as Carmen draws near and watches them. José remains at the side of the stage.

MERCÉDÈS: Mêlons!

FRASQUITA: Mêlons!

MERCÉDÈS: Coupons!

FRASQUITA: Coupons!

MERCÉDÈS: Bien! c'est cela!

FRASQUITA: Bien, c'est cela!

MERCÉDÈS: Trois cartes ici—

FRASQUITA: Trois cartes ici—

MERCÉDÈS: Quatre là!

FRASQUITA: Quatre là:

FRASQUITA, MERCÉDÈS: Et maintenant, parlez, mes belles, de l'avenir, donnez-nous des nouvelles—

FRASQUITA: Dites-nous qui nous trahira!

MERCÉDÈS: Dites-nous qui nous trahira!

MERCEDES: Let's shuffle!

FRASQUITA: Let's shuffle.

MERCEDES: Let's cut!

FRASQUITA: Let's cut!

MERCEDES: Good! That's it!

FRASQUITA: Good! That's it!

MERCEDES: Three cards here—

FRASQUITA: Three cards here—

MERCEDES: Four there!

FRASQUITA: Four there!

FRASQUITA, MERCEDES: And now, speak, darlings, give us news about the future—

FRASQUITA: Tell us who'll double-cross us!

MERCEDES: Tell us who'll double-cross us!

FRASQUITA: Dites-nous qui nous aimera!

MERCÉDÈS: Dites-nous qui nous aimera!

FRASQUITA, MERCEDES: Parlez, parlez! Parlez, parlez! Dites-nous qui nous trahira, dites-nous qui nous aimera!

FRASQUITA: Parlez!

MERCÉDÈS: Parlez!

FRASQUITA: Parlez!

MERCÉDÈS: Parlez!

FRASQUITA: Moi, je vois un jeune amoureux qui m'aime on ne peut davantage!

MERCÉDÈS: Le mien est très riche et très vieux; mais il parle de mariage!

FRASQUITA: Je me campe sur son cheval, et dans la montagne il m'entraîne!

MERCÉDÈS: Dans un château presque royal, le mien m'installe en souveraine!

FRASQUITA: De l'amour à n'en plus finir, tous les jours, nouvelles folies!

MERCÉDÈS: De l'or tant que j'en puis tenir, des diamants, des pierreries!

FRASQUITA: Le mien devient un chef fameux, cent hommes marchent à sa suite!

MERCÉDÈS: Le mien—le mien—en croirai-je mes yeux? Oui—il meurt! Ah! je suis veuve et j'hérite!

FRASQUITA: Tell us who'll love us!

MERCEDES: Tell us who'll love us!

FRASQUITA, MERCEDES: Speak, speak! Speak, speak! Tell us who'll double-cross us, tell us who'll love us!

FRASQUITA: Speak!

MERCEDES: Speak!

FRASQUITA: Speak!

MERCEDES: Speak!

FRASQUITA: I see a young lover who is crazy about me!

MERCEDES: Mine is very rich and very old; but he's talking about marriage!

FRASQUITA: I sit on his horse and he sweeps me off into the mountains!

MERCEDES: Mine is setting me up in a castle, almost as good as the King's, and I'm like a Queen!

FRASQUITA: His love never ends; every day he shows he's crazy about me!

MERCEDES: As much gold as I can carry, diamonds, jewels!

FRASQUITA: Mine is becoming a famous leader, a hundred men march behind him!

MERCEDES: Mine—mine—can I believe my eyes? Yes—he dies! Ah! I'm his widow and I inherit his money!

FRASQUITA: Ah!—

FRASQUITA, MERCÉDÈS: Parlez encore, parlez, mes belles; de l'avenir, donnez-nous des nouvelles ...

FRASQUITA: Dites-nous qui nous trahira!

MERCÉDÈS: Dites-nous qui nous trahira!

FRASQUITA: Dites-nous qui nous aimera!

MERCÉDÈS: Dites-nous qui nous aimera!

FRASQUITA, MERCÉDÈS: Parlez, parlez! Parlez, parlez! Dites-nous qui nous trahira, dites-nous qui nous aimera!

They examine the cards again.

MERCÉDÈS: Fortune!

FRASQUITA: Amour!

CARMEN: Voyons, que j'essaie à mon tour.

She starts to turn over the cards.

Carreau! Pique! La mort! J'ai bien lu—moi d'abord, ensuite lui, pour tous les deux, la mort! En vain pour éviter les réponses amères, en vain tu mêleras; cela ne sert à rien, les cartes sont sincères, et ne mentiront pas! Dans le livre d'en haut si ta page est heureuse, mêle et coupe sans peur: la carte sous tes doigts se tournera joyeuse, t'annonçant le bonheur! Mais si tu dois

FRASQUITA: Ah!—

FRASQUITA, MERCEDES: Speak more, speak, darlings; give us news about the future ...

FRASQUITA: Tell us who will double-cross us!

MERCEDES: Tell us who will double-cross us!

FRASQUITA: Tell us who will love us!

MERCEDES: Tell us who will love us!

FRASQUITA, MERCEDES: Speak, speak! Speak, speak! Tell us who will double-cross us, tell us who will love us!

MERCEDES: Money!

FRASQUITA: Love!

CARMEN: Let's see, let me try my turn.

Diamond! Spade! Death! I've read it right. First me, then him, for both of us, death. It's useless to shuffle the cards to avoid bad answers, it's useless. That doesn't help at all, the cards are honest and don't lie. If your page in the book up there is happy, shuffle and cut without fear; the card will turn up happy under your fingers, telling you of good luck! But if you have to die, if

mourir, si le mot redoutable est écrit par le sort, recommence vingt fois, la carte impitoyable répétera: la mort! (*Shuffling and reshuffling the cards:*) Oui, si tu dois mourir, recommence vingt fois, la carte impitoyable répétera: la mort! Encor! Encor! Toujours la mort!

FRASQUITA, MERCÉDÈS: Parlez encor, parlez, mes belles; de l'avenir donnez-nous des nouvelles ...

CARMEN: Encor!

FRASQUITA: Dites-nous qui nous trahira!

MERCÉDÈS: Dites-nous qui nous trahira!

CARMEN: Encor!

FRASQUITA: Dites-nous qui nous aimera!

MERCÉDÈS: Dites-nous qui nous aimera!

CARMEN: Le désespoir! La mort! la mort! Encor la mort!

FRASQUITA, MÉRCÈDES: Parlez encor! Parlez encor! Dites-nous qui nous trahira! Dites-nous qui nous aimera!

MERCÉDÈS: Fortune!

FRASQUITA: Amour!

CARMEN: Toujours la mort!

MERCÉDÈS: Fortune!

FRASQUITA: Amour!

CARMEN: Toujours la mort!

MERCÉDÈS: Encor!

the great word is written by fate, you can start again twenty times and the pitiless card will repeat: "Death!" (*Shuffling and reshuffling the cards:*) Yes, if you have to die, you can start again twenty times and the pitiless card will repeat: "Death!" Again! Again! Always death!

FRASQUITA, MERCEDES: Speak again, speak, darlings! Give us news about the future ...

CARMEN: Again!

FRASQUITA: Tell us who will double-cross us!

MERCEDES: Tell us who will double-cross us!

CARMEN: Again!

FRASQUITA: Tell us who will love us!

MERCEDES: Tell us who will love us!

CARMEN: It's hopeless! Death! Death! Death again!

FRASQUITA, MERCEDES: Speak again! Speak again! Tell us who will double-cross us! Tell us who will love us!

MERCEDES: Money!

FRASQUITA: Love!

CARMEN: Always death!

MERCEDES: Money!

FRASQUITA: Love!

CARMEN: Always death!

MERCEDES: Again!

FRASQUITA, MERCÉDÈS: Encor!

CARMEN, FRASQUITA, MERCÉDÈS: Encor! encor!

FRASQUITA, MERCEDES: Again!

CARMEN, FRASQUITA, MERCEDES: Again, again!

Scene Three

Reenter El Dancaïro and El Remendado.

CARMEN: Eh bien?

LE DANCAÏRE: Eh bien, nous essayerons de passer—et nous passerons. Reste là-haut, José, garde les marchandises.

FRASQUITA: La route est-elle libre?

LE DANCAÏRE: Oui, mais gare aux surprises! J'ai sur la brèche où nous devons passer vu trois douaniers: Il faut nous en débarrasser.

CARMEN: Prenez les ballots, et partons; il faut passer—nous passerons!

FRASQUITA, MERCÉDÈS: Quant au douanier, c'est notre affaire! Tout comme un autre il aime à plaire, il aime à faire le galant.

CARMEN: Quant au douanier, quant au douanier, c'est notre affaire! Tout comme un autre, il aime à plaire, il aime à plaire, il aime à faire le galant.

CARMEN, FRASQUITA, MERCÉDÈS: Ah! Laissez-nous passer en avant!

CARMEN: Well?

EL DANCAÏRO: Well, we'll try to get through—and we'll get through. Stay up there, José, guard the merchandise.

FRASQUITA: Is the way clear?

EL DANCAÏRO: Yes, but look out for surprises. I saw three customs men at the gap where we have to pass. We have to get rid of them.

CARMEN: Take up your packs and let's go. We have to get through—we'll get through!

FRASQUITA, MERCEDES: As for the customs man, that's our business! Just like everyone else, he likes to please, he likes to be gallant.

CARMEN: As for the customs man, as for the customs man, that's our business! Just like everyone else, he likes to please, he likes to please, he likes to be gallant.

CARMEN, FRASQUITA, MERCEDES: Ah! Let us go first!

FRASQUITA, MERCÉDÈS: Quant au douanier, c'est notre affaire! Tout comme un autre il aime à plaire, il aime à faire le galant!

CARMEN: Quant au douanier, quant au douanier, c'est notre affaire! Tout comme un autre, il aime à plaire, il aime à plaire, il aime à faire le galant!

FIRST SOPRANOS: Quant au douanier, c'est leur affaire! Tout comme un autre, il aime à plaire, il aime à faire le galant!

SECOND SOPRANOS: Quant au douanier, quant au douanier, c'est leur affaire! Tout comme un autre il aime à plaire, il aime à plaire, il aime à faire le galant!

CARMEN, FRASQUITA, MERCÉDÈS: Ah! Laissez-nous passer en avant!

SOPRANOS: Ah! Laissez-les passer en avant!

CARMEN, FRASQUITA, MERCÉDÈS, LE REMENDADO, LE DANCAÏRE, SOPRANOS, TENORS, BASSES: Il aime à plaire!

MERCÉDÈS: Le douanier sera clément!

CARMEN, FRASQUITA, MERCÉDÈS, LE REMENDADO, LE DANCAÏRE, SOPRANOS, TENORS, BASSES: —il est galant!

CARMEN: Le douanier sera charmant!

FRASQUITA, MERCEDES: As for the customs man, that's our business! Just like everyone else he likes to please, he likes to be gallant!

CARMEN: As for the customs man, as for the customs man, that's our business! Just like everyone else, he likes to please, he likes to please, he likes to be gallant!

FIRST SOPRANOS: As for the customs man, that's their business! Just like everyone else, he likes to please, he likes to be gallant!

SECOND SOPRANOS: As for the customs man, as for the customs man, that's their business! Just like everyone else, he likes to please, he likes to be gallant!

CARMEN, FRASQUITA, MERCEDES: Ah! Let us go first!

SOPRANOS: Ah! Let them go first!

CARMEN, FRASQUITA, MERCEDES, EL REMENDADO, EL DANCAÏRO, SOPRANOS, TENORS, BASSES: He likes to please!

MERCEDES: The customs man will be charitable!

CARMEN, FRASQUITA, MERCEDES, EL REMENDADO, EL DANCAÏRO, SOPRANOS, TENORS, BASSES: —he is gallant!

CARMEN: The customs man will be charming!

CARMEN, FRASQUITA, MERCÉDÈS, LE REMENDADO, LE DANCAÏRE, SOPRANOS, TENORS, BASSES: Il aime à plaire!

FRASQUITA: Le douanier sera galant!

MERCÉDÈS: Oui, le douanier sera même entreprenant!

FRASQUITA, MERCÉDÈS: Oui, le douanier, c'est notre affaire! Tout comme un autre, il aime à plaire, il aime à faire le galant, laissez-nous passer en avant!

CARMEN: Oui, le douanier, oui, le douanier, c'est notre affaire! Tout comme un autre il aime à plaire, il aime à plaire, il aime à faire le galant, laissez-nous passer en avant!

BASSES: Quant au douanier, c'est leur affaire! Tout comme un autre, il aime à plaire! Il aime à faire le galant! Laissez-les passer en avant! Oui, passer en avant!

LE REMENDADO, LE DANCAÏRE, TENORS: ———Quant au douanier, c'est leur affaire! Tout comme un autre, il aime à plaire! Il aime à faire le galant!

CARMEN, FRASQUITA, MERCÉDÈS: Il ne s'agit pas de bataille; non, il s'agit tout simplement de se laisser prendre la taille et d'écouter un compliment. S'il faut aller jusqu'au sourire, que voulez-vous, on sourira!

CARMEN, FRASQUITA, MERCEDES, EL REMENDADO, EL DANCAÏRO, SOPRANOS, TENORS, BASSES: He likes to please!

FRASQUITA: The customs man will be gallant!

MERCEDES: Yes, the customs man will even be daring!

FRASQUITA, MERCEDES: Yes, the customs man, that's our business! Just like everyone else, he likes to please, he likes to be gallant! Let us go first!

CARMEN: Yes, the customs man, yes, the customs man, that's our business! Just like everyone else, he likes to please, he likes to please, he likes to be gallant! Let us go first!

BASSES: As for the customs man, that's their business! Just like everyone else, he likes to please, he likes to be gallant! Let them go first! Yes, go first!

EL REMENDADO, EL DANCAÏRO, TENORS: ———As for the customs man, that's their business! Just like everyone else, he likes to please, he likes to be gallant!

CARMEN, FRASQUITA, MERCEDES: It's not a question of a battle; no, it's quite simply a question of letting an arm be put around your waist and listening to a compliment. If you have to go as far as smiling, so what? You'll smile!

FIRST SOPRANOS, SECOND SOPRA-NOS: Et d'avance—

CARMEN, FRASQUITA, MERCÉDÈS: Et d'avance—

SOPRANOS: —je puis le dire—

CARMEN, FRASQUITA, MERCÉDÈS: —je puis le dire—

CARMEN, FRASQUITA, MERCÉDÈS, SOPRANOS: —la contrebande passera!

SOPRANOS: —la contrebande passera!

FRASQUITA: En avant!

{ MERCÉDÈS: En avant!
  FRASQUITA: Marchons!

{ FRASQUITA: Allons!
  MERCÉDÈS: Marchons!
  CARMEN: En avant!

FRASQUITA, MERCÉDÈS, FIRST SOPRANOS: En avant! Le douanier, c'est notre affaire! Tout comme un autre, il aime à plaire, il aime à faire le galant!

CARMEN: Marchons, oui, le douanier, oui, le douanier, c'est notre affaire! Tout comme un autre, il aime à plaire, il aime à plaire, il aime à faire le galant!

SECOND SOPRANOS: Oui, le douanier, oui, le douanier, c'est leur affaire! Tout comme un autre, il aime à plaire, il aime à plaire, il aime à faire le galant!

LE REMENDADO, LE DANCAÏRE, TENORS, BASSES: Le douanier,

FIRST SOPRANOS, SECOND SOPRA-NOS: And in advance—

CARMEN, FRASQUITA, MERCEDES: And in advance—

SOPRANOS: —I can tell you—

CARMEN, FRASQUITA, MERCEDES: —I can tell you—

CARMEN, FRASQUITA, MERCEDES, SOPRANOS: —the contraband will go through!

SOPRANOS: —the contraband will go through!

FRASQUITA: Forward!

MERCEDES: Forward!

FRASQUITA: Let's go!

FRASQUITA: Let's go!

MERCEDES: Let's go!

CARMEN: Forward!

FRASQUITA, MERCEDES, FIRST SOPRANOS: Forward! The customs man, that's our business! Just like everyone else, he likes to please, he likes to be gallant!

CARMEN: Let's go! Yes, the customs man, yes, the customs man, that's our business! Just like everyone else, he likes to please, he likes to please, he likes to be gallant!

SECOND SOPRANOS: Yes, the customs man, yes, the customs man, that's their business! Just like everyone else, he likes to please, he likes to please, he likes to be gallant!

EL REMENDADO, EL DANCAÏRO, TENORS, BASSES: The customs

c'est leur affaire! Comme un autre, il aime à plaire, il aime à faire le galant!

man, that's their business! Just like everyone else, he likes to please, he likes to be gallant!

CARMEN, FRASQUITA, MERCÉDÈS: Ah! Laissez-nous passer en avant! Marchons en avant! Ah! Marchons, marchons! en avant!

CARMEN, FRASQUITA, MERCEDES: Ah! Let us go first! Let's go first! Ah! Let's go, let's go, forward!

LE REMENDADO, LE DANCAÏRE, TENORS: Oui, passez en avant! En avant! en avant! Oui! Oui! en avant!

EL REMENDADO, EL DANCAÏRO, TENORS: Yes, go first! Forward! Forward! Yes! Yes! Forward!

BASSES: Oui, passez en avant, en avant, en avant! Oui, en avant!

BASSES: Yes! Go first, forward, forward! Yes, forward!

SOPRANOS: ———Ah! Laissons-les passer en avant! Marchez en avant! Marchez, marchez, en avant!

SOPRANOS: ———Ah! Let them go first! Go on ahead! Go on, go on, on ahead!

The smugglers pick up their bales and leave. Last to leave is Don José, who is to act as sentinel for the band; he examines his carbine as he walks off the stage. As he is leaving, Micaëla timidly appears on the other side of the stage.

Scene Four

MICAËLA: C'est des contre-bandiers le refuge ordinaire. Il est ici, je le verrai— et le devoir que m'imposa sa mère, sans trembler je l'accomplirai.

Je dis, que rien ne m'épou-vante, je dis, hélas, que je réponds de moi; mais j'ai beau

MICAËLA: This is the place where the smugglers usually hide out. He is here; I'll see him—and I'll carry out the task that his mother gave me, without being afraid.

I say that nothing frightens me, I say that I'll answer for myself; but it's in vain for me to

faire la vaillante, au fond du cœur je meurs d'effroi! Seule en ce lieu sauvage, toute seule j'ai peur, mais j'ai tort d'avoir peur; vous me donnerez du courage, vous me protègerez, Seigneur! Je vais voir de près cette femme dont les artifices maudits ont fini par faire un infâme de celui que j'aimais jadis! Elle est dangereuse, elle est belle! Mais je ne veux pas avoir peur! Non, non, je ne veux pas avoir peur! Je parlerai haut devant elle— Ah! Seigneur, vous me protègerez, Seigneur, vous me protègerez! Ah! Je dis que rien ne m'épouvante, je dis, hélas! que je réponds de moi; mais j'ai beau faire la vaillante, au fond du cœur je meurs d'effroi! Seule en ce lieu sauvage, toute seule j'ai peur, mais j'ai tort d'avoir peur; vous me donnerez du courage, vous me protègerez, Seigneur! Protégez-moi! Ô Seigneur! donnez-moi du courage! Protégez-moi! Ô Seigneur! protégez-moi! Seigneur!

Je ne me trompe pas, c'est lui sur ce rocher— À moi, José, José! je ne puis approcher. Mais que fait-il? il ajuste— il fait feu— Ah! j'ai trop présumé de mes forces, mon Dieu.

act brave, in my heart I'm dying of fright! Alone in this savage place, all alone, I'm afraid, but I'm wrong to be afraid. You will give me courage, you will protect me, Lord. I'm going to get a close look at this woman whose vile tricks have finally made a scoundrel out of the man I formerly loved. She's dangerous, she's beautiful! But I will not be afraid! No, no, I will not be afraid! I'll speak up right in front of her— Ah! Lord, you will protect me, Lord, you will protect me! Ah! I said that nothing frightens me, I said that I'll answer for myself; but it's in vain for me to act brave, in my heart I'm dying of fright! Alone in this savage place, all alone, I'm afraid, but I'm wrong to be afraid. You will give me courage, you will protect me, Lord! Protect me, O Lord! Give me courage! Protect me! O Lord, protect me, Lord!

I'm not mistaken! That's José on that rock— Over here, José! José! I can't come closer. But what's he doing? He's taking aim, he's firing. Ah! I overestimated my strength.

She rushes to hide behind a rock as a rifle shot is heard. Don José enters, holding his rifle. Escamillo also enters, holding his hat in his hands, staring at it.

Scene Five

ESCAMILLO: Quelques lignes plus bas et tout était fini.

DON JOSÉ: Votre nom! répondez!

ESCAMILLO: Eh! doucement, l'ami! Je suis Escamillo, toréro de Grenade.

DON JOSÉ: Escamillo!

ESCAMILLO: C'est moi!

DON JOSÉ: Je connais votre nom. Soyez le bienvenu, mais vraiment, camarade, vous pouviez y rester.

ESCAMILLO: Je ne vous dis pas non. Mais je suis amoureux, mon cher, à la folie! Et celui-là serait un pauvre compagnon qui pour voir ses amours ne risquerait sa vie!

DON JOSÉ: Celle qui vous aimez est ici?

ESCAMILLO: Justement. C'est une Zingara, mon cher.

DON JOSÉ: Elle s'appelle?

ESCAMILLO: Carmen!

DON JOSÉ (*almost to himself*): Carmen!

ESCAMILLO: Carmen! Oui, mon cher. Elle avait pour amant, elle avait pour amant, un soldat qui jadis a déserté pour elle.

DON JOSÉ (*to himself*): Carmen!

ESCAMILLO: A hair or two lower and it would have been the end of me.

DON JOSÉ: Your name! Answer!

ESCAMILLO: Ah! Easy, my friend! I'm Escamillo, torero from Granada.

DON JOSÉ: Escamillo!

ESCAMILLO: Right!

DON JOSÉ: I know your name. You're welcome, but to tell the truth, friend, you should have stayed there.

ESCAMILLO: I don't say you're wrong. But I'm in love, my friend, madly in love. And it would be a poor sort of fellow who wouldn't risk his life to see his girl.

DON JOSÉ: The girl you love is here?

ESCAMILLO: Right! A Gypsy, my friend!

DON JOSÉ: What's her name?

ESCAMILLO: Carmen!

DON JOSÉ (*almost to himself*): Carmen!

ESCAMILLO: Carmen! Yes, my friend. She had for a lover, she had for a lover a soldier who deserted a while ago for her.

DON JOSÉ (*to himself*): Carmen!

ESCAMILLO: Ils s'adoraient! Mais c'est fini, je crois, les amours de Carmen ne durent pas six mois.

DON JOSÉ: Vous l'aimez, cependant!

ESCAMILLO: Je l'aime!

DON JOSÉ: Vous l'aimez, cependant!

ESCAMILLO: Je l'aime, oui, mon cher, je l'aime, je l'aime à la folie!

DON JOSÉ: Mais pour nous enlever nos filles de Bohême, savez-vous bien qu'il fait payer?

ESCAMILLO: Soit! on paiera— soit! on paiera.

DON JOSÉ (*menacingly*): Et que le prix se paie à coups de navaja!

ESCAMILLO (*surprised*): À coups de navaja!

DON JOSÉ: Comprenez-vous?

ESCAMILLO: Le discours est très net. Ce déserteur, ce beau soldat qu'elle aime, ou du moins qu'elle aimait, c'est donc vous?

DON JOSÉ: Oui, c'est moi-même!

ESCAMILLO: J'en suis ravi, mon cher! j'en suis ravi, mon cher, et le tour est complet!

DON JOSÉ: Enfin ma colère trouve à qui parler! Le sang, oui, le sang, je l'espère, va bientôt couler! Enfin ma colère trouve à qui parler, le

ESCAMILLO: They were madly in love! But that's over, I understand; Carmen's love affairs don't last six months.

DON JOSÉ: But you love her just the same!

ESCAMILLO: I love her.

DON JOSÉ: But you love her just the same!

ESCAMILLO: I love her, yes, my friend, I love her, I love her madly!

DON JOSÉ: But do you know that to carry off one of our Gypsy girls you have to pay the price?

ESCAMILLO: All right! It'll be paid! All right! It'll be paid!

DON JOSÉ (*menacingly*): And the price is paid with knives!

ESCAMILLO (*surprised*): With knives?

DON JOSÉ: You understand?

ESCAMILLO: The speech is very clear. This deserter, this fine soldier she loves, or at least that she used to love—that's you, is it?

DON JOSÉ: Yes, I myself.

ESCAMILLO: I'm delighted, my friend, I'm delighted, my friend, and the cycle is finished!

DON JOSÉ: At last my rage finds a focus! Blood, yes, blood, I hope will soon flow! At last my rage finds a focus! Blood, yes, blood, I hope will soon flow!

sang, oui, le sang, je l'espère, va bientôt couler!

ESCAMILLO: Quelle maladresse, j'en rirais vraiment! Chercher la maîtresse et trouver, trouver l'amant! Quelle maladresse, j'en rirais vraiment! Chercher la maîtresse et trouver, trouver l'amant!

ESCAMILLO: How awkward—I could really laugh. To go looking for the mistress and find, find the lover. How awkward—I could really laugh. To go looking for the mistress, and find, find the lover!

DON JOSÉ, ESCAMILLO: Mettez-vous en garde, et veillez sur vous! Mettez-vous en garde, et veillez sur vous! Tant pis pour qui tarde à parer les coups! Mettez-vous en garde, veillez sur vous!

DON JOSÉ, ESCAMILLO: On guard and take care of yourself! On guard, and take care of yourself! Too bad about the man who's slow in parrying! On guard and take care of yourself!

ESCAMILLO: En garde! allons! en garde! veillez sur vous!

ESCAMILLO: On guard! Come on! On guard! Take care of yourself!

DON JOSÉ: Allons, en garde! veillez sur vous!

DON JOSÉ: Come on! On guard! Take care of yourself!

DON JOSÉ, ESCAMILLO: Veillez sur vous!

DON JOSÉ, ESCAMILLO: Take care of yourself!

They rush together and battle furiously until the blade of Escamillo's knife breaks. Don José is about to stab Escamillo when the Gypsies reenter, Carmen among them; Carmen rushes over and stops Don José.

CARMEN: Holà! Holà! José!

CARMEN: Hey, Hey, José!

ESCAMILLO: Vrai! j'ai l'âme ravie que ce soit vous, Carmen, qui me sauviez la vie! (*To José:*) Quant à toi, beau soldat, nous sommes manche à manche, et nous jouerons la belle, oui, nous jouerons la belle, le jour où tu voudras reprendre le combat!

ESCAMILLO: Phew! I'm overjoyed that it's you, Carmen, who saved my life! (*To José:*) As for you, fine soldier, we're even, and we'll play the deciding game, yes, we'll play the deciding game any day you want to take up the fight again!

El Dancaïro steps between José and Escamillo.

Act 3, Scene 5. Escamillo leaves the Gypsy camp as the smugglers restrain Don José.
(Courtesy Bolshoi Theater, Moscow)

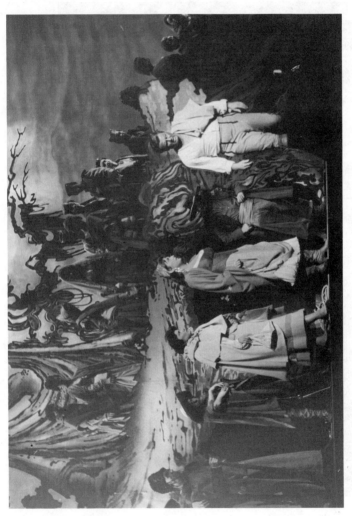

Act 3, Scene 5. Don José (Jon Vickers) is torn between Carmen (Gloria Lane) and Micaëla (Lucine Amara). *(Courtesy San Francisco Opera; photo by Bill Cogan)*

LE DANCAÏRE: C'est bon, c'est bon! plus de querelle! Nous, nous allons partir; et toi, et toi, l'ami, bonsoir.

EL DANCAÏRO: Come on, come on; no more fighting! We are going to leave, and to you, to you, my friend, good evening.

ESCAMILLO: Souffrez au moins qu'avant de vous dire au revoir, je vous invite tous aux courses de Séville. Je compte pour ma part y briller de mon mieux. Et qui m'aime y viendra! (*He ogles Carmen.*) Et qui m'aime y viendra!

ESCAMILLO: At least permit me, before saying goodbye to you, to invite you all to the corridas at Seville. For my part, I count on being at my very best. And anyone who loves me will come! (*He ogles Carmen.*) And anyone who loves me will come!

Don José makes threatening motions, and Escamillo looks at him nonchalantly.

L'ami, tiens-toi tranquille! J'ai tout dit—oui, j'ai tout dit! et je n'ai plus ici qu'à faire mes adieux!

Calm down, my friend. I'm finished speaking, yes, I'm finished speaking, and there's no more left for me here but to say goodbye.

Escamillo walks slowly away, with deliberate casualness. Don José lunges at him, but is held back by El Remendado and El Dancaïro. José then turns to Carmen.

DON JOSÉ: Prends garde à toi, Carmen. Je suis las de souffrir!

DON JOSÉ: Watch your step, Carmen. I'm tired of suffering!

LE DANCAÏRE: En route, en route, il faut partir!

EL DANCAÏRO: Get going, get going, we have to leave.

SOPRANOS, TENORS, BASSES: En route, en route, il faut partir!

SOPRANOS, TENORS, BASSES: Get going, get going, we have to leave.

LE REMENDADO: Halte! quelqu'un est là qui cherche à se cacher.

EL REMENDADO: Stop! There's someone trying to hide over there.

He goes over to the side and brings Micaëla from behind the rocks.

CARMEN: Une femme!

CARMEN: A woman!

LE DANCAÏRE: Pardieu! la surprise est heureuse!

EL DANCAÏRO: By God—this is a pleasant surprise!

DON JOSÉ (*with a start of recognition*): Micaëla!

MICAËLA: Don José!

DON JOSÉ: Malheureuse! Que viens-tu faire ici?

MICAËLA: Moi, je viens te chercher. Là-bas est la chaumière où sans cesse priant, une mère, ta mère, pleure, hélas! sur son enfant! Elle pleure et t'appelle, elle pleure et te tend les bras! Tu prendras pitié d'elle, José, ah! José, tu me suivras, tu me suivras!

CARMEN (*to Don José*): Va-t'en, va-t'en, tu feras bien. Notre métier ne te vaut rien.

DON JOSÉ (*to Carmen*): Tu me dis de la suivre!

CARMEN: Oui, tu devrais partir!

DON JOSÉ: Tu me dis de la suivre! Pour que toi, tu puisses courir après ton nouvel amant! Non! Non vraiment! Dût-il m'en coûter la vie, non, Carmen, je ne partirai pas! Et la chaîne qui nous lie nous liera jusqu'au trépas! Dût-il m'en coûter la vie, non, non, non, je ne partirai pas!

MICAËLA: Écoute-moi, je t'en prie. Ta mère te tend les bras! Cette chaîne qui te lie, José, tu la briseras!

FRASQUITA, MERCÉDÈS, LE REMEN-DADO, LE DANCAÏRE, SOPRANOS,

DON JOSÉ (*with a start of recognition*): Micaëla!

MICAËLA: Don José!

DON JOSÉ: Poor girl! What are you doing here?

MICAËLA: I have come looking for you. Down there is the cottage where a mother, your mother, prays without stop, weeps for her child. She weeps and she calls you, she weeps and she holds out her arms to you. Take pity on her, José, ah! come along with me, come along with me!

CARMEN (*to Don José*): Go on, go on, you'll be doing the right thing. Our trade doesn't suit you at all.

DON JOSÉ (*to Carmen*): You tell me to go along with her!

CARMEN: Yes, you might as well go.

DON JOSÉ: You tell me to go along with her! So that you, you can run after your new lover! No! Certainly not! Even if it costs me my life, no, Carmen, I'm not leaving! And the chain that binds us together will bind us together until death! Even if it costs me my life, no, no, no, I'm not leaving!

MICAËLA: Listen to me, I beg you. Your mother holds out her arms to you! Break that chain that binds you, José.

FRASQUITA, MERCEDES, EL REMEN-DADO, EL DANCAÏRO, SOPRANOS,

TENORS, BASSES: Il t'en coûtera la vie, José, si tu ne pars pas, et la chaîne qui vous lie se rompra par ton trépas.

DON JOSÉ (*to Micaëla*): Laisse-moi!

MICAËLA: Hélas! José!

DON JOSÉ: Car je suis condamné!

Carried away by emotion, he embraces Carmen.

FRASQUITA, MERCÉDÈS, LE REMEN-DADO, LE DANCAÏRE, SOPRANOS, TENORS, BASSES: José! prends garde!

DON JOSÉ: Ah! je te tiens, fille damnée, je te tiens, et je te forcerai bien à subir la destinée qui rive ton sort au mien! Dût-il m'en coûter la vie, non, non, non, je ne partirai pas!

FRASQUITA, MERCÉDÈS, LE REMEN-DADO, LE DANCAÏRE, SOPRANOS, TENORS, BASSES: Ah! prends garde, prends garde, Don José!

MICAËLA (*with sad dignity*): Une parole encor, ce sera la dernière! Hélas! José, ta mère se meurt, et ta mère ne voudrait pas mourir sans t'avoir pardonné!

DON JOSÉ: Ma mère! Elle se meurt!

MICAËLA: Oui, Don José!

DON JOSÉ: Partons! ah! partons! (*Starts to leave, then turns to Carmen:*) Sois contente ... je pars, mais nous nous reverrons!

TENORS, BASSES: It will cost you you life, José, if you don't leave, and the chain that binds you will be snapped by your death.

DON JOSÉ (*to Micaëla*): Get away from me!

MICAËLA: José!

DON JOSÉ: I'm an outlaw!

FRASQUITA, MERCEDES, EL REMEN-DADO, EL DANCAÏRO, SOPRANOS, TENORS, BASSES: José! Watch out!

DON JOSÉ: Ah! I'm holding on to you, damn you, I'm holding on to you, and I am going to make you submit to the fate that welds your lot to mine. Even if it costs me my life, no, no, no, I'm not leaving!

FRASQUITA, MERCEDES, EL REMEN-DADO, EL DANCAÏRO; SOPRANOS, TENORS, BASSES: Ah! Watch out, watch out, Don José!

MICAËLA (*with sad dignity*): One more word, it will be the last! José, your mother is dying, and your mother does not want to die without forgiving you.

DON JOSÉ: My mother! She's dying!

MICAËLA: Yes, Don José!

DON JOSÉ: Let's go! Ah! Let's go! (*Starts to leave, then turns to Carmen:*) Be satisfied ... I'm leaving, but we'll see each other again!

He follows Micaëla off the stage. Escamillo's voice is heard from the distance. Carmen listens, looking down over the rocky cliffs.

ESCAMILLO: Toréador, en garde! Toréador! Toréador! Et songe bien, oui, songe en combattant, qu'un œil noir te regarde, et que l'amour t'attend, Toréador, l'amour t'attend!

ESCAMILLO: Toreador, look out! Toreador! Toreador! And dream, yes, dream while fighting that dark eyes are watching you and that love is waiting for you! Toreador, love is waiting for you!

The Gypsies take up their packs and march off the stage, Carmen with them.

Act Four

IMPORTANT NOTE

As explained on page 75, there are two equally frequently performed sets of words for the opening number of Act Four. If you are listening to the ballet scene, follow the text on the first three left-hand pages of this act. If you are listening to Bizet's original crowd scene, follow the text on the first three right-hand pages. Beginning with page 162, the normal sequence of pages resumes.

ACT FOUR

Scene One (ballet version)

A square in Seville. In the background of the stage are the thick, high walls of the old arena. The entrance to the amphitheater is closed by a long canvas. It is the day of the bullfight, and the square is bustling with people. Vendors are selling water, oranges, fans, etc.

BASSES: Dansez, dansez, dansez, dansez …

BASSES, TENORS: Dansez, dansez, dansez, dansez …

BASSES: Dance, dance, dance, dance …

BASSES, TENORS: Dance, dance, dance, dance …

ACT FOUR

Scene One (crowd version)

A square in Seville. In the background of the stage are the thick, high walls of the old arena. The entrance to the amphitheater is closed by a long canvas. It is the day of the bullfight, and the square is bustling with people. Vendors are selling water, oranges, fans, etc.

BASSES: À deux cuartos! À deux cuartos!

TENORS, BASSES: À deux cuartos! À deux cuartos!

SECOND SOPRANOS, TENORS, BASSES: À deux cuartos! À deux cuartos!

FIRST SOPRANOS, TENORS, BASSES: À deux cuartos! À deux cuartos!

FIRST SOPRANOS: Des éventails pour s'éventer!

SECOND SOPRANOS: Des oranges pour grignoter!

FIRST TENORS: Le programme avec les détails!

SECOND BASSES: Du vin!

SECOND TENORS: De l'eau!

FIRST BASSES: Des cigarettes!

FIRST SOPRANOS: Des éventails pour s'éventer!

BASSES: For two coppers! For two coppers!

TENORS, BASSES: For two coppers! For two coppers!

SECOND SOPRANOS, TENORS, BASSES: For two coppers! For two coppers!

FIRST SOPRANOS, TENORS, BASSES: For two coppers! For two coppers!

FIRST SOPRANOS: Fans to fan yourself with!

SECOND SOPRANOS: Oranges to eat!

FIRST TENORS: Program with details!

SECOND BASSES: Wine!

SECOND TENORS: Water!

FIRST BASSES: Cigarettes!

FIRST SOPRANOS: Fans to fan yourself with!

SECOND SOPRANOS, TENORS, BASSES: Dansez, dansez, dansez, dansez ...

ALL SOPRANOS, TENORS, BASSES: Tournez, tournez, tournez, tournez ...

FIRST SOPRANOS: Danseuses et danseurs tournez ...

SECOND SOPRANOS: Au joyeux bruit du tambourin ...

FIRST TENORS: Au joyeux bruit du tambourin ...

SECOND BASSES: Au bruit—

SECOND TENORS: Dansez!

FIRST BASSES: —des castagnettes.

FIRST SOPRANOS: Allons, prenez-vous par la main—

SECOND SOPRANOS: Beaux garçons et jeunes fillettes.

FIRST TENORS: Allons, prenez-vous par la main!

SECOND BASSES: Garçons!

SECOND TENORS: Dansez!

FIRST BASSES: Jeunes fillettes!

FIRST SOPRANOS: Dansez, dansez!

ALL SOPRANOS: Dansez, dansez!

SOPRANOS, TENORS: Dansez, dansez!

SOPRANOS, TENORS, BASSES: Dansez, dansez, dansez, jeunes garçons, oui, dansez, jeunes fillettes!

SECOND SOPRANOS: De la vigueur, de la vigueur, et de la grâce. Señoras et caballeros, après, vous céderez la place aux toréros!

SECOND SOPRANOS, TENORS, BASSES: Dance, dance, dance, dance ...

ALL SOPRANOS, TENORS, BASSES: Turn, turn, turn turn ...

FIRST SOPRANOS: Men and women dancers, turn ...

SECOND SOPRANOS: To the gay noise of the tambourine ...

FIRST TENORS: To the gay noise of the tambourine ...

SECOND BASSES: To the noise—

SECOND TENORS: Dance!

FIRST BASSES: —of the castanets.

FIRST SOPRANOS: Come, take each other by the hand—

SECOND SOPRANOS: Handsome boys and pretty girls.

FIRST TENORS: Come on, take each other by the hand!

SECOND BASSES: Boys!

SECOND TENORS: Dance!

FIRST BASSES: Young girls!

FIRST SOPRANOS, Dance, dance!

ALL SOPRANOS: Dance, dance!

SOPRANOS, TENORS: Dance, dance!

SOPRANOS, TENORS, BASSES: Dance, dance, dance, young boys, yes, dance, young girls!

SECOND SOPRANOS: Lively now, lively now, gracefully now. Señoras and caballeros, later you'll give way to the toreros!

Set design for Act 4 by Nicola Benois. (*Courtesy Teatro di San Carlo, Naples*)

Act 4, Scene 1. Carmen takes leave of Escamillo before the *corrida*. (*Courtesy Royal Opera House, Covent Garden, London; photo by Roger Wood*)

SECOND SOPRANOS: Des oranges pour grignoter!

SECOND SOPRANOS: Oranges to eat!

FIRST TENORS: Le programme avec les détails!

FIRST TENORS: Program with details!

SECOND BASSES: Du vin!

SECOND BASSES: Wine!

SECOND TENORS: De l'eau!

SECOND TENORS: Water!

FIRST BASSES: Des cigarettes!

FIRST BASSES: Cigarettes!

FIRST SOPRANOS: À deux cuartos!

FIRST SOPRANOS: For two coppers!

FIRST, SECOND SOPRANOS: À deux cuartos!

FIRST, SECOND SOPRANOS: For two coppers!

SOPRANOS, TENORS: À deux cuartos! À deux cuartos!

SOPRANOS, TENORS: For two coppers! For two coppers!

SOPRANOS, TENORS, BASSES: Voyez! À deux cuartos! Señoras et caballeros!

SOPRANOS, TENORS, BASSES: Look! Two coppers! Señoras and caballeros!

Zuñiga and another officer appear, escorting Mercedes and Frasquita.

ZUÑIGA: Des oranges, vite!

ZUÑIGA: Oranges! Fast!

SECOND SOPRANOS (*to Frasquita and Mercedes*): En voici, prenez, prenez, mesdemoiselles.

SECOND SOPRANOS (*to Frasquita and Mercedes*): Here they are; take them, take them, ladies.

Zuñiga pays the girl for the oranges.

GIRL VENDOR: Merci, mon officier, merci!

GIRL VENDOR: Thank you, Señor Officer, thank you!

ALL OTHER VENDORS (*to Zuñiga*): Celles-ci, señor, sont plus belles!

ALL OTHER VENDORS (*to Zuñiga*): Señor, these are better!

FIRST SOPRANOS: Des éventails pour s'éventer!

FIRST SOPRANOS: Fans to fan yourself with!

SECOND SOPRANOS: Des oranges pour grignoter!

SECOND SOPRANOS: Oranges to eat!

FIRST SOPRANOS: Le programme avec les détails!

FIRST SOPRANOS: Program with details!

SECOND BASSES: Du vin!

SECOND BASSES: Wine!

FIRST SOPRANOS: Danseuses et danseurs tournez ...

SECOND SOPRANOS: Au joyeux bruit du tambourin—

FIRST SOPRANOS: Au joyeux bruit du tambourin!

SECOND BASSES: Au bruit—

SECOND SOPRANOS: Dansez!

FIRST BASSES: —des castagnettes! Après vous céderez la place au cortège des toréros!

FIRST SOPRANOS: Dansez, dansez!

ALL SOPRANOS: Dansez, dansez!

TENORS AND SOPRANOS: Dansez, dansez!

TENORS, SOPRANOS, BASSES: Dansez, dansez, dansez, jeunes garçons, oui, dansez, jeunes fillettes! Dansez, dansez, dansez, dansez, dansez, dansez, tournez, tournez!*

FIRST SOPRANOS: Men and women dancers turn ...

SECOND SOPRANOS: To the gay noise of the tambourine—

FIRST SOPRANOS: To the gay noise of the tambourine!

SECOND BASSES: To the noise—

SECOND SOPRANOS: Dance!

FIRST BASSES: —of the castanets! Later you'll give way to the parade of the toreros!

FIRST SOPRANOS: Dance, dance!

ALL SOPRANOS: Dance, dance!

TENORS, SOPRANOS: Dance, dance!

TENORS, SOPRANOS, BASSES: Dance, dance, dance, young boys, yes, dance, young girls, Dance, dance, dance, dance, dance, dance, turn turn!

* Sometimes a reprise follows from the words "De la vigueur" to this point.

SECOND SOPRANOS: Des oranges pour grignoter!

SECOND SOPRANOS: Oranges to eat!

FIRST TENORS: Le programme avec les détails!

FIRST TENORS: Program with details!

SECOND BASSES: Du vin!

SECOND BASSES: Wine!

SECOND TENORS: De l'eau!

SECOND TENORS: Water!

FIRST BASSES: Des cigarettes!

FIRST BASSES: Cigarettes!

FIRST SOPRANOS: À deux cuartos!

FIRST SOPRANOS: For two coppers!

FIRST, SECOND SOPRANOS: À deux cuartos!

FIRST, SECOND SOPRANOS: For two coppers!

SOPRANOS, TENORS: À deux cuartos! À deux cuartos!

SOPRANOS, TENORS: For two coppers! For two coppers!

SOPRANOS, TENORS, BASSES: Voyez! À deux cuartos! Señoras et caballeros!

SOPRANOS, TENORS, BASSES: Look! Two coppers! Señoras and caballeros!

Zuñiga and another officer appear, escorting Mercedes and Frasquita.

ZUÑIGA: Des oranges, vite!

ZUÑIGA: Oranges! Fast!

SECOND SOPRANOS (*to Frasquita and Mercedes*): En voici, prenez, prenez, mesdemoiselles.

SECOND SOPRANOS (*to Frasquita and Mercedes*): Here they are; take them, take them, ladies.

Zuñiga pays the girl for the oranges.

GIRL VENDOR: Merci, mon officier, merci!

GIRL VENDOR: Thank you, Señor Officer, thank you!

ALL OTHER VENDORS (*to Zuñiga*): Celles-ci, señor, sont plus belles!

ALL OTHER VENDORS (*to Zuñiga*): Señor, these are better!

FIRST SOPRANOS: Des éventails pour s'éventer!

FIRST SOPRANOS: Fans to fan yourself with!

SECOND SOPRANOS: Des oranges pour grignoter!

SECOND SOPRANOS: Oranges to eat!

FIRST SOPRANOS: Le programme avec les détails!

FIRST SOPRANOS: Program with details!

SECOND BASSES: Du vin!

SECOND BASSES: Wine!

FIRST SOPRANOS: Danseuses et danseurs tournez ...

SECOND SOPRANOS: Au joyeux bruit du tambourin—

FIRST SOPRANOS: Au joyeux bruit du tambourin!

SECOND BASSES: Au bruit—

SECOND SOPRANOS: Dansez!

FIRST BASSES: —des castagnettes! Après vous céderez la place au cortège des toréros!

FIRST SOPRANOS: Dansez, dansez!

ALL SOPRANOS: Dansez, dansez!

TENORS AND SOPRANOS: Dansez, dansez!

TENORS, SOPRANOS, BASSES: Dansez, dansez, dansez, jeunes garçons, oui, dansez, jeunes fillettes! Dansez, dansez, dansez, dansez, dansez, dansez, tournez, tournez!*

FIRST SOPRANOS: Men and women dancers turn ...

SECOND SOPRANOS: To the gay noise of the tambourine—

FIRST SOPRANOS: To the gay noise of the tambourine!

SECOND BASSES: To the noise—

SECOND SOPRANOS: Dance!

FIRST BASSES: —of the castanets! Later you'll give way to the parade of the toreros!

FIRST SOPRANOS: Dance, dance!

ALL SOPRANOS: Dance, dance!

TENORS, SOPRANOS: Dance, dance!

TENORS, SOPRANOS, BASSES: Dance, dance, dance, young boys, yes, dance, young girls, Dance, dance, dance, dance, dance, dance, turn turn!

---

* Sometimes a reprise follows from the words "De la vigueur" to this point.

SECOND SOPRANOS: De l'eau!

FIRST BASSES: Des cigarettes!

ZUÑIGA: Holà! des éventails!

A Gypsy comes up to Zuñiga, who pushes him aside.

GYPSY: Voulez-vous aussi des lorgnettes?

FIRST SOPRANOS: À deux cuartos!

FIRST, SECOND SOPRANOS: À deux cuartos!

SOPRANOS, TENORS: À deux cuartos!

SOPRANOS, TENORS, BASSES: À deux cuartos! Voyez! À deux cuartos! Señoras et caballeros! À deux cuartos! À deux cuartos! À deux cuartos! Voyez! Voyez!

SECOND SOPRANOS: Water!

FIRST BASSES: Cigarettes!

ZUÑIGA: Hey! Fans!

GYPSY: Do you want glasses, too?

FIRST SOPRANOS: For two coppers!

FIRST, SECOND SOPRANOS: For two coppers!

SOPRANOS, TENORS: For two coppers!

SOPRANOS, TENORS, BASSES: For two coppers! Look! For two coppers! Señoras and caballeros! For two coppers! For two coppers! For two coppers! Look! Look!

This is the end of the ballet/crowd-scene variant. The normal sequence of pages will now resume.

A crowd of excited children enters. Loud cries, fanfare.

CHILDREN: Les voici! Les voici! Voici la quadrille!

BASSES: Les voici!

TENORS: Les voici!

SECOND SOPRANOS: Les voici!

SOPRANOS, TENORS: Oui, les voici!

SOPRANOS, TENORS, BASSES: Voici la quadrille!

SOPRANOS, TENORS, BASSES, CHILDREN: Les voici! voici la quadrille, la quadrille des toréros! Sur les lances le soleil brille!

CHILDREN, SOPRANOS: En l'air, en l'air, en l'air, en l'air toques et sombréros!

TENORS: ––En l'air, en l'air, en l'air toques et sombréros!

BASSES: ––––En l'air, en l'air toques et sombréros!

CHILDREN, SOPRANOS, TENORS, BASSES: Les voici, voici la quadrille, la quadrille des toréros!

BASSES: Les voici!

BASSES, TENORS: Les voici!

BASSES, TENORS, SOPRANOS, CHILDREN: Les voici!

CHILDREN: Here they are! Here they are! Here's the cuadrilla!

BASSES: Here they are!

TENORS: Here they are!

SECOND SOPRANOS: Here they are!

SOPRANOS, TENORS: Yes, here they are!

SOPRANOS, TENORS, BASSES: Here's the cuadrilla!

SOPRANOS, TENORS, BASSES, CHILDREN: Here they are! Here's the cuadrilla! The cuadrilla of the toreros! The sun sparkles on their lances!

CHILDREN, SOPRANOS: In the air, in the air, in the air, in the air with caps and hats!

TENORS: ––In the air, in the air, in the air with caps and hats!

BASSES: ––––In the air, in the air with caps and hats!

CHILDREN, SOPRANOS, TENORS, BASSES: Here they are, here's the cuadrilla, the cuadrilla of the toreros!

BASSES: Here they are!

BASSES, TENORS: Here they are!

BASSES, TENORS, SOPRANOS, CHILDREN: Here they are!

The ceremonial procession which precedes a bullfight begins to enter the arena. The chorus comments as the procession passes. The alguazils enter.

CHILDREN: Voici, débouchant sur la place, voici d'abord,

CHILDREN: Here, coming into the square, here in first place,

marchant au pas, voici d'abord, marchant au pas, l'alguazil à vilaine face. À bas! à bas! à bas! à bas!

TENORS: À bas l'alguazil! à bas!

CHILDREN: À bas! à bas! à bas! à bas!

TENORS: Oui! à bas! à bas! à bas! à bas!

BASSES: À bas! à bas! à bas! à bas! à bas!

SOPRANOS: À bas! à bas! à bas!

CHILDREN: À bas!

The chulos and banderilleros pass through.

TENORS, BASSES: Et puis saluons au passage, saluons les hardis chulos! Bravo! Viva! gloire au courage! Voici les hardis chulos!

SOPRANOS: Voyez, les banderilléros, voyez quel air de crânerie!

BASSES: Voyez!

TENORS: Voyez!

CHILDREN: Voyez!

SOPRANOS: Voyez! quels regards, et de quel éclat étincelle la broderie de leur costume de combat!

BASSES: Voyez!

TENORS: Voyez!

CHILDREN: Voyez!

CHILDREN, SOPRANOS, TENORS, BASSES: Voici les banderilléros!

---

marching in step, in first place, marching in step, is the alguazil with the ugly face! Down! Down! Down! Down with him!

TENORS: Down with the alguazil! Down with him!

CHILDREN: Down! Down! Down! Down!

TENORS: Yes, down! Down! Down! Down!

BASSES: Down! Down! Down! Down! Down!

SOPRANOS: Down! Down! Down!

CHILDREN: Down!

TENORS, BASSES: And now let's cheer as they go by, cheer the brave chulos! Bravo! Viva! Glory to courage! Here are the brave chulos!

SOPRANOS: Look, the banderilleros, look how they swagger!

BASSES: Look!

TENORS: Look!

CHILDREN: Look!

SOPRANOS: Look! What a fine air, and how brightly the gold embroidery on their fighting costume sparkles!

BASSES: Look!

TENORS: Look!

CHILDREN: Look!

CHILDREN, SOPRANOS, TENORS, BASSES: Here are the banderilleros!

CHILDREN: Une autre quadrille s'avance!

SOPRANOS: Une autre quadrille s'avance!

TENORS: Voyez les picadors!

CHILDREN: Voyez les picadors!

BASSES: Voyez les picadors!

FIRST SOPRANOS, TENORS: Comme ils sont beaux!

CHILDREN, SECOND SOPRANOS: Ah! Comme ils sont beaux!

BASSES: Comme ils sont beaux!

FIRST SOPRANOS, TENORS: Comme ils vont du fer de leur lance harceler le flanc des taureaux!

CHILDREN: Ah! voyez, comme ils sont beaux!

SECOND SOPRANOS, BASSES: Comme il vont du fer de leur lance harceler le flanc des taureaux!

Escamillo finally marches in; near him is Carmen, proud and joyful, gaudily dressed.

BASSES: L'espada!

SECOND SOPRANOS: L'espada!

TENORS: L'espada!

FIRST SOPRANOS: L'espada!

CHILDREN: Escamillo!

BASSES: Escamillo!

SECOND SOPRANOS: Escamillo!

TENORS: Escamillo!

ALL: Escamillo! C'est l'espada, la fine lame, celui qui vient terminer tout, qui paraît à la fin du drame et qui frappe le

CHILDREN: Another cuadrilla is coming!

SOPRANOS: Another cuadrilla is coming!

TENORS: Look at the picadors!

CHILDREN: Look at the picadors!

BASSES: Look at the picadors!

FIRST SOPRANOS, TENORS: How handsome they are!

CHILDREN, SECOND SOPRANOS: Ah! How handsome they are!

BASSES: How handsome they are!

FIRST SOPRANOS, TENORS: How they are going to torment the bulls' sides with the iron of their pikes!

CHILDREN: Ah! Look! How handsome they are!

SECOND SOPRANOS, BASSES: How they are going to torment the bulls' sides with the iron of their pikes!

BASSES: The espada!

SECOND SOPRANOS: The espada!

TENORS: The espada!

FIRST SOPRANOS: The espada!

CHILDREN: Escamillo!

BASSES: Escamillo!

SECOND SOPRANOS: Escamillo!

TENORS: Escamillo!

ALL: Escamillo! It's the espada, the fine swordsman, the one who's going to end it all, who appears at the end of the

dernier coup! Vive Escamillo!
Vive Escamillo! Ah! bravo!
Les voici! voici la quadrille, la
quadrille des toréros! Sur les
lances le soleil brille!

CHILDREN, FIRST SOPRANOS: En
l'air—

CHILDREN, FIRST SOPRANOS,
TENORS: En l'air—

CHILDREN, SOPRANOS, TENORS: En
l'air—

CHILDREN, SOPRANOS, TENORS,
BASSES: En l'air toques et sombréros! Les voici! Voici la quadrille, la quadrille des toréros!

CHILDREN: Vive Escamillo!

BASSES: Vive Escamillo!

TENORS: Vive Escamillo!

ALL: Ah!—

CHILDREN, SOPRANOS: Vive
Escamillo! Vive Escamillo!

TENORS, BASSES: Vive Escamillo!
Bravo!

CHILDREN, SOPRANOS: Bravo!

TENORS, BASSES: Viva!

CHILDREN, SOPRANOS: Viva!

TENORS, BASSES: Bravo!

CHILDREN, SOPRANOS: Bravo!

CHILDREN, SOPRANOS, TENORS,
BASSES: Bravo!

ESCAMILLO (*to Carmen*): Si tu
m'aimes, Carmen, si tu
m'aimes, Carmen, tu pourras,
tout à l'heure, être fière de moi!
Si tu m'aimes, si tu m'aimes!

drama and strikes the last
blow! Viva Escamillo! Viva
Escamillo! Ah! bravo! Here
they are! Here's the cuadrilla,
the cuadrilla of the toreros! On
their lances the sun sparkles!

CHILDREN, FIRST SOPRANOS: In
the air—

CHILDREN, FIRST SOPRANOS,
TENORS: In the air—

CHILDREN, SOPRANOS, TENORS: In
the air—

CHILDREN, SOPRANOS, TENORS,
BASSES: In the air with caps
and hats! Here they are! Here's
the cuadrilla, the cuadrilla of
the toreros!

CHILDREN: Viva Escamillo!

BASSES: Viva Escamillo!

TENORS: Viva Escamillo!

ALL: Ah!—

CHILDREN, SOPRANOS: Viva
Escamillo! Viva Escamillo!

TENORS, BASSES: Viva Escamillo!
Bravo!

CHILDREN, SOPRANOS: Bravo!

TENORS, BASSES: Viva!

CHILDREN, SOPRANOS: Viva!

TENORS, BASSES: Bravo!

CHILDREN, SOPRANOS: Bravo!

CHILDREN, SOPRANOS, TENORS,
BASSES: Bravo!

ESCAMILLO (*to Carmen*): If you
love me, Carmen, if you love
me, Carmen, you will soon be
proud of me. If you love me, if
you love me!

CARMEN: Ah! je t'aime, Escamillo, je t'aime et que je
meure, si j'ai jamais aimé quelqu'un autant que toi!

ESCAMILLO, CARMEN: Ah! je
t'aime, oui, je t'aime!

BASSES (ALGUAZILS): Place, place!
place au seigneur Alcade!

CARMEN: Ah! I love you, Escamillo! I love you and may I
die if I have ever loved anyone as much as you!

ESCAMILLO, CARMEN: Ah! I love
you, yes, I love you!

BASSES (ALGUAZILS): Make way!
Make way! Make way for the
alcalde!

*A march by the orchestra. The alcalde, preceded and followed
by alguazils, marches very slowly to the background of the stage.
Frasquita and Mercedes approach Carmen.*

FRASQUITA (*in a low voice*): Carmen, un bon conseil, ne reste
pas ici.

CARMEN: Et pourquoi, s'il te
plaît?

MERCÉDÈS: Il est là!

CARMEN: Qui donc?

MERCÉDÈS: Lui! Don José! dans
la foule il se cache, regarde.

CARMEN: Oui, je le vois.

FRASQUITA: Prends garde!

CARMEN: Je ne suis pas femme à
trembler devant lui. Je l'attends, et je vais lui parler.

MERCÉDÈS: Carmen, crois-moi,
prends garde!

CARMEN: Je ne crains rien!

FRASQUITA: Prends garde!

FRASQUITA (*in a low voice*): Carmen, some good advice, don't
stay here.

CARMEN: And why, please?

MERCEDES: *He* is there!

CARMEN: Who's there?

MERCEDES: He! Don José. He's
hiding in the crowd, look!

CARMEN: Yes, I see him.

FRASQUITA: Watch out!

CARMEN: I'm not the woman to
be afraid of him. I'll wait for
him and I'm going to talk to
him.

MERCEDES: Carmen, take my
word for it, watch out!

CARMEN: I'm not afraid of anything!

FRASQUITA: Watch out!

*The alcalde has entered the arena. Behind him the procession of
the "cuadrilla" resumes its march and enters the arena, the crowd
following. The orchestra plays the motive "Les voici! Les voici!
Voici la quadrille!" and as the mob disappears into the arena,*

*Don José and Carmen are left alone on the stage. They look at
each other as the mob disappears and the music dies in the distance,
and come together.*

Scene Two

CARMEN: C'est toi?

DON JOSÉ: C'est moi!

CARMEN: L'on m'avait avertie que tu n'étais pas loin, que tu devais venir; l'on m'avait même dit de craindre pour ma vie; mais je suis brave, et n'ai pas voulu fuir.

DON JOSÉ: Je ne menace pas, j'implore, je supplie! Notre passé, Carmen, notre passé, je l'oublie! Oui, nous allons tous deux commencer une autre vie, loin d'ici sous d'autres cieux!

CARMEN: Tu demandes l'impossible! Carmen jamais n'a menti; son âme reste inflexible; entre elle et toi, tout est fini. Jamais je n'ai menti; entre nous tout est fini!

DON JOSÉ (*visibly shocked*): Carmen, il est temps encore, oui, il est temps encore— Ô ma Carmen, laisse-moi te sauver, toi que j'adore. (*Excitedly*): Ah! laisse-moi te sauver, et me sauver avec toi!

CARMEN: Non! je sais bien que c'est l'heure. Je sais bien que tu me tueras; mais que je vive

CARMEN: It's you!

DON JOSÉ: That's right!

CARMEN: I was warned that you weren't far away, that you'd come. They even told me to fear for my life. But I'm brave and I didn't want to run away!

DON JOSÉ: I'm not threatening, I'm pleading, I'm begging! What's past, Carmen, what's past, I forget. Yes, let's the two of us start a new life, far from here under other skies!

CARMEN: You're asking the impossible! Carmen has never lied. Her mind can't be changed. Everything is over between her and you. I have never lied. Everything is over between us!

DON JOSÉ (*visibly shocked*): Carmen, there is still time, yes, there's still time— O my Carmen, let me save you, you that I adore! (*Excitedly*): Ah! Let me save you, and save myself with you!

CARMEN: No! I know very well that this is the hour. I know very well you'll kill me; but if

ou que je meure, non, non! non, je ne te cèderai pas!

DON JOSÉ: Carmen! il est temps encore, oui, il est temps encore. Ô ma Carmen, laisse-moi te sauver, toi que j'adore! Ah! laisse-moi te sauver, et me sauver avec toi. Ô ma Carmen, il est temps encore. Ah! laisse-moi te sauver, Carmen, ah! laisse-moi te sauver, toi que j'adore! Et me sauver avec toi!

CARMEN: Pourquoi t'occuper encore d'un cœur qui n'est plus à toi! Non, ce cœur n'est plus à toi. En vain tu dis: "Je t'adore!" Tu n'obtiendras rien, non, rien de moi! Ah! c'est en vain. Tu n'obtiendras rien, rien de moi!

I live or if I die, no, no! no, I will not give in to you!

DON JOSÉ: Carmen! There's still time, yes, there's still time. O my Carmen, let me save you, you that I adore! Ah! Let me save you and save myself with you. O my Carmen, there's still time. Ah! Let me save you, Carmen. Ah! let me save you, you that I adore! And save myself with you!

CARMEN: Why do you still bother with a heart that is no longer yours? No, this heart is no longer yours. You're wasting your time saying: "I adore you!" You won't get anything from me, no, nothing from me! Ah! It's no use! You won't get anything, nothing from me!

Don José is almost beside himself with rage.

DON JOSÉ: Tu m'aimes donc plus?

DON JOSÉ: You don't love me any more then?

Carmen is silent.

DON JOSÉ: Tu ne m'aimes donc plus?

CARMEN (*serenely*): Non, je ne t'aime plus.

DON JOSÉ: Mais, moi, Carmen, je t'aime encore, Carmen, hélas, moi, je t'adore!

CARMEN: À quoi bon tout cela? que de mots superflus!

DON JOSÉ: Carmen, je t'aime, je t'adore! Eh bien! s'il faut

DON JOSÉ: You don't love me any more then?

CARMEN (*serenely*): No, I don't love you any more.

DON JOSÉ: But I, Carmen, I still love you, Carmen. I, I adore you!

CARMEN: What good is all this? So many useless words!

DON JOSÉ: Carmen, I love you, I adore you! All right! If I

pour te plaire, je resterai bandit, tout ce que tu voudras— Tout! tu m'entends, tout, tu m'entends, tout! Mais ne me quitte pas, ô ma Carmen. Ah! souviens-toi, souviens-toi du passé! Nous nous aimions, naguère! Ah ne me quitte pas, Carmen, ah! ne me quitte pas!

CARMEN: Jamais Carmen ne cédera! Libre elle est née et libre elle mourra!

SOPRANOS, TENORS, BASSES: Viva! viva! la course est belle! Viva! sur le sable sanglant, le taureau, le taureau s'élance!

FIRST SOPRANOS: Voyez!

FIRST SOPRANOS, TENORS: Voyez!

ALL SOPRANOS, TENORS: Voyez!

SOPRANOS, TENORS, BASSES: Voyez! Le taureau qu'on harcèle en bondissant s'élance, voyez, frappe juste, juste en plein cœur!

BASSES: Voyez!

BASSES, TENORS: Voyez!

BASSES, TENORS, SOPRANOS: Voyez!

SOPRANOS, TENORS, BASSES: Victoire!

have to, to please you, I'll remain a bandit, anything you want—anything! Do you hear me? Anything! Do you hear me? But don't leave me, O my Carmen. Ah! Remember, remember the past! We used to love each other, not long ago! Ah! Don't leave me, Carmen! Ah! Don't leave me!

CARMEN: Carmen will never give in! Free she was born and free she will die!

SOPRANOS, TENORS, BASSES: Viva! Viva! A beautiful corrida! Viva! On the bloody sand, the bull, the bull charges!

FIRST SOPRANOS: Look!

FIRST SOPRANOS, TENORS: Look!

ALL SOPRANOS, TENORS: Look!

SOPRANOS, TENORS, BASSES: Look! The bull that they're goading is rushing and charging! Look! Struck exactly, right through the heart!

BASSES: Look!

BASSES, TENORS: Look!

BASSES, TENORS, SOPRANOS: Look!

SOPRANOS, TENORS, BASSES: Victory!

During the chorus, Carmen and Don José remain silent. Cries of "Victoire, victoire!" are heard, and Carmen sighs with joy and pride. Don José watches her fixedly. When the chorus ends, Carmen takes a step toward the side of the arena.

DON JOSÉ (*stepping in front of her*): Où vas-tu?

DON JOSÉ (*stepping in front of her*): Where are you going?

CARMEN: Laisse-moi!

DON JOSÉ: Cet homme qu'on acclame, c'est ton nouvel amant!

CARMEN: Laisse-moi! Laisse-moi!

DON JOSÉ: Sur mon âme, tu ne passeras pas, Carmen—c'est moi que tu suivras!

CARMEN: Laisse-moi, Don José, je ne te suivrai pas.

DON JOSÉ: Tu vas le retrouver, dis—tu l'aimes donc?

Don José becomes angrier and angrier.

CARMEN: Je l'aime! je l'aime et devant la mort même je répéterai que je l'aime!

Again Carmen tries to enter the arena and is kept back by Don José as fanfares and cheers come from inside.

CHORUS: Viva! Viva! La course est belle! Viva! sur le sable sanglant, le taureau s'élance!

FIRST SOPRANOS: Voyez!

FIRST SOPRANOS, TENORS: Voyez!

ALL SOPRANOS, TENORS: Voyez!

SOPRANOS, TENORS, BASSES: Voyez! Le taureau qu'on harcèle en bondissant s'élance, voyez!

DON JOSÉ: Ainsi, le salut de mon âme je l'aurai perdu pour que toi—pour que tu t'en ailles, infâme, entre ses bras rire de moi! Non, par le sang, tu n'iras pas! Carmen, c'est moi que tu suivras!

CARMEN: Let me go!

DON JOSÉ: That man they're cheering—he's your new lover!

CARMEN: Let me go! Let me go!

DON JOSÉ: By my soul, you won't pass, Carmen—I'm the one you're going with!

CARMEN: Let me go, Don José, I'm not going with you!

DON JOSÉ: You're going to meet him! Tell me: Do you love him?

CARMEN: I love him! I love him and I'll repeat in the face of death itself that I love him!

CHORUS: Viva! Viva! A beautiful corrida! Viva! On the bloody sand the bull charges!

FIRST SOPRANOS: Look!

FIRST SOPRANOS, TENORS: Look!

ALL SOPRANOS, TENORS: Look!

SOPRANOS, TENORS, BASSES: Look! The bull they're goading is rushing and charging! Look!

DON JOSÉ: So! I've lost my very soul so that you, so that you can run away, you bitch, and laugh at me from his arms! No! By my blood! You will not go! Carmen, it's me you're coming with!

Act 4, Scene 2. Don José (Mario Del Monaco) and Carmen (Giulietta Simionato) are left alone in front of the arena. Set and costumes by Georges Wakhevitch. *(Courtesy Teatro alla Scala, Milan; photo by E. Piccagliani)*

Act 4, Scene 2. Carmen (Giulietta Simionato) is threatened by Don José (*left*: Giuseppe Di Stefano; *right*: Franco Corelli). Set and costumes by Georges Wakhevitch. (*Courtesy Teatro alla Scala, Milan; photos by E. Piccagliani*)

Act 4, Scene 2. Don José (Jon Andrew) pleads with Carmen (Joyce Blackham) to return to him. *(Courtesy Sadler's Wells Opera, London; photo by Donald Southern)*

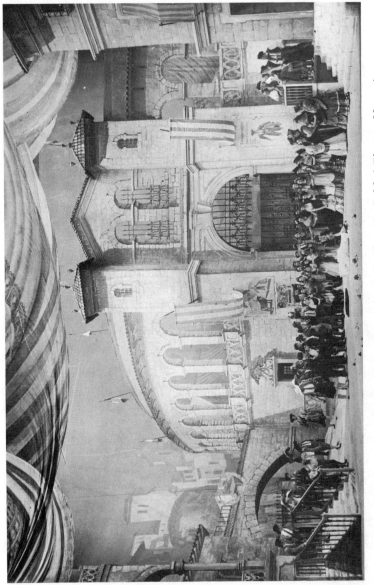

Act 4, Scene 2. Don José bends over Carmen's body. *(Courtesy Bolshoi Theater, Moscow)*

CARMEN: Non, non, jamais!

CARMEN: No! No! Never!

DON JOSÉ: Je suis las de te menacer!

DON JOSÉ: I'm tired of threatening you!

CARMEN (*violently*): Eh bien! Frappe-moi donc, ou laisse-moi passer!

CARMEN (*violently*): All right! Then strike or let me by!

CHORUS: Victoire!

CHORUS: Victory!

DON JOSÉ: Pour la dernière fois, démon, veux-tu me suivre?

DON JOSÉ: For the last time, you devil, are you going to come with me?

CARMEN: Non, non! Cette bague, autrefois, tu me l'avais donnée, tiens!

CARMEN: No! No! You once gave me this ring! Take it back!

She tears a ring off her finger and throws it at Don José.

DON JOSÉ: Eh bien! damnée!

DON JOSÉ: All right! Damn you!

José, knife in hand, advances on Carmen. She recoils, but José blocks her way. During this action fanfares and chorus are heard from the amphitheater.

CHORUS: Toréador, en garde! Toréador! Toréador! Et songe bien, oui, songe en combattant qu'un œil noir te regarde, et que l'amour t'attend, Toréador, l'amour t'attend!

CHORUS: Toreador! Look out! Toreador! Toreador! And dream, yes, dream while you're fighting that dark eyes are watching you, and that love is waiting for you, toreador, love is waiting for you!

Don José stabs Carmen, who falls down dead. The canvas opens and the mob pours out of the arena.

DON JOSÉ: Vous pouvez m'arrêter. C'est moi qui l'ai tuée!

DON JOSÉ: Come on! Arrest me! I'm the one that killed her!

Escamillo appears on the steps of the arena. Don José throws himself upon Carmen's corpse.

DON JOSÉ: Ah Carmen! ma Carmen adorée!

DON JOSÉ: Ah, Carmen! My darling Carmen!

APPENDIX:
OTHER VERSIONS OF "CARMEN"

As explained on pages 74 and 75, the original 1875 libretto of *Carmen* and the one used at the Opéra-Comique in Paris differ in many respects from the grand opera version that was the basis of the main text in this volume. Those passages (only) which differ, mostly spoken parts, are printed on the following pages, with indications of the place in the main text to which they correspond. (As may be seen, the Opéra-Comique text is essentially a condensation of that of 1875.)

The French column of the main text has been used as the basis for line counts. Separate stage directions do not enter into the count. In this appendix no heed has been paid to repetitions of words or phrases for musical reasons, nor to slight differences of punctuation.

I. THE 1875 VERSION

P. 83; add before stage directions to Scene Two:

MORALÈS: Attention! chut! Taisons-nous! Voici venir un vieil époux, œil soupçonneux, mine jalouse! Il tient au bras sa jeune épouse; l'amant sans doute n'est pas loin; il va sortir de quelque coin.

MORALES: Attention! Shh! Let's be quiet! Here comes an old husband, suspicious eyes, jealous expression! He has his young wife on his arm; her lover, no doubt, is not far away; he'll come out of some corner.

At that moment a young man rapidly comes into the square.

Ah! ah! ah! ah! Le voilà. Voyons comment ça tournera.

Ah! Ah! Ah! Ah! There he is! Let's see how it comes out.

The second verse continues and adapts itself faithfully to the actions of the three actors who are mimicked. The young man approaches the old gentleman and the young lady, and exchanges some words in a low voice, etc.

MORALÈS: Vous trouver ici, quel bonheur! Je suis bien votre serviteur. Il salue, il parle avec grâce. Le vieux mari fait la grimace; mais d'un air fort encourageant la dame accueille le galant.

MORALES (*imitating the eager greeting of the young man*): How fortunate to come upon you here! (*Assuming the surly manner of the elderly husband:*) Indeed, your servant, sir. (*Reassuming the manner of the young man:*) Oh so gracefully he makes his salutation and talks. (*In the manner of the old man:*) The elderly husband makes a sour face. (*Imitating the smiles of the lady:*) But the lady greets the young man very encouragingly.

At this point the young man surreptitiously takes a note out of his pocket, and manages to let the lady see it.

Ah! ah! ah! ah! L'y voilà. Ah! ah! ah! ah! L'y voilà; voyons comment ça tournera. Ah! ah! ah! ah! Voyons comment ça tournera.

Ah! Ah! Ah! Ah! He's at it now. Ah! Ah! Ah! Ah! He's at it now. Now let's see how it comes out. Ah! Ah! Ah! Ah! Now let's see how it comes out.

All three—the husband, the wife and the lover—promenade slowly around the place. The young man tries to pass his note to the lady.

Ils font ensemble quelques pas; notre amoureux, levant le bras, fait voir au mari quelque chose, et le mari toujours morose regarde en l'air. ... Le tour est fait, car la dame a pris le billet.

They take a few steps together; our lover, lifting his hand, makes the husband look at something, and the husband, always sour, looks into the air. ... The trick is done, for the lady has taken the letter.

With one hand the young man points out something in the sky to the old man, while with the other hand he passes the note to the lady.

MORALÈS: Ah! ah! ah! ah! Et voilà, on voit comment ça tournera.

MORALES: Ah! Ah! Ah! Ah! And there it is; you see how it will come out.

ALL: Ah! ah! ah! ah! Et voilà, on voit comment ça tournera.

ALL: Ah! Ah! Ah! Ah! And there it is; you see how it will come out.

From the far distance is heard a military march, clarions and fifes. The new guard is approaching. The young man and the elderly husband shake hands cordially. The young man respectfully salutes the lady. An officer emerges from the post. The soldiers of the post take up their lances and form a line in front of the guardhouse. The military march comes closer and closer. The new guard finally enters from the left and crosses the bridge. Two bugles and two fifes first. Then a band of little street boys who are trying to take long strides to march at the pace of the dragoons. The children as small as possible. Behind the boys Lieutenant Zuñiga and Corporal Don José, then the dragoons with their lances.

P. 84; in place of lines 5 from bottom to bottom:

MORALÈS: Il y a une jolie fille qui est venue te demander. Elle a dit qu'elle reviendrait. ...

MORALES (*to Don José*): A pretty girl was just here looking for you. She said she would return. ...

DON JOSÉ: Une jolie fille?

DON JOSÉ: A pretty girl?

MORALÈS: Oui, et gentiment habillée, une jupe bleue, des nattes tombant sur les épaules ...

MORALES: Yes, and nicely dressed, a blue skirt and braids falling down over her shoulders.

DON JOSÉ: C'est Micaëla. Ce ne peut être que Micaëla.

DON JOSÉ: That's Micaëla. It could only be Micaëla.

MORALÈS: Elle n'a pas dit son nom.

MORALES: She didn't tell her name.

P. 85; in place of passage from line 15 to p. 86, line 3:

ZUÑIGA: Dites-moi, brigadier?

ZUÑIGA: Tell me something, corporal.

DON JOSÉ: Mon lieutenant?

DON JOSÉ (*getting up*): Yes, lieutenant?

ZUÑIGA: Je ne suis dans le régiment que depuis deux jours

ZUÑIGA: I've only been in this regiment for two days and I've

et jamais je n'étais venu à Séville. Qu'est-ce que ce grand bâtiment?

DON JOSÉ: C'est la manufacture de tabacs ...

ZUÑIGA: Ce sont des femmes qui travaillent là?

DON JOSÉ: Oui, mon lieutenant. Elles n'y sont pas maintenant; tout à l'heure, après leur dîner, elles vont revenir. Et je vous réponds qu'alors il y aura du monde pour les voir passer.

ZUÑIGA: Elles sont beaucoup?

DON JOSÉ: Ma foi, elles sont bien quatre ou cinq cents qui roulent des cigares dans une grande salle ...

ZUÑIGA: Ce doit être curieux.

DON JOSÉ: Oui, mais les hommes ne peuvent pas entrer dans cette salle sans une permission.

ZUÑIGA: Ah!

DON JOSÉ: Parce que, lorsqu'il fait chaud, ces ouvrières se mettent à leur aise, surtout les jeunes.

ZUÑIGA: Il y en a de jeunes?

DON JOSÉ: Mais oui, mon lieutenant.

ZUÑIGA: Et de jolies?

DON JOSÉ: Je le suppose. ... Mais à vous dire vrai, et bien que j'aie été de garde ici plusieurs fois déjà, je n'en suis pas bien sûr, car je ne les ai jamais beaucoup regardées. ...

ZUÑIGA: Allons donc ...

never been to Seville before. What is that big building?

DON JOSÉ: That's the tobacco factory.

ZUÑIGA: Are there women working there?

DON JOSÉ: Yes, lieutenant. They're not in there now; in a little while, after their dinner, they'll come back. And I'd tell you that then there will be a mob here watching them go by.

ZUÑIGA: Are there a lot of them?

DON JOSÉ: Oh, there are certainly four or five hundred who roll cigars in one big room.

ZUÑIGA: That must be something to see.

DON JOSÉ: Yes, but men cannot go into this room without a pass.

ZUÑIGA: Ah!

DON JOSÉ: Because when it gets hot, they take off their clothing to keep comfortable, especially the young ones.

ZUÑIGA: There are young ones there?

DON JOSÉ: Yes, lieutenant.

ZUÑIGA: Goodlooking ones, too?

DON JOSÉ (*laughing*): I suppose so. But to tell you the truth, even though I've already been on guard here several times, I am not sure, because I've never really looked at them much.

ZUÑIGA: Come on!

DON JOSÉ: Que voulez-vous? ...
ces Andalouses me font peur.
Je ne suis pas fait à leurs
manières, toujours à railler ...
jamais un mot de raison ...

ZUÑIGA: Et puis nous avons un
faible pour les jupes bleues, et
pour les nattes tombant sur les
épaules ...

DON JOSÉ: Ah! Mon lieutenant a
entendu ce que me disait
Moralès? ...

ZUÑIGA: Oui ...

DON JOSÉ: Je ne le nierai pas ...
la jupe bleue, les nattes ...
c'est le costume de la Navarre
... ça me rappelle le pays ...

ZUÑIGA: Vous êtes Navarrais?

DON JOSÉ: Et vieux chrétien.
Don José Lizzarabengoa, c'est
mon nom ... On voulait que je
fusse d'église, et l'on m'a fait
étudier. Mais je ne profitais
guère, j'aimais trop jouer à la
paume. Un jour que j'avais
gagné, un gars de l'Alava me
chercha querelle; j'eus encore
l'avantage, mais cela m'obligea
de quitter le pays. Je me fis
soldat! Je n'avais plus mon
père; ma mère me suivit et vint
s'établir à dix lieues de Séville
... avec la petite Micaëla ...
c'est une orpheline que ma
mère a recueillie, et qui n'a pas
voulu se séparer d'elle ...

ZUÑIGA: Et quel âge a-t-elle, la
petite Micaëla?

DON JOSÉ: Why not? I'm afraid
of these Andalusian women.
I'm not cut out for their ways,
always jeering—never a
straight word.

ZUÑIGA: And then we have a
weakness for blue skirts and for
braids that fall down over the
shoulders.

DON JOSÉ: Ah, the lieutenant
heard what Morales was telling
me?

ZUÑIGA: Yes.

DON JOSÉ: I don't deny it. Blue
skirt and braids—that's the
costume of Navarre. It reminds
me of my homeland.

ZUÑIGA: You're a Navarrese?

DON JOSÉ: And an Old Christian.
Don José Lizzarabengoa is my
name. They wanted me to to
into the church and they made
me study. But it didn't do me
any good; I would much rather
play *paume*.* One day when I
won, a fellow from Alava
picked a fight with me. I still
had the better of it, but I had
to leave the country. I became
a soldier! My father was dead;
my mother has followed me
and has settled about ten miles
from Seville ... with little
Micaëla; she's an orphan that
my mother took in, and
Micaëla doesn't want to be
separated from her.

ZUÑIGA: How old is she, this
little Micaëla?

* A game like tennis.

DON JOSÉ: Dix-sept ans. ...

ZUÑIGA: Il fallait dire cela tout de suite ... Je comprends maintenant pourquoi vous ne pouvez pas me dire si les ouvrières de la manufacture sont jolies ou laides ...

DON JOSÉ: Seventeen.

ZUÑIGA: You should have said so right away. Now I understand why you can't tell me if the girls in the factory are good-looking or ugly.

The factory bell is heard.

DON JOSÉ: Voici la cloche qui sonne, mon lieutenant, et vous allez pouvoir juger par vous-même ... Quant à moi je vais faire une chaîne pour attacher mon épinglette.

DON JOSÉ: That's the bell, lieu-tenant, and you can go judge for yourself. As for me, I'm going to make a chain for my priming pin.

P. 87, to follow line 3 from bottom:

SOLDIERS: Sans faire les cruelles, écoutez-nous, les belles, vous que nous adorons, que nous idolâtrons. [*Followed by repeat of cigarette girls' chorus.*]

SOLDIERS: Don't be cruel, listen to us, we adore you, we idolize you!

P. 91; to follow line 11:

CARMEN: Eh! Compère, qu'est-ce que tu fais là? ...

DON JOSÉ: Je fais une chaîne avec du fil de laiton, une chaîne pour attacher mon épinglette.

CARMEN: Ton   épinglette, vraiment. Ton épinglette ... épinglier de mon âme ...

CARMEN: Hey, pal, what are you doing there?

DON JOSÉ: I'm making a chain out of brass wire, a chain to attach my priming pin to.

CARMEN (*laughing*): Your prim-ing pin, that's good! Your priming pin! You're my darling pinmaker.

She pulls a cassia-flower out of her corsage and darts it at Don José. He leaps to his feet. The cassia-flower has fallen in front of him. A burst of laughter comes from the onlookers; the factory bell rings a second time. The factory girls and the onlookers leave.

P. 91; in place of passage from line 4 from bottom to p. 92, line 4:

DON JOSÉ: Qu'est-ce que cela veut dire, ces façons-là? ... Quelle effronterie! ... (*Smiling*:) Tout ça parce que je ne faisais pas attention à elle! ... Alors, suivant l'usage des femmes et des chats qui ne viennent pas quand on les appelle, et qui viennent quand on ne les appelle pas, elle est venue ... Avec quelle adresse elle me l'a lancée, cette fleur ... là, juste entre les deux yeux ... ça m'a fait l'effet d'une balle qui m'arrivait ...

DON JOSÉ: What does this mean, behavior like this? What brazenness! (*Smiling*:) All because I didn't pay any attention to her. Well, that's just like women and cats: they don't come when you call them, and they do come when you don't call them—and she came. (*Looking at the cassia-flower on the ground by his feet:*) The way she threw that flower at me was very good. She struck me right between the eyes with it, and I felt as if a bullet hit me.

He breathes the perfume of the flower.

Comme c'est fort! ... Certainement s'il y a des sorcières, cette fille-là en est une.

Really strong. If there are such things as witches, that girl surely is one.

P. 92; instead of lines 5 to 8:

MICAËLA: Monsieur le brigadier?
DON JOSÉ: Quoi? ... Qu'est-ce que c'est? ... Micaëla! ... c'est toi ...
MICAËLA: C'est moi! ...
DON JOSÉ: Et tu viens de là-bas? ...
MICAËLA: Et je viens de là-bas ...

MICAËLA: Corporal?
DON JOSÉ (*hastily hiding the cassia-flower*): What? What is it? Micaela! It's you!
MICAËLA: It is I.
DON JOSÉ: And you have come from over there?
MICAËLA: And I have come from over there.

P. 94; instead of lines 12 from bottom and 11 from bottom:

et la vénère et qu'il se conduit aujourd'hui en bon sujet, pour que [sa mère soit contente de lui ...]

and respects her and that he is conducting himself well, so that [his mother will be satisfied with him ...]

P. 96; instead of lines 1 to 18:

DON JOSÉ: Attends un peu maintenant ... je vais lire sa lettre ...

MICAËLA: J'attendrai, monsieur le brigadier, j'attendrai ...

DON JOSÉ: Ah! "Continue à te bien conduire, mon enfant. L'on t'a promis de te faire maréchal-des-logis. Peut-être alors pourrais-tu quitter le service, te faire donner une petite place et revenir près de moi. Je commence à me faire bien vieille. Tu reviendrais près de moi et tu te marierais, nous n'aurions pas, je pense, grand'peine à te trouver une femme, et je sais bien, quant à moi, celle que je te conseillerais de choisir; c'est tout justement celle qui te porte ma lettre ... Il n'y en a pas de plus sage ni de plus gentille ..."

MICAËLA: Il vaut mieux que je ne sois pas là!

DON JOSÉ: Pourquoi donc? ...

MICAËLA: Je viens de me rappeler que votre mère m'a chargée de quelques petits achats: je vais m'en occuper tout de suite.

DON JOSÉ: Attends un peu, j'ai fini ...

MICAËLA: Vous finirez quand je ne serai plus là ...

DON JOSÉ: Wait a minute. I'm going to read her letter.

MICAËLA: I'll wait, corporal, I'll wait.

DON JOSÉ (*holding the letter to his heart before reading it*): Ah! (*Reading:*) "Keep on doing well, my child. They have promised to make you a sergeant. Perhaps then you will be able to quit the service, get yourself a job, and come back near me. I'm beginning to get very old. You would come back near me and you would get married; we won't have any great trouble, I think, in finding you a wife, and I know well, as far as I am concerned, the one that I would advise you to pick: it's no one but the girl who is carrying my letter to you ... There are none better-behaved or nicer ..."

MICAËLA (*interrupting him*): It would be better if I weren't here.

DON JOSÉ: Why?

MICAËLA: I've just remembered that your mother asked me to make a few small purchases; I'm going to attend to them right away.

DON JOSÉ: Wait a minute, I've almost finished.

MICAËLA: You'll finish when I'm not here.

DON JOSÉ: Mais la réponse? ...

MICAËLA: Je viendrai la prendre avant mon départ et je la porterai à votre mère ... Adieu.

DON JOSÉ: Micaëla!

MICAËLA: Non, non ... je reviendrai, j'aime mieux cela ... je reviendrai, je reviendrai ... (*Exit*).

DON JOSÉ: Il n'y en a pas de plus sage, ni de plus gentille ... il n'y en a pas surtout qui t'aime davantage ... et si tu voulais ..." Oui, ma mère, oui, je ferai ce que tu désires ... j'épouserai Micaëla, et quant à cette bohémienne, avec ses fleurs qui ensorcellent ...

DON JOSÉ: But my answer?

MICAËLA: I'll come back and pick it up before I leave and I'll take it to your mother. Goodbye.

DON JOSÉ: Micaëla!

MICAËLA: No, no, I'll be back, I'd rather have it that way, I'll be back, I'll be back. (*Exit*.)

DON JOSÉ (*reading*): "There are none better-behaved, none nicer ... above all, there are none that love you better ... and if you are willing ..." Yes, mother, yes, I'll do what you want. I'll marry Micaëla, and as for that Gypsy with her witch flowers ...

Just as he is about to tear the flowers from his jacket, an uproar from the factory. The lieutenant enters, followed by soldiers.

ZUÑIGA: Eh bien! eh bien! qu'est-ce qui arrive? ...

ZUÑIGA: All right! All right! What's going on?

P. 100; instead of lines 1 to 9:

ZUÑIGA: Voyons, brigadier ... Maintenant que nous avons un peu de silence ... qu'est-ce que vous avez trouvé là-dedans? ...

DON JOSÉ: J'ai d'abord trouvé trois cents femmes, criant, hurlant, gesticulant, faisant un tapage à ne pas entendre Dieu tonner ... D'un côté il y en avait une les quatre fers en l'air, qui criait: Confession! confession! je suis morte ... Elle avait sur la figure un X qu'on venait

ZUÑIGA: All right, corporal. Now that we have a little quiet, what did you find in there?

DON JOSÉ: First of all I found three hundred women shrieking, howling, waving their arms around, making such a racket that you couldn't have heard God thunder. On one side one of the girls was down on her back screaming, "Get a priest, get a priest, I'm dying." There

de lui marquer en deux coups de couteau ... en face de la blessée j'ai vu ...

was an "x" on her face, made by two knife-cuts, and opposite the wounded woman I saw ...

A look from Carmen stops him.

ZUÑIGA: Eh bien? ...

DON JOSÉ: J'ai vu mademoiselle...

ZUÑIGA: Mademoiselle Carmencita?

DON JOSÉ: Oui, mon lieutenant ...

ZUÑIGA: Et qu'est-ce qu'elle disait, mademoiselle Carmencita?

DON JOSÉ: Elle ne disait rien, mon lieutenant, elle serrait les dents et roulait des yeux comme un caméléon.

CARMEN: On m'avait provoquée ... je n'ai fait que me défendre ... Monsieur le brigadier vous le dira ... N'est-ce pas, monsieur le brigadier?

DON JOSÉ: Tout ce que j'ai pu comprendre au milieu du bruit, c'est qu'une discussion s'était élevée entre ces deux dames, et qu'à la suite de cette discussion, mademoiselle, avec le couteau dont elle coupait le bout des cigares, avait commencé à dessiner des croix de saint André sur le visage de sa camarade ...

ZUÑIGA: Well?

DON JOSÉ: I saw this girl.

ZUÑIGA: Señorita Carmencita?

DON JOSÉ: Yes, lieutenant.

ZUÑIGA: And what did Señorita Carmencita have to say?

DON JOSÉ: She didn't say anything, lieutenant; she was clenching her teeth and rolling her eyes like a chameleon.

CARMEN: They started it. All I did was defend myself. The corporal will tell you so. (*To José:*) Isn't that right, Corporal?

DON JOSÉ (*hesitating a moment*): All that I could understand in the midst of the noise was that an argument started between the two girls, and that following this argument, the señorita, with the knife that she was using to trim the cigar ends, started to carve a St. Andrew's cross on her friend's face.

The lieutenant looks at Carmen; Carmen, after a glance at Don José and a slight shrug of her shoulders, assumes an expression of impassiveness.

Le cas m'a paru clair. J'ai prié mademoiselle de me suivre ...

The case seemed clear to me. I asked the señorita to come

Elle d'abord fait un mouvement comme pour résister ... puis elle s'est résignée ... et m'a suivi, douce comme un mouton!

ZUÑIGA: Et la blessure de l'autre femme?

DON JOSÉ: Très-légère, mon lieutenant, deux balafres à fleur de peau.

ZUÑIGA: Eh bien, la belle, vous avez entendu le brigadier? ... Je n'ai pas besoin de vous demander si vous avez dit la vérité.

DON JOSÉ: Foi de Navarrais, mon lieutenant!

Carmen turns abruptly and looks again at José.

ZUÑIGA: Eh bien ... vous avez entendu? ... Avez-vous quelque chose à répondre? ... parlez, j'attends ...

Carmen, instead of answering, starts to sing.

P. 100; instead of lines 15 to 17:

ZUÑIGA: Ce ne sont pas des chansons que je te demande, c'est une réponse.

P. 100; instead of lines 24 from top to 4 from bottom:

ZUÑIGA: Ah! ah! nous le prenons sur ce ton-là ... Ce qui est sûr, n'est-ce pas, c'est qu'il y a eu des coups de couteau, et que c'est elle qui les a donnés ...

At this moment five or six girls on the right break through the line of guards and throw themselves into the scene, screaming:

CHORUS: Oui, oui, c'est elle! ...

---

along with me. At first she made a movement as if to resist, but then she resigned herself ... she came along with me as sweet as a lamb.

ZUÑIGA: And the other girl's wound?

DON JOSÉ: Very light, Lieutenant. Two skin cuts.

ZUÑIGA (*to Carmen*): Well, good-looking, you've heard the corporal. (*To José:*) I don't have to ask you if you've told the truth.

DON JOSÉ: On the word of a Navarrese, Lieutenant.

ZUÑIGA (*to Carmen*): Very well. You have heard this. Do you have any answer? Speak, I'm waiting.

ZUÑIGA: I'm not asking you for songs. I want an answer.

ZUÑIGA: Ah! Ah! So that's the attitude we're taking! (*To Jose:*) It is certain, isn't it, that there were knife cuts and she was the one who did it ...

CHORUS: Yes, yes, she's the one!

ZUÑIGA: Eh! eh! vous avez la main leste décidément. Trouvez-moi une corde.

ZUÑIGA: Eh, eh? You've really got a fast hand. (*To the soldiers:*) Find me a piece of rope.

P. 101; instead of lines 1 to 5:

A moment of quiet, then Carmen starts to sing in the most insolent way, staring at the officer.

SOLDIER: Voilà, mon lieutenant.

SOLDIER (*carrying a rope*): Here it is, lieutenant.

ZUÑIGA: Prenez, et attachez-moi ces deux jolies mains.

ZUÑIGA (*to Don José*): Take it, and tie those two pretty hands.

Carmen, without making the least resistance, holds out her two hands to Don José with a smile.

C'est dommage vraiment, car elle est gentille ... Mais si gentille que vous soyez, vous n'irez pas moins faire un tour à la prison. Vous pourrez y chanter vos chansons de bohémienne. Le porte-clefs vous dira ce qu'il en pense.

It's too bad, really, because she's nice-looking ... But no matter how goodlooking you are, you're not getting away without a stay in prison. You can sing your Gypsy songs there. The turnkey will tell you what he thinks of them.

Carmen's hands are tied. They make her sit down on a stool in front of the guardhouse. She sits there, motionless, eyes cast to the ground.

Je vais écrire l'ordre. C'est vous qui la conduirez ...

I'm going to write the order. (*To Don José:*) You take her there ...

Zuñiga leaves.

P. 101; instead of lines 6 from top to 3 from bottom:

A brief moment of silence. Carmen raises her eyes and looks at Don José. He turns away, goes away a few steps, then turns back to Carmen, who watches him steadily.

CARMEN: Où me conduirez-vous? ...

CARMEN: Where are you going to take me?

DON JOSÉ: À la prison, ma pauvre enfant ...

DON JOSÉ: To prison.

CARMEN: Hélas! que deviendrai-je? Seigneur officier, ayez pitié de moi ... Vous êtes si jeune, si gentil ...

CARMEN: Oh, what will become of me? Señor Officer, have pity on me. You are so young, so nice.

José does not answer; he walks back and forth, while Carmen continues to watch him.

Cette corde, comme vous l'avez serrée, cette corde ... j'ai les poignets brisés.

This rope, you've tied it so tight, this rope ... my wrists are broken.

DON JOSÉ: Si elle vous blesse, je puis la desserrer ... Le lieutenant m'a dit de vous attacher les mains ... il ne m'a pas dit ...

DON JOSÉ (*coming near to Carmen*): If it hurts you, I can loosen it. The lieutenant told me to tie your hands. He didn't tell me ...

He loosens the rope.

CARMEN: Laisse-moi m'échapper, je te donnerai un morceau de la bar lachi, une petite pierre qui te fera aimer de toutes les femmes.

CARMEN: Let me escape and I'll give you a piece of bar lachi,* a little stone that will make all the women fall in love with you.

DON JOSÉ: Nous ne sommes pas ici pour dire des balivernes ... il faut aller à la prison. C'est la consigne, et il n'y a pas de remède.

DON JOSÉ (*drawing back*): We're not here to talk foolishness. You have to go to jail. It's orders. There's nothing can be done about it.

CARMEN: Tout à l'heure vous avez dit: foi de Navarrais ... vous êtes des Provinces? ...

CARMEN: You just said: "On the word of a Navarrese." Are you from the Provinces?

DON JOSÉ: Je suis d'Elizondo ...

DON JOSÉ: I'm from Elizondo.

CARMEN: Et moi d'Etchalar ...

CARMEN: And I'm from Etchalar.

DON JOSÉ: D'Etchalar! ... c'est à quatre heures d'Elizondo, Etchalar.

DON JOSÉ (*stopping*): Etchalar? That's about four hours from Elizondo.

CARMEN: Oui, c'est là que je suis née ... J'ai été emmenée par des Bohémiens à Séville. Je travaillais à la manufacture

CARMEN: Yes, that's where I was born. I was kidnapped by Gypsies and brought to Seville. I was working in the factory to

* Lodestone.

pour gagner de quoi retourner en Navarre, près de ma pauvre mère qui n'a que moi pour soutien ... On m'a insultée parce que je ne suis pas de ce pays de filous, de marchands d'oranges pourries, et ces coquines se sont mises toutes contre moi parce que je leur ai dit que tous leurs Jacques de Séville avec leurs couteaux ne feraient pas peur à un gars de chez nous avec son béret bleu et son maquila. Camarade, mon ami, ne ferez-vous rien pour une payse?

DON JOSÉ: Vous êtes Navarraise, vous? ...

CARMEN: Sans doute.

DON JOSÉ: Allons donc ... il n'y a pas un mot de vrai ... vos yeux seuls, votre bouche, votre teint ... Tout vous dit Bohémienne ...

CARMEN: Bohémienne, tu crois?

DON JOSÉ: J'en suis sûr ...

CARMEN: Au fait, je suis bien bonne de me donner la peine de mentir ... Oui, je suis Bohémienne, mais tu n'en feras pas moins ce que je te demande ... Tu le feras parce que tu m'aimes ...

DON JOSÉ: Moi!

CARMEN: Eh! oui, tu m'aimes ... ne me dis pas non, je m'y connais! tes regards, la façon dont tu me parles. Et cette fleur que tu as gardée. Oh! tu

* A sort of quarterstaff.

get the money to get back to Navarre, to my poor mother who has only me to support her. They insulted me because I don't belong to this country of cheats and rotten-orange sellers; and these sluts are all against me because I told them that all their Jack o' Sevilles with their knives wouldn't frighten one of our boys with blue berets and maquilas.* Comrade, friend, won't you do anything for a fellow Basque?

DON JOSÉ: You're a Navarrese? You ...

CARMEN: Absolutely!

DON JOSÉ: Come on ... there's not a word of truth in it. Your eyes alone, your mouth, your complexion ... they all say Gypsy ...

CARMEN: You think I'm a Gypsy?

DON JOSÉ: I know it.

CARMEN: Actually, I'm silly to go to the trouble of lying ... Yes, I'm a Gypsy, but you will still do what I ask you, You'll do it because you love me.

DON JOSÉ: Me?

CARMEN: Eh! Yes, you love me ... don't tell me you don't. I know it. The way you look at me, the way you talk to me. And this flower that you've

peux la jeter maintenant … cela n'y fera rien. Elle est restée assez de temps sur ton cœur; le charme a opéré …

kept. Oh, you can throw it away now; that will not make any difference. it's been there long enough over your heart; the charm has worked.

DON JOSÉ: Ne me parle plus, tu entends, je te défends de me parler …

DON JOSÉ (*with anger*): Don't talk to me any more, do you hear, I forbid you to talk to me.

CARMEN: C'est très-bien, seigneur officier, c'est très-bien. Vous me défendez de parler, je ne parlerai plus …

CARMEN: That's all right, Señor Officer; that's all right. You forbid me to talk. I won't talk any more.

She looks at José, who draws back.

Près de la Porte de [Séville, chez …]

Near the gate of [Seville, at my friend …]

P. 102; instead of lines 5 from bottom to 3 from bottom:

officier qui m'aime et que l'un de ces jours je pourrai bien aimer.

officer who loves me, and one of these days I could love him well.

P. 103; add after line 6 from bottom:

DON JOSÉ: Le lieutenant! … Prenez garde.

DON JOSÉ: The lieutenant! Watch out!

Carmen seats herself on the stool, her hands behind her back. The lieutenant reënters.

P. 103; instead of line 2 from bottom and 1 from bottom:

CARMEN: Sur le pont je te pousserai, je te

CARMEN: On the bridge I'll give you a push, I'll

P. 108; instead of passage from line 4 from bottom to p. 109, line 10 from bottom:

A very rapid, very violent dance. Carmen herself dances, and with the last notes of the orchestra flings herself panting upon a tavern bench. After the dance Lillas Pastia begins to pace around the officers with an embarrassed air.

ZUÑIGA: Vous avez quelque chose à nous dire, maître Lillas Pastia?

PASTIA: Mon Dieu, messieurs ...

MORALÈS: Parle, voyons ...

PASTIA: Il commence à se faire tard ... et je suis, plus que personne, obligé d'observer les règlements. Monsieur le corrégidor étant assez mal disposé à mon égard, je ne sais pas pourquoi il est mal disposé ...

ZUÑIGA: Je le sais très-bien, moi. C'est parce que ton auberge est le rendez-vous ordinaire de tous les contrebandiers de la province.

PASTIA: Que ce soit pour cette raison ou pour une autre, je suis obligé de prendre garde ... or, je vous le répète, il commence à se faire tard.

MORALÈS: Cela veut dire que tu nous mets à la porte!

PASTIA: Oh, non, messieurs les officiers ... oh! non ... je vous fais seulement observer que mon auberge devrait être fermée depuis dix minutes ...

ZUÑIGA: Dieu sait ce qui s'y passe dans ton auberge une fois qu'elle est fermée ...

PASTIA: Oh, mon lieutenant ...

ZUÑIGA: Enfin! Nous avons encore, avant l'appel, le temps d'aller passer une heure au théâtre ... vous y viendrez avec nous, n'est-ce pas, les belles?

ZUÑIGA: Do you have something to say to us, Lillas Pastia?

PASTIA: Gentlemen ...

MORALES: Talk, let us have it.

PASTIA: It's beginning to get late ... and more than anyone else I have to obey the rules. The Corregidor has it in for me ... I don't know why he has it in for me ...

ZUÑIGA: I know very well. It's because your tavern is the usual hangout for all the smugglers in the province.

PASTIA: No matter if it's for that reason, or another, I have to watch my step ... and so I repeat, it's beginning to get late.

MORALES: That means you're showing us the door!

PASTIA: Oh, no, gentlemen ... oh no, I just call it to your attention that my tavern should have been closed ten minutes ago.

ZUÑIGA: God knows what happens in your tavern once it is closed!

PASTIA: Oh, lieutenant!

ZUÑIGA: Enough! We have time before roll call to spend an hour at the theater. Will you come there with us, girls?

Pastia signals the Gypsies to refuse.

FRASQUITA: Non, messieurs les officiers, non, nous restons ici, nous.

ZUÑIGA: Comment, vous ne viendrez pas …

MERCÉDÈS: C'est impossible …

MORALÈS: Mercédès! …

MERCÉDÈS: Je regrette …

MORALÈS: Frasquita!

FRASQUITA: Je suis désolée …

ZUÑIGA: Mais toi, Carmen … je suis bien sûr que tu ne refuseras pas …

CARMEN: C'est ce qui vous trompe, mon lieutenant … je refuse et encore plus nettement qu'elles deux, si c'est possible …

FRASQUITA: No, gentlemen, we shall stay here.

ZUÑIGA: What? You won't come?

MERCEDES: It's impossible.

MORALES: Mercedes!

MERCEDES: I'm so sorry …

MORALES: Frasquita!

FRASQUITA: I'm heartbroken …

ZUÑIGA: How about you, Carmen? I'm sure you won't say no.

CARMEN: That's where you're wrong, lieutenant. I refuse and even more flatly than the other two girls, if that's possible.

While the lieutenant is talking to Carmen, Andres and the other two soldiers try to persuade Frasquita and Mercedes.

ZUÑIGA: Tu m'en veux?

CARMEN: Pourquoi vous en voudrais-je?

ZUÑIGA: Parce qu'il y a un mois j'ai eu la cruauté de t'envoyer à la prison …

CARMEN: À la prison? …

ZUÑIGA: J'étais de service, je ne pouvais pas faire autrement.

CARMEN: À la prison … je ne me souviens pas d'être allée à la prison …

ZUÑIGA: Je le sais pardieu bien que tu n'y es pas allée … le brigadier qui était chargé de te conduire ayant jugé à propos de te laisser échapper … et de se

ZUÑIGA: Do you hold it against me?

CARMEN: Why should I hold anything against you?

ZUÑIGA: Because a month ago I was so heartless as to send you to prison …

CARMEN (*as if she doesn't remember anything about it*): To prison?

ZUÑIGA: I was on duty and couldn't do any different.

CARMEN (*still pretending*): To prison … I don't remember anything about going to prison.

ZUÑIGA: I know damned well you didn't go to prison. The corporal who was supposed to take you there decided to let you get away … and got

faire dégrader et emprisonner pour cela ...

CARMEN: Dégrader et emprisonner?

ZUÑIGA: Mon Dieu oui ... on n'a pas voulu admettre qu'une aussi petite main ait été assez forte pour renverser un homme ...

CARMEN: Oh!

ZUÑIGA: Cela n'a pas paru naturel ...

CARMEN: Et ce pauvre garçon est redevenu simple soldat?...

ZUÑIGA: Oui ... et il a passé un mois en prison...

CARMEN: Mais il en est sorti? ...

ZUÑIGA: Depuis hier seulement!

CARMEN: Tout est bien puisqu'il en est sorti, tout est bien.

ZUÑIGA: À la bonne heure, tu te consoles vite ...

CARMEN: Et j'ai raison ... Si vous m'en croyez, vous ferez comme moi, vous voulez nous emmener, nous ne voulons pas vous suivre ... vous vous con- solerez ...

MORALÈS: Il faudra bien.

---

broken and put in the stockade.

CARMEN (*seriously*): Broken and in the stockade?

ZUÑIGA: Why, of course ... No one was willing to believe that a hand as small as yours could be strong enough to knock a man down.

CARMEN: Oh!

ZUÑIGA: It didn't look right.

CARMEN: And the poor kid has become a private again?

ZUÑIGA: Yes ... and he's spent a month in the stockade.

CARMEN: But he's out now?

ZUÑIGA: Only since yesterday.

CARMEN (*clicking her castanets*): Everything's all right since he's out again, everything's all right.

ZUÑIGA: Good, you don't suffer long.

CARMEN (*aside*): And I'm right. (*Aloud:*) If you take my advice, you will do exactly the same. You want to take us along; we don't want to go; you won't suffer.

MORALES: That's right.

P. 110; instead of lines 1 to 8:

ZUÑIGA: Qu'est-ce que c'est que ça?

MERCÉDÈS: Une promenade aux flambeaux ...

MORALÈS: Et qui promène-t-on?

ZUÑIGA: What's that?

MERCEDES: A parade with torches.

MORALES: Who is it that they're parading?

FRASQUITA: Je le reconnais ... c'est Escamillo ... un toréro qui s'est fait remarquer aux dernières courses de Grenade et qui promet d'égaler la gloire de Montes et de Pepe Illo ...

MORALÈS: Pardieu, il faut le faire venir ... nous boirons en son honneur!

ZUÑIGA: C'est cela, je vais l'inviter. Monsieur le toréro ... voulez-vous nous faire l'amitié de monter ici? Vous y trouverez des gens qui aiment fort tous ceux qui comme vous, ont de l'adresse et du courage ... Il vient ...

PASTIA: Messieurs les officiers, je vous avais dit ...

ZUÑIGA: Ayez la bonté de nous laissez tranquille, maître Lillas Pastia, et faites-nous apporter de quoi boire ...

FRASQUITA: I recognize him ... it's Escamillo ... a bullfighter who attracted a lot of attention in the last corridas in Granada and promises to equal the glory of Montes and Pepe Illo.

MORALES: By God, he must come here! We'll have a drink in his honor.

ZUÑIGA: Right! I'm going to invite him (*Goes to the window.*) Señor Torero, would you do us the honor of coming in? You'll find people who love skilled, brave men like you. (*Leaving the window:*) He is coming.

PASTIA (*whining*): Gentlemen, gentlemen, as I have told you...

ZUÑIGA: Be so kind as to let us alone, Lillas Pastia, and bring us something to drink.

P. 110; add before line 14 from bottom:

ZUÑIGA: Ces dames et nous, vous remercions d'avoir accepté notre invitation; nous n'avons pas voulu vous laisser passer sans boire avec nous au grand art de la tauromachie ...

ESCAMILLO: Messieurs les officiers, je vous remercie.

ZUÑIGA: These ladies and we thank you for accepting our invitation; we were unwilling to let you go by without drinking a toast with us to the grand art of tauromachy.

ESCAMILLO: Gentlemen, I thank you.

P. 113; instead of passage from line 13 from bottom to page 114, line 7:

PASTIA: Messieurs les officers, je vous en prie.

ZUÑIGA: C'est bien, c'est bien, nous partons.

PASTIA: Gentlemen, gentlemen, I beg you ...

ZUÑIGA: All right, all right. We're going.

The officers get ready to leave. Escamillo is near Carmen.

ESCAMILLO: Dis-moi ton nom, et la première fois que je frapperai le taureau, ce sera ton nom que je prononcerai.

CARMEN: Je m'appelle la Carmencita.

ESCAMILLO: La Carmencita?

CARMEN: Carmen, la Carmencita, comme tu voudras.

ESCAMILLO: Eh bien, Carmen, ou la Carmencita, si je m'avisais de t'aimer et de vouloir être aimé de toi, qu'est-ce que tu me répondrais?

CARMEN: Je répondrais que tu peux m'aimer tout à ton aise, mais que quant à être aimé de moi pour le moment, il n'y faut pas songer.

ESCAMILLO: Ah.

CARMEN: C'est comme ça.

ESCAMILLO: J'attendrai alors et je me contenterai d'espérer ...

CARMEN: Il n'est pas défendu d'attendre et il est toujours agréable d'espérer.

MORALÈS: Vous ne venez pas décidément?

MERCÉDÈS, FRASQUITA: Mais, non, mais non ...

MORALÈS: Mauvaise campagne, lieutenant.

ZUÑIGA: Bah. La bataille n'est pas encore perdue ... Écoutemoi, Carmen, puisque tu ne veux pas venir avec nous, c'est

ESCAMILLO: Tell me your name, and the next time that I strike the bull I will say your name.

CARMEN: My name is Carmencita.

ESCAMILLO: Carmencita?

CARMEN: Carmen, Carmencita, as you like.

ESCAMILLO: Well, Carmen, or Carmencita, if I were to think of falling in love with you and of wishing to be loved by you, what would you say?

CARMEN: I'd say that you can love me as much as you want, but as for me loving you, for the time being, don't dream of it.

ESCAMILLO: Ah.

CARMEN: That's the way it is.

ESCAMILLO: Then I'll wait, and I'll content myself with hoping ...

CARMEN: I can't stop you from waiting, and it's always nice to hope.

MORALES (*to Frasquita and Mercedes*): You're really not coming?

MERCEDES, FRASQUITA (*upon a new signal from Pastia*): No, no!

MORALES (*to Zuñiga*): A bad campaign, Lieutenant!

ZUÑIGA: Bah. The battle isn't lost yet. (*In a low voice to Carmen:*) Listen, Carmen, since you won't come with us, I'm

moi qui dans une heure reviendrai ici …

CARMEN: Ici … ?

ZUÑIGA: Oui, dans une heure … après l'appel.

CARMEN: Je ne vous conseille pas de revenir …

ZUÑIGA: Je reviendrai tout de même. Nous partons avec vous, toréro, et nous nous joindrons au cortége qui vous accompagne.

ESCAMILLO: C'est un grand honneur pour moi, je tâcherai de ne pas m'en montrer indigne lorsque je combattrai sous vos yeux. [*Chorus repeats: " Toréador, etc."*]

going to come back here in an hour.

CARMEN: Here?

ZUÑIGA: Yes, in an hour. After roll call.

CARMEN: I don't advise you to.

ZUÑIGA: I'm coming back just the same (*Aloud:*) We'll leave with you, Señor Torero, and will join the retinue that accompanies you.

ESCAMILLO: It is a great honor for me; I will try to show myself not unworthy of it when I fight before your eyes.

P. 114; instead of lines 8 from top to 7 from bottom:

FRASQUITA: Pourquoi étais-tu si pressé de les faire partir, et pourquoi nous as-tu fait signe de ne pas les suivre? …

PASTIA: Le Dancaïre et le Remendado viennent d'arriver … ils ont à vous parler de vos affaires, des affaires d'Égypte.

CARMEN: Le Dancaïre et le Remendado? …

PASTIA: Oui, les voici … tenez …

FRASQUITA (*to Pastia*): Why were you in such a hurry to make them leave, and why did you signal us not to go with them?

PASTIA: El Dancaïro and El Remendado have just arrived. They have business to talk over with you, Egyptian business.

CARMEN: El Dancaïro and El Remendado?

PASTIA (*opening a door and beckoning*): Yes, they're here.

El Dancaïro and El Remendado enter. Pastia shuts and locks all the doors, closes the shutters, etc.

FRASQUITA: Eh bien, les nouvelles?

LE DANCAÏRE: Pas trop mauvaises les nouvelles; nous arrivons de Gibraltar …

FRASQUITA: Well, what's new?

EL DANCAÏRO: The news is not too bad. We've just come from Gibraltar.

LE REMENDADO: Jolie ville, Gibraltar! ... On y voit des Anglais, beaucoup d'Anglais, de jolis hommes les Anglais; un peu froids, mais distingués.

LE DANCAÏRE: Remendado! ...

LE REMENDADO: Patron.

LE DANCAÏRE: Vous comprenez?

LE REMENDADO: Parfaitement, patron ...

LE DANCAÏRE: Taisez-vous alors. Nous arrivons de Gibraltar, nous avons arrangé avec un patron de navire l'embarquement de marchandises anglaises. Nous irons les attendre pres de la côte, nous en cacherons une partie dans la montagne et nous ferons passer le reste. Tous nos camarades ont été prévenus ... ils sont ici, cachés, mais c'est de vous trois surtout que nous avons besoin ... vous allez partir avec nous ...

CARMEN: Pour quoi faire? Pour vous aider à porter les ballots? ...

LE REMENDADO: Oh! non ... faire porter des ballots à des dames ... ça ne serait pas distingué.

LE DANCAÏRE: Remendado?

LE REMENDADO: Oui, patron.

LE DANCAÏRE: Nous ne vous ferons pas porter des ballots, mais nous aurons besoin de vous pour autre chose.

EL REMENDADO: Pretty town, Gibraltar! You see Englishmen there, a lot of Englishmen. Nice men, the English; a little cold, but elegant ...

EL DANCAÏRO: Remendado!

EL REMENDADO: Boss.

EL DANCAÏRO (*laying his hand upon his knife*): Understand?

EL REMENDADO: Perfectly, Boss.

EL DANCAÏRO: Then shut up. We've come from Gibraltar, we have made arrangements with the master of a merchantman to take off some English goods. We're going to wait for them near the coast; we're going to cache part of them in the mountains and get rid of the rest. All our comrades have been tipped off; they're here, in hiding, but we need you three most of all ... you're going to come with us.

CARMEN (*laughing*): To do what? To help you carry the bales?

EL REMENDADO: Oh, no. To make women carry the bales ... that wouldn't be elegant.

EL DANCAÏRO (*threateningly*): Remendado!

EL REMENDADO: Yes, boss.

EL DANCAÏRO: We won't make you carry bales, but we will need you for something else.

P. 119; instead of line 25:

CARMEN: Pardonnez-moi.   CARMEN: Sorry.

P. 120; instead of passage from line 2 from bottom to p. 121, line 9:

LE DANCAÏRE: En voilà assez; je t'ai dit qu'il fallait venir, et tu viendras ... je suis le chef ...

EL DANCAÏRO: That's enough. I've told you that you have to come, and you will come. I'm the boss.

CARMEN: Comment dis-tu ça?

CARMEN: What's that you say?

LE DANCAÏRE: Je te dis que je suis le chef ...

EL DANCAÏRO: I tell you that I'm the boss.

CARMEN: Et tu crois que je t'obéirai? ...

CARMEN: And you think I'll do what you tell me?

LE DANCAÏRE: Carmen! ...

EL DANCAÏRO (furious): Carmen!

CARMEN: Eh bien! ...

CARMEN: (very calm): So?

LE REMENDADO: Je vous en prie ... des personnes si distinguées ...

EL REMENDADO (throwing himself between El Dancaïro and Carmen): I beg of you ... such elegant people ...

LE DANCAÏRE: Attrape ça, toi ...

EL DANCAÏRO (aiming a kick at El Remendado, who avoids it): Take this, you!

LE REMENDADO: Patron ...

EL REMENDADO (standing up): Boss ...

LE DANCAÏRE: Qu'est-ce que c'est?

EL DANCAÏRO: What do you want?

LE REMENDADO: Rien, patron!

EL REMENDADO: Nothing, boss.

LE DANCAÏRE: Amoureuse ... ce n'est pas une raison, cela.

EL DANCAÏRO: In love ... that's no reason.

LE REMENDADO: Le fait est que ce n'en est pas une ... moi aussi je suis amoureux et ça ne m'empêche pas de me rendre utile.

EL REMENDADO: As a matter of fact, it isn't at all; I'm in love, too, but it doesn't stop me from being useful.

CARMEN: Partez sans moi ... j'irai vous rejoindre demain. Mais pour ce soir je reste ...

CARMEN: Go on without me. I'll join you tomorrow. But tonight I stay here.

FRASQUITA: Je ne t'ai jamais vue comme cela; qui attends-tu donc? ...

FRASQUITA: I've never seen you like this. Who is it you're waiting for?

CARMEN: Un pauvre diable de soldat qui m'a rendu service ...

MERCÉDÈS: Ce soldat qui était en prison?

CARMEN: Oui ...

FRASQUITA: Et à qui, il y a quinze jours, le geôlier a remis de ta part un pain dans lequel il y avait une pièce d'or et une lime? ...

CARMEN: Oui.

LE DANCAÏRE: Il s'en est servi de cette lime? ...

CARMEN: Non.

LE DANCAÏRE: Tu vois bien! ton soldat aura eu peur d'être puni plus rudement qu'il ne l'avait été; ce soir encore il aura peur ... tu auras beau entr'ouvrir les volets et regarder s'il vient, je parierais qu'il ne viendra pas.

CARMEN: Ne parie pas, tu perdrais ...

CARMEN: A poor devil of a soldier who did me a favor.

MERCEDES: That soldier who was in jail?

CARMEN: Yes ...

FRASQUITA: The same one that the jailer gave a loaf of bread from you, about two weeks ago, with a gold piece and a file in it?

CARMEN (going to the window): Yes.

EL DANCAÏRO: He used the file?

CARMEN (turning away from the window): No.

EL DANCAÏRO: There you go! Your soldier was probably afraid of being punished worse than he already was; he'll be afraid tonight, too. It's a waste of time to open the shutters and see if he's coming. I'll bet he doesn't come.

CARMEN: Don't bet, you'd lose.

P. 121; lines 11, 14 and 22 (also p. 122, lines 8, 9 and 15):
Read "d'Almanza" instead of "d'Alcala."

P. 121; instead of passage from line 5 from bottom to p. 122, line 6:

MERCÉDÈS: C'est un dragon, ma foi.

FRASQUITA: Et un beau dragon.

LE DANCAÏRE: Eh bien, puisque tu ne veux venir que demain, sais-tu au moins ce que tu devrais faire?

MERCEDES: It's a dragoon.

FRASQUITA: And a goodlooking dragoon.

EL DANCAÏRO (to Carmen): All right, since you don't want to come until tomorrow, do you know at least what you should do?

CARMEN: Qu'est-ce que je devrais faire? ...

CARMEN: What should I do?

LE DANCAÏRE: Tu devrais décider ton dragon à venir avec toi et à se joindre à nous.

EL DANCAÏRO: You should convince your dragoon to come with you and join our band.

CARMEN: Ah! Si cela se pouvait ... mais il n'y faut pas penser ... ce sont des bêtises ... il est trop niais.

CARMEN: Ah ... if that could be! But there's no point thinking about it. It's a foolish idea. He's too simple.

LE DANCAÏRE: Pourquoi l'aimes-tu puisque tu conviens toi-même ...

EL DANCAÏRO: Why do you love him then, since you yourself admit it?

CARMEN: Parce qu'il est joli garçon donc et qu'il me plaît.

CARMEN: Because he's a handsome boy and I like him.

LE REMENDADO: Le patron ne comprend pas ça, lui ... qu'il suffise d'être joli garçon pour plaire aux femmes ...

EL REMENDADO (*fatuously*): The boss doesn't understand that, not he, that it's enough to be a handsome boy to make the women like you.

LE DANCAÏRE: Attends un peu, toi, attends un peu ...

EL DANCAÏRO: Wait a minute, you, wait a minute ...

El Remendado saves himself by running out and El Dancaïro runs after him. Mercedes and Frasquita follow them, trying to calm El Dancaïro.

P. 122; instead of passage from line 9 from bottom to p. 123, line 17:

CARMEN: Enfin ... te voilà ... C'est bien heureux!

CARMEN: At last you're here. This is really nice!

DON JOSÉ: Il y a deux heures seulement que je suis sorti de prison.

DON JOSÉ: It's just two hours ago that I got out of prison.

CARMEN: Qui t'empêchait de sortir plus tôt? Je t'avais envoyé une lime et une pièce d'or ... avec la lime il fallait scier le plus gros barreau de ta prison ... avec la pièce d'or il fallait, chez le premier fripier venu, changer ton uniforme pour un habit bourgeois.

CARMEN: Who stopped you from getting out before? I sent you a file and a gold piece ... With the file you could have sawn the thickest bar in the prison; with the gold piece you could have changed your uniform for civvies at the first used-clothes store you came to.

DON JOSÉ: En effet tout cela était possible.

CARMEN: Pourquoi ne l'as-tu pas fait?

DON JOSÉ: Que veux-tu? j'ai encore mon honneur de soldat, et déserter me semblerait un grand crime ... Oh! je ne t'en suis pas moins reconnaissant ... Tu m'as envoyé une lime et une pièce d'or ... La lime me servira pour affiler ma lance et je la garde comme souvenir de toi. Quant à l'argent ...

CARMEN: Tiens, il l'a gardé! ... ça se trouve à merveille ... Holà! ... Lillas Pastia, holà! ... nous mangerons tout ... tu me régales ... holà! holà! ...

Pastia enters.

PASTIA: Prenez donc garde ...

CARMEN: Tiens, attrape ... et apporte-nous des fruits confits; apporte-nous des bonbons, apporte-nous des oranges, apporte-nous du manzanilla ... apporte-nous de tout ce que tu as, de tout, de tout ...

PASTIA: Tout de suite, mademoiselle Carmencita.

He leaves.

CARMEN: Tu m'en veux alors et tu regrettes de t'être fait mettre en prison pour mes beaux yeux?

DON JOSÉ: Actually, that was all possible.

CARMEN: Why didn't you do it?

DON JOSÉ: What do you expect? I've still got my honor as a soldier, and deserting would seem to be a real crime to me. Oh, I'm not any less grateful to you. You sent me a file and a gold piece. I can use the file to sharpen my lance and I will keep it as a souvenir of you. (*Handing her money:*) As for the money ...

CARMEN: He kept it! This comes at the right time! (*Shouting and thumping on the table:*) Hey! Lillas Pastia! Hey! We'll eat everything. You can treat me. Hey! Hey!

PASTIA (*stopping her shouting*): Be careful!

CARMEN: (*throwing him the gold piece*): Here, catch it ... and bring us some candied fruit, bring us some bonbons, bring us some oranges, bring us some manzanilla ... bring us everything you've got, everything, everything ...

PASTIA: Right away, Carmencita.

CARMEN (*to Don José*): You hold it against me, then, and you're sorry you were put in prison for my beautiful eyes?

DON JOSÉ: Quant à cela non, par exemple.

CARMEN: Vraiment?

DON JOSÉ: L'on m'a mis en prison, l'on m'a ôté mon grade, mais ça m'est égal.

CARMEN: Parce que tu m'aimes?

DON JOSÉ: Oui, parce que je t'aime, parce que je t'adore.

CARMEN: Je paie mes dettes ... c'est notre loi à nous autres bohémiennes ... je paie mes dettes ... je paie mes dettes ...

DON JOSÉ: Certainly not!

CARMEN: Really?

DON JOSÉ: They threw me in jail, they broke me, but I don't care.

CARMEN: Because you love me?

DON JOSÉ: Yes, because I love you, because I adore you.

CARMEN (*putting her two hands in José's hands*): I pay my debts ... that's the law between us Gypsies ... I pay my debts ... I pay my debts ...

Lillas Pastia reënters carrying on a platter oranges, bonbons, sugared fruit, manzanilla.

CARMEN: Mets tout cela ici ... d'un seul coup, n'aie pas peur...

CARMEN: Put it all here. All at once, don't be afraid.

Pastia obeys and half of the things roll onto the floor.

Ça ne fait rien, nous ramasserons tout ça nous-mêmes ... sauve-toi maintenant, sauve-toi, sauve-toi.

So what? We'll pick it all up ourselves. Out, now, out, out!

Pastia leaves.

Mets-toi là et mangeons de tout! de tout! de tout!

Sit down there and let's eat it all up! all! all!

She is seated; José sits facing her.

DON JOSÉ: Tu croques les bonbons comme un enfant de six ans ...

CARMEN: C'est que je les aime ... Ton lieutenant était ici tout à l'heure, avec d'autres officiers, ils nous ont fait danser la Romalis ...

DON JOSÉ: Tu as dansé?

DON JOSÉ: You bolt those bonbons like a six-year-old.

CARMEN: It's because I love them ... Your lieutenant was just here, with some other officers, they had us dance the Romali for them.

DON JOSÉ: Did you dance?

CARMEN: Oui, et quand j'ai eu dansé, ton lieutenant s'est permis de me dire qu'il m'adorait ...

DON JOSÉ: Carmen! ...

CARMEN: Qu'est-ce que tu as? ... Est-ce que tu serais jaloux, par hasard? ...

DON JOSÉ: Mais certainement, je suis jaloux ...

CARMEN: Ah bien! ... Canari, va! ... tu es un vrai canari d'habit et de caractère ... allons, ne te fâche pas ... pourquoi es-tu jaloux? parce que j'ai dansé tout à l'heure pour ces officiers? ... Eh bien, si tu le veux, je danserai pour toi maintenant, pour toi tout seul.

DON JOSÉ: Si je le veux, je crois bien que je le veux ...

CARMEN: Ou sont mes castagnettes? ... qu'est-ce que j'ai fait de mes castagnettes? C'est toi qui me les as prises, mes castagnettes?

DON JOSÉ: Mais non!

CARMEN: Mais si, mais si ... je suis sûre que c'est toi ... ah! bah! en voilà des castagnettes.

CARMEN: Yes, and when I was done dancing, the lieutenant took the liberty of telling me that he adored me.

DON JOSÉ: Carmen!

CARMEN: What's wrong with you? You wouldn't be jealous, by any chance?

DON JOSÉ: Of course I am jealous.

CARMEN: All right. Go on, canary. You're a real canary in the way you dress* and the way you act. Come on, don't get angry. What are you jealous for? Because I just danced for those officers? All right, if you want, I'll dance for you now, for you alone.

DON JOSÉ: If I want ... yes, I really want you to!

CARMEN: Where are my castanets? What have I done with my castanets? (*Laughing:*) Did you take them from me, my castanets?

DON JOSÉ: Of course not.

CARMEN (*tenderly*): Oh, yes. Oh, yes. I'm sure it was you. Ah! Bah! Here are some castanets.

She breaks a plate, takes up two pieces and uses them as castanets.

Ah! ça ne vaudra jamais mes castagnettes ... Où sont-elles donc?

DON JOSÉ: Tiens! les voici.

Ah! This will never be as good as my castanets. Where are they?

DON JOSÉ (*finding the castanets on the table at the right*): Ah, here they are.

---

* The dragoons wore yellow uniforms.

CARMEN: Ah! tu vois bien … c'est toi qui les avais prises …

CARMEN (*laughing*): Ah! There you go! It was you who took them.

DON JOSÉ: Ah! que je t'aime, Carmen, que je t'aime!

DON JOSÉ: Ah! How I love you, Carmen, how I love you!

CARMEN: Je l'espère bien. Je vais en ton honneur danser la Romalis, et tu verras, mon fils, comment je sais moi-même accompagner ma danse. Mettez-vous là, don José, je commence.

CARMEN: I hope so. I'm going to dance the Romali in your honor, and, my friend, you'll see how I can accompany my dance myself. Sit down there, Don José, I'm starting.

P. 129; instead of line 13 from bottom:

CARMEN: Mon officier, […]

CARMEN: My good officer, […]

P. 129; instead of lines 2 from bottom to bottom:

Nous allons, cher monsieur [*repeated*].

We are going, my dear sir, […]

P. 137; instead of passage from line 13 to p. 138, line 10:

LE DANCAÏRE: Halte! nous allons nous arrêter ici … ceux qui ont sommeil pourront dormir pendant une demi-heure …

EL DANCAÏRO: Halt! We're going to stop here. Those who are sleepy can sleep for a half hour.

LE REMENDADO: Ah!

EL REMENDADO (*stretching himself out luxuriously*): Ah!

LE DANCAÏRE: Je vais, moi, voir s'il y a moyen de faire entrer les marchandises dans la ville… une brèche s'est faite dans le mur d'enceinte et nous pourrions passer par là: malheureusement on a mis un factionnaire pour garder cette brèche.

EL DANCAÏRO: I'm going to see if there is a way of getting the goods into the city. There's a gap in the city wall, and we can get in through it. Unfortunately, they've put a guard to watch it.

DON JOSÉ: Lillas Pastia nous a fait savoir que, cette nuit, ce factionnaire serait un homme à nous …

DON JOSÉ: Lillas Pastia gave us to think that tonight the guard would be a man of ours.

LE DANCAÏRE: Oui, mais Lillas Pastia a pu se tromper ... le factionnaire qu'il veut dire a pu être changé ... Avant d'aller plus loin je ne trouve pas mauvais de m'assurer par moi-même ... Remendado! ...

LE REMENDADO: Hé?

LE DANCAÏRE: Debout, tu vas venir avec moi ...

LE REMENDADO: Mais, patron ...

LE DANCAÏRE: Qu'est-ce que c'est? ...

LE REMENDADO: Voilà, patron, voilà! ...

LE DANCAÏRE: Allons, passe de-vant.

LE REMENDADO: Et moi qui rêvais que j'allais pouvoir dormir ... C'était un rêve, hélas, c'était un rêve! ...

EL DANCAÏRO: Yes, but Lillas Pastia could be wrong. The guard that he talked about might have been changed. Before I go any farther I think it's not a bad idea to make sure myself. (*Calling:*) Remendado!

EL REMENDADO (*waking*): What?

EL DANCAÏRO: On your feet, you're coming with me.

EL REMENDADO: But, boss ...

EL DANCAÏRO: What is it?

EL REMENDADO (*getting up*): All right, boss, all right.

EL DANCAÏRO: Come on, go on ahead.

EL REMENDADO: And I dreaming that I'd be able to sleep. It was a dream, all a dream.

He follows El Dancaïro. During the scene between Carmen and José, some of the Gypsies light a fire, near which Mercedes and Frasquita come and sit; the others roll themselves in their cloaks and lie down to sleep.

DON JOSÉ: Voyons, Carmen ... si je t'ai parlé trop durement, je t'en demande pardon, faisons la paix.

CARMEN: Non.

DON JOSÉ: Tu ne m'aimes plus alors?

CARMEN: Ce qui est sûr c'est que je t'aime beaucoup moins qu'autrefois ... et que si tu continues à t'y prendre de cette façon-là, je finirai par ne plus t'aimer du tout ... Je ne veux pas être tourmentée ni

DON JOSÉ: Look, Carmen ... If I spoke too harshly, I apologize. Let's make up.

CARMEN: No.

DON JOSÉ: Don't you love me any more then?

CARMEN: One thing that I'm sure of is that I love you much less than I used to, and that if you keep on acting in this way, I'm going to end up not loving you at all. I don't want to be tormented and most of all I

surtout commandée. Ce que je veux, c'est être libre et faire ce qui me plaît.

DON JOSÉ: Tu es le diable, Carmen?

CARMEN: Oui, Qu'est-ce que tu regardes là, a quoi penses-tu?…

DON JOSÉ: Je me dis que là-bas … à sept ou huit lieues d'ici tout au plus, il y a un village, et dans ce village une bonne vieille femme qui croit que je suis encore un honnête homme …

CARMEN: Une bonne vieille femme?

DON JOSÉ: Oui; ma mère.

CARMEN: Ta mère … Eh bien là, vrai, tu ne ferais pas mal d'aller la retrouver, car décidément tu n'es pas fait pour vivre avec nous … chien et loup ne font pas longtemps bon ménage …

DON JOSÉ: Carmen …

CARMEN: Sans compter que le métier n'est pas sans péril pour ceux qui, comme toi, refusent de se cacher quand ils entendent les coups de fusil … plusieurs des nôtres y ont laissé leur peau, ton tour viendra.

DON JOSÉ: Et le tien aussi … si tu me parles encore de nous séparer et si tu ne te conduis pas avec moi comme je veux que tu te conduises …

CARMEN: Tu me tuerais, peut-être?…

don't want to be ordered around. What I want is to be free and do what I want.

DON JOSÉ: Are you the Devil, Carmen?

CARMEN: Yes. What are you looking at there, and what are you thinking about?

DON JOSÉ: I am just telling myself that down there … seven or eight leagues away from here at most, there is a village, and in that village there is a good old lady who thinks that I am still an honest man.

CARMEN: A good old lady?

DON JOSÉ: Yes, my mother.

CARMEN: Your mother. Oh yes. It wouldn't be a bad idea at all if you went back to her, for you're certainly not cut out for living with us. Dog and wolf don't keep house together very long.

DON JOSÉ: Carmen!

CARMEN: I won't even count the fact that our trade is dangerous for people like you who refuse to take cover when they hear a gunshot … many of our people have lost their skins, and your turn will come.

DON JOSÉ: And yours too, if you talk to me again about separating and if you don't behave with me the way I want you to.

CARMEN: You'll kill me, I suppose?

Don José doesn't answer.

À la bonne heure ... j'ai vu plusieurs fois dans les cartes que nous devions finir ensemble. Bah! arrive qui plante ...

DON JOSÉ: Tu es le diable, Carmen? ...

CARMEN: Mais oui, je te l'ai déjà dit ...

All right. Many times I've seen in the cards that we would finish together. (*Clicking her castanets:*) Bah! Let what's going to happen, happen.

DON JOSÉ: Are you the Devil, Carmen?

CARMEN: Of course, I've already told you so.

P. 140; instead of lines 15 from bottom and 14 from bottom:

CARMEN: Donnez que j'essaie à mon tour.

CARMEN: Give them to me, let me try my turn.

P. 141; insert after line 10:

CARMEN: Bah! qu'importe après tout, qu'importe? Carmen bravera tout, Carmen est la plus forte.

CARMEN: Bah! So what does it matter after all, what does it matter? Carmen can take anything, Carmen is the toughest.

P. 142; instead of lines 4 to 18:

CARMEN: Eh bien? ...

LE DANCAÏRE: Eh bien, j'avais raison de ne pas me fier aux renseignements de Lillas Pastia; nous n'avons pas trouvé son factionnaire, mais en revanche nous avons aperçu trois douaniers qui gardaient la brèche et qui la gardaient bien, je vous assure ...

CARMEN: Savez-vous leurs noms à ces douaniers? ...

LE REMENDADO: Certainement nous savons leurs noms; qui est-ce qui connaîtrait les douaniers si nous ne les connaissions pas? il y avait Eusebio, Perez et Bartolomé ...

CARMEN: Well?

EL DANCAÏRO: Well, I was right not to trust Lillas Pastia's information. We didn't find our guard; instead we saw three customs officers watching the gap and watching it well, I can assure you.

CARMEN: Do you know the names of these customs men?

EL REMENDADO: Certainly we know their names; if we didn't know the customs men, who would? They're Eusebio, Perez and Bartolomé.

FRASQUITA: Eusebio ...

MERCÉDÈS: Perez ...

CARMEN: Et Bartolomé ... N'ayez pas peur, Dancaïre, nous vous en répondons de vos trois douaniers ...

DON JOSE: Carmen! ...

LE DANCAÏRE: Ah! toi, tu vas nous laisser tranquilles avec ta jalousie ... le jour vient et nous n'avons pas de temps à perdre ... En route, les enfants ...

They start to take up their packs.

Quant à toi, je te confie la garde des marchandises que nous n'emporterons pas ... Tu vas te placer là, sur cette hauteur ... tu y seras à merveille pour voir si nous sommes suivis ...; dans le cas où tu apercevrais quelqu'un, je t'autorise a passer ta colère sur l'indiscret. — Nous y sommes? ...

LE REMENDADO: Oui, patron.

LE DANCAÏRE: En route alors... Mais vous ne vous flattez pas, vous me répondez vraiment de ces trois douaniers?

CARMEN: N'ayez pas peur, Dancaïre.

FRASQUITA: Eusebio ...

MERCEDES: Perez ...

CARMEN: And Bartolomé. (*Laughing:*) Don't be afraid, El Dancaïro, we'll answer for your three customs men.

DON JOSÉ (*furiously*): Carmen!

EL DANCAÏRO: Ah! You! You never let us have a minute of peace with your jealousy. It's getting light and we have no time to lose. Let's go.

(*To Don José:*) As for you, I'm trusting you to guard the goods that we don't take along. Get up there, on that height ... you'll be well placed there to see if anyone is following us. In case you see anyone, I authorize you to work off your anger on him. Are we all here?

EL REMENDADO: Yes, boss.

EL DANCAÏRO: Let's go then. (*To the women:*) You're not flattering yourselves now. You will really answer to me for these three customs agents?

CARMEN: Don't worry, El Dancaïro.

P. 146; instead of lines 8 from bottom to 4 from bottom:

LE GUIDE: Nous y sommes.

MICAËLA: C'est ici.

GUIDE (*advancing cautiously, then making a sign to Micaëla, who is not visible yet*): Here we are.

MICAËLA (*entering*): Here.

LE GUIDE: Oui, vilain endroit, n'est-ce pas, et pas rassurant du tout?

MICAËLA: Je ne vois personne.

LE GUIDE: Ils viennent de partir, mais ils reviendront bientôt car ils n'ont pas emporté toutes leurs marchandises ... je connais leurs habitudes ... prenez garde ... l'un des leurs doit être sentinelle quelque part et si l'on nous apercevait...

MICAËLA: Je l'espère bien qu'on m'apercevra ... puisque je suis venue ici tout justement pour parler à ... pour parler à un de ces contrebandiers ...

LE GUIDE: Eh bien là, vrai, vous pouvez vous vanter d'avoir du courage ... tout à l'heure quand nous nous sommes trouvés au milieu de ce troupeau de taureaux savages que conduisait le célèbre Escamillo, vous n'avez pas tremblé ... Et maintenant venir ainsi affronter ces Bohémiens ...

MICAËLA: Je ne suis pas facile à effrayer.

LE GUIDE: Vous dites cela parce que je suis près de vous, mais si vous étiez toute seule ...

MICAËLA: Je n'aurais pas peur, je vous assure.

LE GUIDE: Bien vrai? ...

MICAËLA: Bien vrai ...

LE GUIDE: Alors je vous demanderai la permission de m'en aller. — J'ai consenti à vous servir de guide parce que

GUIDE: Yes, a nasty place, isn't it, and not at all reassuring.

MICAËLA: I don't see anyone.

GUIDE: They've just left, but they'll come back again soon, for they haven't carried away all their goods. I know their ways. Watch out. One of them is bound to be set out somewhere as a sentinel, and if they saw us ...

MICAËLA: I really hope I'm seen. Since I've come here for just that reason, to talk to ... to talk to one of the smugglers.

GUIDE: Well, then, it's true, you can really boast of being brave. A while ago, when we found ourselves in the middle of that herd of wild bulls that the famous Escamillo was driving along, you didn't even tremble. And now, to come here to face these Gypsies ...

MICAËLA: I do not frighten easily.

GUIDE: You say that just because I am near you, but if you were alone ...

MICAËLA: I wouldn't be afraid, I assure you.

GUIDE: Is that really true?

MICAËLA: That's really true.

GUIDE (naively): Then I will ask your permission to leave. I consented to act as your guide because you paid me well; but

vous m'avez bien payé; mais maintenant que vous êtes arrivée … si ça ne vous fait rien, j'irai vous attendre là, où vous m'avez pris … à l'auberge qui est au bas de la montagne.

MICAËLA: C'est cela, allez m'attendre!

LE GUIDE: Vous restez décidément?

MICAÉLA: Oui, je reste!

LE GUIDE: Que tous les saints du paradis vous soient en aide alors, mais c'est une drôle d'idée que vous avez là …

MICAËLA: Mon guide avait raison … l'endroit n'a rien de bien rassurant …

now that you are here … if it doesn't make any difference to you, I will go and wait for you where you hired me … the inn at the foot of the mountain.

MICAËLA: That's right; go and wait for me.

GUIDE: You are definitely staying here?

MICAËLA: Yes, I am staying here.

GUIDE: May all the saints in Paradise help you then, but it's a strange idea that you have …

MICAËLA (looking around her): The guide was right … this place has nothing reassuring about it.

P. 147; instead of lines 6 from bottom to bottom of French text:

MICAËLA: Mais … je ne me trompe pas … à cent pas d'ici … sur ce rocher, c'est don José. José, José! Mais que fait-il? Il ne regarde pas de mon côté … il arme sa carabine, il ajuste … il fait feu …

MICAËLA: But … I'm not wrong … a hundred paces from here … on that rock, it's Don José … (Calling:) José, José! (With terror:) But what's he doing? He's not looking in my direction … he is taking up his rifle, he's aiming, he's firing.

A gunshot is heard.

Ah! mon Dieu, j'ai trop présumé de mon courage … j'ai peur … j'ai peur.

Ah! God! I overestimated my courage … I'm frightened, I'm frightened.

P. 148; instead of lines 1 to 3:

She disappears behind the rocks. At the same moment Escamillo enters with his hat in his hand. Don José follows.

ESCAMILLO: Quelques lignes plus bas ... et ce n'est pas moi qui, à la course prochaine, aurais eu le plaisir de combattre les taureaux que je suis en train de conduire ...

DON JOSÉ Qui êtes-vous? répondez.

ESCAMILLO (*fingering his hat*): A hair or two lower ... and I wouldn't have been the one to have the pleasure of fighting these bulls that I'm driving, in the next corrida.

DON JOSÉ: Who are you? Answer.

P. 150; insert after line 22:

ESCAMILLO: Je la connais ta garde navarraise, et je te préviens en ami, qu'elle ne vaut rien ...

ESCAMILLO: I know your Navarre defense, and like a friend I warn you that it's worthless ...

Without replying Don José advances toward the bullfighter.

À ton aise. Je t'aurais du moins averti.

As you like. I wanted to warn you, at least.

They fight. The toreador very calmly only tries to defend himself.

DON JOSÉ: Tu m'épargnes, maudit.

ESCAMILLO: À ce jeu de couteau je suis trop fort pour toi.

DON JOSÉ: Voyons cela.

DON JOSÉ: You're sparing me, damn you!

ESCAMILLO: In this knife-play I'm too strong for you.

DON JOSÉ: We'll see.

Rapid and very lively hand-to-hand struggle. Don José finds himself at the mercy of Escamillo, who does not strike.

ESCAMILLO: Tout beau. Ta vie est à moi, mais en somme, j'ai pour métier de frapper le taureau, non de trouer le cœur de l'homme.

DON JOSÉ: Frappe ou bien meurs ... ceci n'est pas un jeu.

ESCAMILLO: Soit, mais au moins respire un peu.

ESCAMILLO: All right! Your life is mine, but, to make a long story short, my trade is killing bulls, not piercing men's hearts.

DON JOSÉ: Strike me or you die ... this is not a game.

ESCAMILLO (*disengaging himself*): As you wish, but at least let's get our breath for a minute.

They resume fighting. Escamillo slips and is momentarily at the mercy of José, who is about to kill him, when Carmen and the other Gypsies enter and save him.

P. 154; add after last line:

DON JOSÉ: Partons, Micaëla, partons.

DON JOSÉ: Let's go, Micaëla, let's go.

P. 162; add before stage direction at top:

ZUÑIGA: Qu'avez-vous donc fait de la Carmencita? Je ne la vois pas.

FRASQUITA: Nous la verrons tout à l'heure ... Escamillo est ici, la Carmencita ne doit pas être loin.

ANDRÈS: Ah, c'est Escamillo, maintenant? ...

MERCÉDÈS: Elle en est folle ...

FRASQUITA: Et son ancien amoureux, José, sait-on ce qu'il est devenu? ...

ZUÑIGA: Il a reparu dans le village où sa mère habitait ... l'ordre avait même été donné de l'arrêter, mais quand les soldats sont arrivés, José n'était plus là ...

MERCÉDÈS: En sorte qu'il est libre?

ZUÑIGA: Oui, pour le moment.

FRASQUITA: Hum! je ne serais pas tranquille à la place de Carmen, je ne serais pas tranquille du tout.

ZUÑIGA: What have you done with la Carmencita? I don't see her.

FRASQUITA: We'll see her soon. Escamillo is here, and Carmencita won't be far away.

ANDRES: Ah, it's Escamillo now?

MERCEDES: She's crazy about him.

FRASQUITA: And her old lover, José, is it known what became of him?

ZUÑIGA: He turned up in the village where his mother lived ... the order had even been given to arrest him, but when the soldïers got there, José was gone.

MERCEDES: And so he is still free?

ZUÑIGA: Yes, for the moment.

FRASQUITA: Hmm! I wouldn't be calm in Carmen's place; I wouldn't be calm at all.

P. 166; add after line 8:

CHORUS: Pas de bousculade, regardons passer et se prélasser le seigneur Alcade.

ALGUAZILS: Place, place, au seigneur alcade!

CHORUS (as the crowd makes a passage for the alcalde): No jostling, let's watch the alcalde go strutting by.

ALGUAZILS: Make way, make way for the alcalde.

P. 169; line 24. Chorus continues:

Le taureau tombe! Gloire au toréro vainqueur! Victoire! Victoire!

The bull falls! Glory for the conquering toreador! Victory! Victory!

II. THE OPÉRA-COMIQUE VERSION

P. 84; instead of lines 5 from bottom to bottom:

MORALÈS: Une jolie fille est venue te demander.

DON JOSÉ: Une jolie fille?

MORALÈS: Oui, une jupe bleue, des nattes tombant sur les épaules.

DON JOSÉ: Ce ne peut être que Micaëla.

MORALES: A pretty girl was here looking for you.

DON JOSÉ: A pretty girl?

MORALES: Yes, a blue skirt, braids falling down over her shoulders.

DON JOSÉ: It must have been Micaëla.

P. 85; instead of passage from line 15 to p. 86, line 3:

ZUÑIGA: Dites-moi, brigadier.

DON JOSÉ: Mon lieutenant?

ZUÑIGA: Qu'est-ce que ce grand bâtiment?

DON JOSÉ: C'est la manufacture de tabacs ...

ZUÑIGA: Les cigarières, sont-elles jeunes et jolies?

DON JOSÉ: À vous dire vrai, je ne les ai pas beaucoup regardées...

ZUÑIGA: Et puis nous avons un faible pour les jupes bleues, et pour les nattes tombant sur les épaules.

DON JOSÉ: Je ne le nierai pas.

ZUÑIGA: Tell me something, corporal.

DON JOSÉ: Yes, lieutenant?

ZUÑIGA: What's that big building?

DON JOSÉ: That's the tobacco factory.

ZUÑIGA: Are the cigarette girls young and goodlooking?

DON JOSÉ: To tell you the truth, I haven't looked at them very much.

ZUÑIGA: And then we have a weakness for blue skirts and for braids that fall down over the shoulders.

DON JOSÉ: I don't deny it.

P. 91; to follow line 11:

CARMEN: Eh! Compère, qu'est-ce que tu fais là?

CARMEN: Hey, pal, what are you doing there?

DON JOSÉ: Je fais une chaîne pour attacher mon épinglette.

CARMEN: Ton épinglette, vraiment. Ton épinglette ... épinglier de mon âme ...

DON JOSÉ: I'm making a chain to attach my priming pin to.

CARMEN: Your priming pin, that's good! Your priming pin! darling pinmaker!

P. 91; in place of passage from line 4 from bottom to p. 92, line 4:

DON JOSÉ: Avec quelle adresse elle me l'a lancée, cette fleur ... Comme c'est fort!

DON JOSÉ: The way she threw that flower at me was very good ... It's really strong!

P. 92; instead of lines 5 to 8:

MICAËLA: Monsieur le brigadier?

DON JOSÉ: Qu'est-ce que c'est? ... Micaëla!

MICAËLA: Corporal?

DON JOSÉ: What is it? Micaëla!

P. 96; instead of lines 1 to 16:

DON JOSÉ: Maintenant ... je vais lire sa lettre.

MICAËLA: J'attendrai, monsieur le brigadier.

DON JOSÉ: "Continue à te bien conduire et tu te marierais avec celle qui te porte ma lettre ..."

MICAËLA: Il vaut mieux que je ne sois pas là!

DON JOSÉ: Attends un peu.

MICAËLA: Non, non ... je reviendrai, j'aime mieux cela.

DON JOSÉ: Oui, ma mère, j'épouserai Micaëla, et quant à cette bohémienne, avec ses fleurs qui ensorcellent ...

DON JOSÉ: Now—I'm going to read her letter.

MICAËLA: I'll wait, corporal.

DON JOSÉ: "Keep on doing well and you should marry the girl who is bringing my letter to you ..."

MICAËLA: It would be better if I weren't here!

DON JOSÉ: Wait a minute.

MICAËLA: No, no ... I'll be back, I'd rather have it that way.

DON JOSÉ: Yes, Mother, I'll marry Micaëla, and as for that Gypsy with her witch flowers ...

P. 100; instead of lines 1 to 9:

ZUÑIGA: Voyons, brigadier ... qu'est-ce que vous avez trouvé là-dedans?

DON JOSÉ: J'ai trouvé trois cents femmes, criant, hurlant ... en

ZUÑIGA: All right, corporal ... What did you find in there?

DON JOSÉ: I found three hundred women shrieking, howling, ...

face d'une femme blessée ...
j'ai vu mademoiselle Carmencita qui serrait les dents et
roulait des yeux comme un
caméléon.

zuñiga: Et la blessure de l'autre
femme?

don josé: Deux balafres à fleur
de peau.

zuñiga: (to Carmen): Eh bien, la
belle, avez-vous quelque chose
à répondre?

opposite a wounded woman ...
I saw Señorita Carmencita
clenching her teeth and rolling
her eyes like a chameleon.

zuñiga: And the other girl's
wound?

don josé: Two skin cuts.

zuñiga (to Carmen): Well, goodlooking, do you have any
answer?

P. 100; instead of lines 15 to 17:

zuñiga: Ce ne sont pas des
chansons que je te demande,
c'est une réponse.

zuñiga: I'm not asking you for
songs. I want an answer.

P. 100; instead of lines 24 from top to 4 from bottom:

zuñiga: Ah! Ah! Nous le prenons sur ce ton-là ... Ce qui est
sûr, n'est-ce pas, c'est qu'il
y a eu des coups de couteau, et
que c'est elle qui les a donnés...

zuñiga: Ah! Ah! So that's the
attitude we're taking! ... It is
certain, isn't it, that there were
knife cuts and she was the
one who did it ...

P. 101; instead of lines 1 to 5:

zuñiga: Si gentille que vous
soyez, vous n'irez pas moins
faire un tour à la prison. Je
vais écrire l'ordre. C'est vous
qui la conduirez ...

zuñiga: No matter how goodlooking you are, you're not getting away without a stay in jail.
I'm going to write the order.
You take her there.

P. 101; instead of lines 6 from top to 4 from bottom:

carmen: Laisse-moi m'échapper.
Tu le feras parce que tu
m'aimes.

don josé: Moi!

carmen: Eh! oui, tu m'aimes ...
ne me dis pas non, je m'y
connais! tes regards, et cette

carmen: Let me escape. You'll
do it because you love me.

don josé: Me!

carmen: Eh! Yes, you love me
... Don't tell me you don't. I
know it. The way you look at

fleur que tu as gardée. Oh! Tu peux la jeter maintenant. Le charme a opéré.

DON JOSÉ: Ne me parle plus, tu entends, je te défends de me parler.

CARMEN: C'est très-bien, je ne parlerai plus …

P. 103; add after line 6 from bottom:

DON JOSÉ: Le lieutenant! … Prenez garde.

P. 108; instead of passage from line 4 from bottom to p. 109, line 10 from bottom:

ZUÑIGA: Vous avez quelque chose à nous dire, maître Lillas Pastia?

PASTIA: Mon lieutenant, mon auberge devrait être fermée depuis dix minutes.

ZUÑIGA: Enfin! Nous avons encore, avant l'appel, le temps d'aller passer une heure au théâtre … vous y viendrez avec nous, n'est-ce pas, les belles?

MERCÉDÈS: Ce n'est pas possible.

MORALÈS: Frasquita!

FRASQUITA: Je suis désolée.

ZUÑIGA: Mais toi, Carmen … je suis bien sûr que tu ne refuseras pas.

CARMEN: C'est ce qui vous trompe, mon lieutenant.

ZUÑIGA: Tu m'en veux? Parce qu'il y a un mois j'ai eu la cruauté de t'envoyer à la prison …

CARMEN: À la prison … je ne me souviens pas d'être allée à la prison.

me, and this flower that you've kept. You can throw it away now; the charm has worked.

DON JOSÉ: Don't talk to me any more, do you hear, I forbid you to talk to me.

CARMEN: That's all right, I won't talk any more …

DON JOSÉ: The lieutenant! Watch out!

ZUÑIGA: Do you have something to say to us, Lillas Pastia?

PASTIA: Lieutenant, my tavern should have been closed ten minutes ago.

ZUÑIGA: Enough! We have time before roll call to spend an hour at the theater … would you like to come with us, girls?

MERCEDES: It's not possible.

MORALES: Frasquita!

FRASQUITA: I'm so sorry …

ZUÑIGA: How about you, Carmen? I'm sure you won't say no.

CARMEN: That's where you're wrong, Lieutenant.

ZUÑIGA: Do you hold it against me? Because a month ago I was so heartless as to send you to prison …

CARMEN: To prison … I don't remember anything about going to prison.

ZUÑIGA: Je le sais pardieu bien que tu n'y es pas allée ... le brigadier qui était chargé de te conduire ayant jugé à propos de te laisser échapper ... et de se faire dégrader et emprisonner pour cela. Il a passé un mois en prison.

CARMEN: Mais il en est sorti?

ZUÑIGA: Depuis hier seulement!

CARMEN: Tout est bien puisqu'il en est sorti.

ZUÑIGA: Don't I know that you didn't go to jail! The corporal who was supposed to take you there decided to let you get away ... and to be broken and be put in the stockade for that. He's spent a month in the stockade.

CARMEN: But he's out now?

ZUÑIGA: Only since yesterday!

CARMEN: Everything's all right since he's out again.

P. 110; instead of lines 1 to 8:

ZUÑIGA: Qu'est-ce que c'est que ça?

MERCÉDÈS: Une promenade aux flambeaux.

MORALÈS: Et qui promène-t-on?

FRASQUITA: Je le reconnais ... c'est Escamillo ... un toréro qui s'est fait remarquer aux dernières courses de Grenade.

MORALÈS: Pardieu, il faut le faire venir ... nous boirons en son honneur!

ZUÑIGA: Maître Lillas Pastia, faites-nous apporter de quoi boire ...

ZUÑIGA: What's that?

MERCEDES: A parade with torches.

MORALES: Who is it they're parading?

FRASQUITA: I recognize him ... it's Escamillo ... a bullfighter who attracted a lot of attention in the last corridas in Granada.

MORALES: By God, he must come here ... we'll have a drink in his honor!

ZUÑIGA: Lillas Pastia, bring us something to drink!

P. 113; instead of line 13 from bottom to bottom:

PASTIA: Messieurs les officiers, je vous en prie.

ZUÑIGA: C'est bien, nous partons.

ESCAMILLO: Dis-moi ton nom, la belle.

CARMEN: Je m'appelle Carmen ou la Carmencita, comme tu voudras.

PASTIA: Gentlemen, gentlemen, I beg you ...

ZUÑIGA: All right, we're going.

ESCAMILLO: Tell me your name, goodlooking.

CARMEN: My name is Carmen or Carmencita, as you like.

ESCAMILLO: Eh bien, Carmen, ou la Carmencita, si je m'avisais de t'aimer et de vouloir être aimé de toi, que me répondrais-tu?

CARMEN: Je répondrais que tu peux m'aimer tout à ton aise, mais que quant à être aimé de moi pour le moment, il n'y faut pas songer.

ESCAMILLO: J'attendrai alors.

ESCAMILLO: Well, Carmen or Carmencita, if I were to think of falling in love with you, and wanted to be loved by you, what would you say?

CARMEN: I'd say that you can love me as much as you want, but as for me loving you, don't dream of it—for the moment.

ESCAMILLO: Then I'll wait.

P. 114; instead of lines 3 to 7:

ZUÑIGA: Écoute-moi, Carmen, puisque tu ne veux pas venir avec nous, c'est moi qui dans une heure reviendrai ici.

CARMEN: Je ne vous conseille pas de revenir.

ZUÑIGA: Je reviendrai tout de même. Nous partons avec vous, toréro!

ZUÑIGA: Listen, Carmen, since you won't come with us, I'll be back in an hour.

CARMEN: I don't advise you to.

ZUÑIGA: I'm coming back just the same. We'll leave with you, Señor torero.

P. 114; instead of lines 8 from top to 7 from bottom:

FRASQUITA: Pourquoi nous as-tu fait signe de ne pas les suivre?

PASTIA: Le Dancaïre et le Remendado viennent d'arriver. Eh, tenez, les voici.

FRASQUITA: Eh bien, les nouvelles?

LE DANCAÏRE: Pas trop mauvaises les nouvelles. Mais c'est de vous trois surtout que nous avons besoin.

CARMEN: Pour vous aider à porter les ballots?

LE REMENDADO: Oh! Ha, ha, patron. Faire porter les ballots

FRASQUITA: Why did you signal us not to go with them?

PASTIA: El Dancaïro and El Remendado are coming. Ah, here they are.

FRASQUITA: Well, what's new?

EL DANCAÏRO: The news is not too bad. But we need you three most of all.

CARMEN: To help you carry the packs?

EL REMENDADO: Oh, ha, ha, boss. To make the women carry the

à des dames ... ça ne serait pas distingué.

LE DANCAÏRE: Remendado! Vous comprenez?

LE REMENDADO: Oui, patron.

LE DANCAÏRE: Bien.

packs ... that wouldn't be elegant.

EL DANCAÏRO: Remendado! Do you understand?

EL REMENDADO: Yes, boss.

EL DANCAÏRO: All right!

P. 120; instead of passage from line 2 from bottom to p. 121, line 9:

LE DANCAÏRE: En voilà assez; je t'ai dit qu'il fallait venir, et tu viendras ... je suis le chef.

CARMEN: Et tu crois que je t'obéirai?

LE DANCAÏRE: Hmmmmm.

CARMEN: Partez sans moi ... j'irai vous rejoindre demain. Mais pour ce soir je reste ...

FRASQUITA: Je ne t'ai jamais vue comme ça; qui attends-tu donc?

CARMEN: Un pauvre diable de soldat qui m'a rendu service.

LE DANCAÏRE: Tu auras beau entr'ouvrir les volets et regarder s'il vient, je parierais qu'il ne viendra pas.

CARMEN: Ne parie pas, tu perdrais.

EL DANCAÏRO: That's enough. I've told you that you have to come, and you will come. I'm the boss.

CARMEN: And you think I'll do what you tell me?

EL DANCAÏRO: Hmmmmm.

CARMEN: Go on without me ... I'll join you tomorrow. But tonight I stay here.

FRASQUITA: I've never seen you like this. Who is it you're waiting for?

CARMEN: A poor devil of a soldier who did me a favor.

EL DANCAÏRO: It'd be a waste of time to open the shutters and see if he's coming. I'll bet he doesn't come.

CARMEN: Don't bet. You'd lose.

P. 121; instead of passage from line 5 from bottom to p. 122, line 6:

MERCEDES: C'est un beau dragon, ma foi.

LE DANCAÏRE: Tu devrais décider ton dragon à te suivre et à se joindre à nous.

CARMEN: Ah! Si cela se pouvait ... mais il n'y faut pas songer ... il est trop niais.

MERCEDES: A handsome dragoon!

EL DANCAÏRO: You should convince your dragoon to come with you and join our band.

CARMEN: Ah! If that could be ... But there's no point dreaming about it. He's too simple.

ALL: Ha, ha, ha.   ALL: Ha, ha, ha.

P. 122; instead of passage from line 9 from bottom to p. 123, line 17:

CARMEN: Enfin ... te voilà ... C'est bien heureux!

CARMEN: At last, you're here! This is really nice!

DON JOSÉ: Il y a deux heures seulement que je suis sorti de prison.

DON JOSÉ: It's just two hours ago that I got out of prison.

CARMEN: Qui t'empêchait de sortir plus tôt? Je t'avais envoyé une lime pour scier les barreaux se ta prison, et une pièce d'or pour acheter un habit bourgeois.

CARMEN: Who stopped you from getting out before? I sent you a file for cutting the bars and a gold piece to buy civvies.

DON JOSÉ: Que veux-tu? Déserter me semblerait un grande crime. La lime me servira pour affiler ma lance; quant à la pièce d'or ...

DON JOSÉ: What do you want? Deserting would seem to be a real crime to me. I can use the file to sharpen my lance; The gold piece ...

CARMEN: Tiens, il l'a gardé. Holà! Lillas Pastia! Apportenous des fruits confits, des bonbons, des oranges, du manzanilla, de tout, de tout, de tout ...

CARMEN: He kept it! Hey, Lillas Pastia! Bring us some candied fruit, some bonbons, oranges, manzanilla ... everything, everything, everything.

PASTIA: Tout de suite, mademoiselle Carmencita.

PASTIA: Right away, Señorita Carmencita.

CARMEN: Tu m'en veux alors et tu regrettes de t'être fait mettre en prison pour mes beaux yeux?

CARMEN: You hold it against me, then, and you're sorry you were put in jail for my beautiful eyes?

DON JOSÉ: L'on m'a mis en prison, l'on m'a ôté mon grade, mais ça m'est égal.

DON JOSÉ: They threw me in prison, they broke me, but I don't care.

CARMEN: Parce que tu m'aimes?

CARMEN: Because you love me?

DON JOSÉ: Oui parce que je t'aime, parce que je t'adore, Carmen.

DON JOSÉ: Yes, because I love you, because I adore you, Carmen.

PASTIA: Voici.

PASTIA: Here you are.

CARMEN: Pose tout cela ici et

CARMEN: Set it all here and get

sauve-toi maintenant. ... Ton lieutenant était ici tout à l'heure, avec d'autres officiers, ils nous ont fait danser la romalis ...

DON JOSÉ: Carmen!

CARMEN: Allons, ne te fâche pas. Es-tu jaloux parce que j'ai dansé tout à l'heure pour ces officiers ... Eh bien, si tu le veux, je danserai pour toi seul maintenant.

DON JOSÉ: Je crois bien que je le veux.

out now. (*To Don José:*) Your lieutenant was just here, with some other officers. They had us dance the Romali for them ...

DON JOSÉ: Carmen!

CARMEN: Go on, don't get angry. Are you jealous because I danced a while ago for those officers? All right, if you want, I'll dance for you alone now.

DON JOSÉ: Yes, I really want you to.

P. 137; instead of passage from line 13 to p. 138; line 10:

LE DANCAÏRE: Nous allons camper ici, Je vais, moi, voir s'il y a moyen de faire entrer les marchandises dans la ville. Remendado!

LE REMENDADO: Hé?

LE DANCAÏRE: Debout, tu vas venir avec moi.

LE REMENDADO: Et moi qui rêvais que j'allais pouvoir dormir.

EL DANCAÏRO: We're going to camp here. I'm going to see if there's a way of getting the goods into the city. Remendado!

EL REMENDADO: What?

EL DANCAÏRO: On your feet, you're coming with me.

EL REMENDADO: And I dreaming that I'd be able to sleep.

They exit.

DON JOSÉ: Voyons, Carmen ... si je t'ai parlé trop durement, je t'en demande pardon, faisons la paix.

CARMEN: Non.

DON JOSÉ: Tu ne m'aimes plus alors?

CARMEN: Ce qui est sûr c'est que je t'aime beaucoup moins qu'autrefois. Je ne veux pas être tourmentée ni surtout

DON JOSÉ: Look, Carmen ... If I spoke too harshly, I apologize. Let's make up.

CARMEN: No.

DON JOSÉ: Don't you love me any more?

CARMEN: One thing that I'm sure of is that I love you much less than I used to. I don't want to be tormented and

commandée. Ce que je veux, c'est être libre et faire ce qui me plaît.

DON JOSÉ: Tu es le diable, Carmen!

CARMEN: Mais oui, je te l'ai déjà dit.

most of all I don't want to be ordered around. What I want is to be free and to do what I want.

DON JOSÉ: You're the Devil, Carmen!

CARMEN: Of course; I've already told you so.

P. 142; instead of lines 4 to 18:

CARMEN: Eh bien?

LE DANCAÏRE: Eh bien. Nous avons aperçu trois douaniers qui gardaient la brèche.

CARMEN: Savez-vous leurs noms à ces douaniers?

LE REMENDADO: Certainement nous savons leurs noms; qui est-ce qui connaîtrait les douaniers si nous ne les connaissions pas? il y avait Eusebio, Perez, et Bartolomé...

FRASQUITA: Eusebio...

MERCÉDÈS: Perez...

CARMEN: Et Bartolomé. N'ayez pas peur, Dancaïre, nous vous en répondons de vos trois douaniers...

DON JOSÉ: Carmen!

LE DANCAÏRE: Ah! Toi, tu vas nous laisser tranquilles avec ta jalousie. Je te confie la garde des marchandises que nous n'emporterons pas... Tu vas te placer là, sur cette hauteur et dans le cas où tu apercevrais quelqu'un, je t'autorise à passer ta colère sur l'indiscret. Y sommes-nous les autres?...

CARMEN: Well?

EL DANCAÏRO: Well, we saw three customs officers watching the gap.

CARMEN: Do you know the names of these customs men?

EL REMENDADO: Of course we know their names; if we didn't know them, who would? They're Eusebio, Perez, and Bartolomé.

FRASQUITA: Eusebio...

MERCEDES: Perez...

CARMEN: And Bartolomé. Don't be afraid, Dancaïro, we'll answer for your three customs men.

DON JOSÉ: Carmen!

EL DANCAÏRO: Ah! You! You never let us have a minute of peace with your jealousy. I'm trusting you to guard the goods we don't take along. Go up there, on that height, and if you see anyone, I authorize you to work off your anger on him. The rest of us, all here?

P. 147; instead of passage from line 6 from bottom to p. 148, line 3:

MICAËLA: Mais ... je ne me trompe pas ... sur ce rocher, c'est José. José! Jose! Il arme sa carabine.

DON JOSÉ: Votre nom!

MICAËLA: But ... I'm not mistaken ... on that rock, it's José. José! José! He's taking up his rifle!

DON JOSÉ: Your name!

BIBLIOGRAPHY

Arditi, Luigi, *My Reminiscences*, Skeffington & Son, London, 1896.

Berton, Pierre, *Souvenirs de la vie de théâtre*, P. Lafitte, Paris [1924].

Bizet, Georges, *Carmen. An Opera in Four Acts*, with prefatory material by Philip Hale, Oliver Ditson, Boston, 1914 [Vocal and piano].

————, *Carmen. Opera in Four Acts*, G. Schirmer, New York [n.d.] [Vocal and piano].

————, *Carmen. Opera in Four Acts*, International Music Publishers, New York [n.d.] [Orchestral score].

————, *Lettres à un ami, 1865–1872*, with Introduction by Edmond Galabert, Calmann-Lévy, Paris [1909].

Calvé, Emma. *My Life*, Appleton, New York, 1922.

Chase, Gilbert, *The Music of Spain*, 2nd ed., Dover, New York, 1959.

Chop, Max, *Georges Bizet: Carmen. Oper in Vier Aufzügen*, Reklam, Berlin [1907?].

Crosten, William, *French Grand Opera, An Art and a Business*, Kings Crown Press, Columbia University, New York, 1948. [Good survey of operatic background in early and middle nineteenth-century France.]

Curtiss, Mina, *Bizet and His World*, Knopf, New York, 1958. [Much the fullest account of Bizet's life, with inexhaustible quotes from primary sources, background material, etc; corrects many details in earlier studies and adds much new material; primarily historical and biographical, though, without very much on Bizet's music.]

Dean, Winton, *Bizet*, Collier Books, New York, 1962. [The best brief survey, with excellent discussions of Bizet's music.]

Delmas, Marc, *Georges Bizet, 1838–1875*, E. Ploix-Musique, Paris, 1930. [Somewhat erratic but important for reproductions of material from the first score of *Carmen*.]

Ferrar, Geraldine, *Such Sweet Compulsion*, Greystone, New York, 1938.

Gallet, Louis, *Notes d'un librettiste*, Musique Contemporaine, Calmann-Lévy, Paris, 1897.

Garden, Mary and Biancolli, Louis, *Mary Garden's Story*, Simon & Schuster, New York, 1951.

Gaudier, Charles, *Carmen de Bizet*, Les Chefs-d'oeuvre de la Musique, Librairies Delaplane, Paris, 1922.

Grout, Donald Jay, *A Short History of Opera*, Columbia University Press, New York, 1947, 2 vols. [The most scholarly English-language history of opera.]

Hauk, Minnie, *Memories of a Singer*, Philpot, London, 1925.

Henry, Stuart, *Paris Days and Evenings*, Unwin, London, 1896.

Istel, Edgar, *Bizet und "Carmen," der Künstler und sein Werk*, Engelhorns Nachf., Stuttgart [1927]. [Full, thorough study of *Carmen*.]

———, *Carmen, die Novelle und das Libretto, Eine dramaturgische Studie*, Die Musik, Stuttgart, 1923.

Kellogg, Clara, *Memoirs of an American Prima Donna*, Putnam, New York, 1913.

Klein, Herman, *The Golden Age of Opera*, Routledge, London, 1933.

———, *Thirty Years of Musical Life in London, 1870–1900*, Heinemann, London, 1903.

———, *The Reign of Patti*, Century, New York, 1920.

Klein, John W., "The Two Versions of Carmen," *Musical Opinion*, London, March, 1949.

———, "Bizet's Admirers and Detractors," *Music and Letters*, London, October, 1938.

Kracauer, Siegfried, *Orpheus in Paris: Offenbach and the Paris of His Time*, Constable, London, 1937. [Excellent cultural and musical coverage of the Second Empire.]

Landormy, Paul, *Bizet*, Gallimard, Paris, 1950.

Malherbe, Henry, *Carmen*, Éditions Albin Michel, Paris [1951]. [Many off-trail topics in Bizet's life and work.]

Mapleson, James H., *The Mapleson Memoirs, 1848–1888*, 2nd ed., Remington, London, 1888. [Lively report on doings of singers and impresarios in England and America.]

Parker, D. C., *Bizet*, Routledge and Kegan Paul, London, 1951.

Pigot, Charles, *Georges Bizet et son œuvre, avec une lettre préface d'Ernest Guiraud*, Librairie de la Société des Gens de Lettres, Paris, 1886. [The basis for most later studies of Bizet.]

Saint-Saëns, Camille, *Portraits et Souvenirs*, Société d'édition artistique, Paris, 1900.

Stefan, Paul, *Georges Bizet*, Atlantis Verlag, Zürich [1952].

Van Vechten, Carl, *The Music of Spain*, Knopf, New York, 1918.

A CATALOGUE OF SELECTED DOVER BOOKS
IN ALL FIELDS OF INTEREST

A CATALOGUE OF SELECTED DOVER BOOKS
IN ALL FIELDS OF INTEREST

THE DEVIL'S DICTIONARY, Ambrose Bierce. Barbed, bitter, brilliant witticisms in the form of a dictionary. Best, most ferocious satire America has produced. 145pp. 20487-1 Pa. $1.50

ABSOLUTELY MAD INVENTIONS, A.E. Brown, H.A. Jeffcott. Hilarious, useless, or merely absurd inventions all granted patents by the U.S. Patent Office. Edible tie pin, mechanical hat tipper, etc. 57 illustrations. 125pp. 22596-8 Pa. $1.50

AMERICAN WILD FLOWERS COLORING BOOK, Paul Kennedy. Planned coverage of 48 most important wildflowers, from Rickett's collection; instructive as well as entertaining. Color versions on covers. 48pp. 8¼ x 11. 20095-7 Pa. $1.35

BIRDS OF AMERICA COLORING BOOK, John James Audubon. Rendered for coloring by Paul Kennedy. 46 of Audubon's noted illustrations: red-winged blackbird, cardinal, purple finch, towhee, etc. Original plates reproduced in full color on the covers. 48pp. 8¼ x 11. 23049-X Pa. $1.35

NORTH AMERICAN INDIAN DESIGN COLORING BOOK, Paul Kennedy. The finest examples from Indian masks, beadwork, pottery, etc. — selected and redrawn for coloring (with identifications) by well-known illustrator Paul Kennedy. 48pp. 8¼ x 11. 21125-8 Pa. $1.35

UNIFORMS OF THE AMERICAN REVOLUTION COLORING BOOK, Peter Copeland. 31 lively drawings reproduce whole panorama of military attire; each uniform has complete instructions for accurate coloring. (Not in the Pictorial Archives Series). 64pp. 8¼ x 11. 21850-3 Pa. $1.50

THE WONDERFUL WIZARD OF OZ COLORING BOOK, L. Frank Baum. Color the Yellow Brick Road and much more in 61 drawings adapted from W.W. Denslow's originals, accompanied by abridged version of text. Dorothy, Toto, Oz and the Emerald City. 61 illustrations. 64pp. 8¼ x 11. 20452-9 Pa. $1.50

CUT AND COLOR PAPER MASKS, Michael Grater. Clowns, animals, funny faces . . . simply color them in, cut them out, and put them together, and you have 9 paper masks to play with and enjoy. Complete instructions. Assembled masks shown in full color on the covers. 32pp. 8¼ x 11. 23171-2 Pa. $1.50

STAINED GLASS CHRISTMAS ORNAMENT COLORING BOOK, Carol Belanger Grafton. Brighten your Christmas season with over 100 Christmas ornaments done in a stained glass effect on translucent paper. Color them in and then hang at windows, from lights, anywhere. 32pp. 8¼ x 11. 20707-2 Pa. $1.75

CREATIVE LITHOGRAPHY AND HOW TO DO IT, Grant Arnold. Lithography as art form: working directly on stone, transfer of drawings, lithotint, mezzotint, color printing; also metal plates. Detailed, thorough. 27 illustrations. 214pp.
21208-4 Pa. $3.00

DESIGN MOTIFS OF ANCIENT MEXICO, Jorge Enciso. Vigorous, powerful ceramic stamp impressions — Maya, Aztec, Toltec, Olmec. Serpents, gods, priests, dancers, etc. 153pp. 6⅛ x 9¼.
20084-1 Pa. $2.50

AMERICAN INDIAN DESIGN AND DECORATION, Leroy Appleton. Full text, plus more than 700 precise drawings of Inca, Maya, Aztec, Pueblo, Plains, NW Coast basketry, sculpture, painting, pottery, sand paintings, metal, etc. 4 plates in color. 279pp. 8⅜ x 11¼.
22704-9 Pa. $4.50

CHINESE LATTICE DESIGNS, Daniel S. Dye. Incredibly beautiful geometric designs: circles, voluted, simple dissections, etc. Inexhaustible source of ideas, motifs. 1239 illustrations. 469pp. 6⅛ x 9¼.
23096-1 Pa. $5.00

JAPANESE DESIGN MOTIFS, Matsuya Co. Mon, or heraldic designs. Over 4000 typical, beautiful designs: birds, animals, flowers, swords, fans, geometric; all beautifully stylized. 213pp. 11⅜ x 8¼.
22874-6 Pa. $4.95

PERSPECTIVE, Jan Vredeman de Vries. 73 perspective plates from 1604 edition; buildings, townscapes, stairways, fantastic scenes. Remarkable for beauty, surrealistic atmosphere; real eye-catchers. Introduction by Adolf Placzek. 74pp. 11⅜ x 8¼.
20186-4 Pa. $2.75

EARLY AMERICAN DESIGN MOTIFS, Suzanne E. Chapman. 497 motifs, designs, from painting on wood, ceramics, appliqué, glassware, samplers, metal work, etc. Florals, landscapes, birds and animals, geometrics, letters, etc. Inexhaustible. Enlarged edition. 138pp. 8⅜ x 11¼.
22985-8 Pa. $3.50
23084-8 Clothbd. $7.95

VICTORIAN STENCILS FOR DESIGN AND DECORATION, edited by E.V. Gillon, Jr. 113 wonderful ornate Victorian pieces from German sources; florals, geometrics; borders, corner pieces; bird motifs, etc. 64pp. 9⅜ x 12¼.
21995-X Pa. $2.50

ART NOUVEAU: AN ANTHOLOGY OF DESIGN AND ILLUSTRATION FROM THE STUDIO, edited by E.V. Gillon, Jr. Graphic arts: book jackets, posters, engravings, illustrations, decorations; Crane, Beardsley, Bradley and many others. Inexhaustible. 92pp. 8⅛ x 11.
22388-4 Pa. $2.50

ORIGINAL ART DECO DESIGNS, William Rowe. First-rate, highly imaginative modern Art Deco frames, borders, compositions, alphabets, florals, insectals, Wurlitzer-types, etc. Much finest modern Art Deco. 80 plates, 8 in color. 8⅜ x 11¼.
22567-4 Pa. $3.00

HANDBOOK OF DESIGNS AND DEVICES, Clarence P. Hornung. Over 1800 basic geometric designs based on circle, triangle, square, scroll, cross, etc. Largest such collection in existence. 261pp.
20125-2 Pa. $2.50

How to Solve Chess Problems, Kenneth S. Howard. Practical suggestions on problem solving for very beginners. 58 two-move problems, 46 3-movers, 8 4-movers for practice, plus hints. 171pp. 20748-X Pa. $2.00

A Guide to Fairy Chess, Anthony Dickins. 3-D chess, 4-D chess, chess on a cylindrical board, reflecting pieces that bounce off edges, cooperative chess, retrograde chess, maximummers, much more. Most based on work of great Dawson. Full handbook, 100 problems. 66pp. 7⅞ x 10¾. 22687-5 Pa. $2.00

Win at Backgammon, Millard Hopper. Best opening moves, running game, blocking game, back game, tables of odds, etc. Hopper makes the game clear enough for anyone to play, and win. 43 diagrams. 111pp. 22894-0 Pa. $1.50

Bidding a Bridge Hand, Terence Reese. Master player "thinks out loud" the binding of 75 hands that defy point count systems. Organized by bidding problem—no-fit situations, overbidding, underbidding, cueing your defense, etc. 254pp. EBE 22830-4 Pa. $2.50

The Precision Bidding System in Bridge, C.C. Wei, edited by Alan Truscott. Inventor of precision bidding presents average hands and hands from actual play, including games from 1969 Bermuda Bowl where system emerged. 114 exercises. 116pp. 21171-1 Pa. $1.75

Learn Magic, Henry Hay. 20 simple, easy-to-follow lessons on magic for the new magician: illusions, card tricks, silks, sleights of hand, coin manipulations, escapes, and more —all with a minimum amount of equipment. Final chapter explains the great stage illusions. 92 illustrations. 285pp. 21238-6 Pa. $2.95

The New Magician's Manual, Walter B. Gibson. Step-by-step instructions and clear illustrations guide the novice in mastering 36 tricks; much equipment supplied on 16 pages of cut-out materials. 36 additional tricks. 64 illustrations. 159pp. 6⅝ x 10. 23113-5 Pa. $3.00

Professional Magic for Amateurs, Walter B. Gibson. 50 easy, effective tricks used by professionals —cards, string, tumblers, handkerchiefs, mental magic, etc. 63 illustrations. 223pp. 23012-0 Pa. $2.50

Card Manipulations, Jean Hugard. Very rich collection of manipulations; has taught thousands of fine magicians tricks that are really workable, eye-catching. Easily followed, serious work. Over 200 illustrations. 163pp. 20539-8 Pa. $2.00

Abbott's Encyclopedia of Rope Tricks for Magicians, Stewart James. Complete reference book for amateur and professional magicians containing more than 150 tricks involving knots, penetrations, cut and restored rope, etc. 510 illustrations. Reprint of 3rd edition. 400pp. 23206-9 Pa. $3.50

The Secrets of Houdini, J.C. Cannell. Classic study of Houdini's incredible magic, exposing closely-kept professional secrets and revealing, in general terms, the whole art of stage magic. 67 illustrations. 279pp. 22913-0 Pa. $2.50

THE FITZWILLIAM VIRGINAL BOOK, edited by J. Fuller Maitland, W.B. Squire. Famous early 17th century collection of keyboard music, 300 works by Morley, Byrd, Bull, Gibbons, etc. Modern notation. Total of 938pp. $8^3/8$ x 11.
ECE 21068-5, 21069-3 Pa., Two vol. set $12.00

COMPLETE STRING QUARTETS, Wolfgang A. Mozart. Breitkopf and Härtel edition. All 23 string quartets plus alternate slow movement to K156. Study score. 277pp. $9^3/8$ x $12^1/4$. 22372-8 Pa. $6.00

COMPLETE SONG CYCLES, Franz Schubert. Complete piano, vocal music of Die Schöne Müllerin, Die Winterreise, Schwanengesang. Also Drinker English singing translations. Breitkopf and Härtel edition. 217pp. $9^3/8$ x $12^1/4$.
22649-2 Pa. $4.00

THE COMPLETE PRELUDES AND ETUDES FOR PIANOFORTE SOLO, Alexander Scriabin. All the preludes and etudes including many perfectly spun miniatures. Edited by K.N. Igumnov and Y.I. Mil'shteyn. 250pp. 9 x 12. 22919-X Pa. $5.00

TRISTAN UND ISOLDE, Richard Wagner. Full orchestral score with complete instrumentation. Do not confuse with piano reduction. Commentary by Felix Mottl, great Wagnerian conductor and scholar. Study score. 655pp. $8^1/8$ x 11.
22915-7 Pa. $10.00

FAVORITE SONGS OF THE NINETIES, ed. Robert Fremont. Full reproduction, including covers, of 88 favorites: Ta-Ra-Ra-Boom-De-Aye, The Band Played On, Bird in a Gilded Cage, Under the Bamboo Tree, After the Ball, etc. 401pp. 9 x 12.
EBE 21536-9 Pa. $6.95

SOUSA'S GREAT MARCHES IN PIANO TRANSCRIPTION: ORIGINAL SHEET MUSIC OF 23 WORKS, John Philip Sousa. Selected by Lester S. Levy. Playing edition includes: The Stars and Stripes Forever, The Thunderer, The Gladiator, King Cotton, Washington Post, much more. 24 illustrations. 111pp. 9 x 12.
USO 23132-1 Pa. $3.50

CLASSIC PIANO RAGS, selected with an introduction by Rudi Blesh. Best ragtime music (1897-1922) by Scott Joplin, James Scott, Joseph F. Lamb, Tom Turpin, 9 others. Printed from best original sheet music, plus covers. 364pp. 9 x 12.
EBE 20469-3 Pa. $6.95

ANALYSIS OF CHINESE CHARACTERS, C.D. Wilder, J.H. Ingram. 1000 most important characters analyzed according to primitives, phonetics, historical development. Traditional method offers mnemonic aid to beginner, intermediate student of Chinese, Japanese. 365pp. 23045-7 Pa. $4.00

MODERN CHINESE: A BASIC COURSE, Faculty of Peking University. Self study, classroom course in modern Mandarin. Records contain phonetics, vocabulary, sentences, lessons. 249 page book contains all recorded text, translations, grammar, vocabulary, exercises. Best course on market. 3 12" $33^1/3$ monaural records, book, album. 98832-5 Set $12.50

THE BEST DR. THORNDYKE DETECTIVE STORIES, R. Austin Freeman. The Case of Oscar Brodski, The Moabite Cipher, and 5 other favorites featuring the great scientific detective, plus his long-believed-lost first adventure — 31 New Inn — reprinted here for the first time. Edited by E.F. Bleiler. USO 20388-3 Pa. $3.00

BEST "THINKING MACHINE" DETECTIVE STORIES, Jacques Futrelle. The Problem of Cell 13 and 11 other stories about Prof. Augustus S.F.X. Van Dusen, including two "lost" stories. First reprinting of several. Edited by E.F. Bleiler. 241pp. 20537-1 Pa. $3.00

UNCLE SILAS, J. Sheridan LeFanu. Victorian Gothic mystery novel, considered by many best of period, even better than Collins or Dickens. Wonderful psychological terror. Introduction by Frederick Shroyer. 436pp. 21715-9 Pa. $4.00

BEST DR. POGGIOLI DETECTIVE STORIES, T.S. Stribling. 15 best stories from EQMM and The Saint offer new adventures in Mexico, Florida, Tennessee hills as Poggioli unravels mysteries and combats Count Jalacki. 217pp. 23227-1 Pa. $3.00

EIGHT DIME NOVELS, selected with an introduction by E.F. Bleiler. Adventures of Old King Brady, Frank James, Nick Carter, Deadwood Dick, Buffalo Bill, The Steam Man, Frank Merriwell, and Horatio Alger — 1877 to 1905. Important, entertaining popular literature in facsimile reprint, with original covers. 190pp. 9 x 12. 22975-0 Pa. $3.50

ALICE'S ADVENTURES UNDER GROUND, Lewis Carroll. Facsimile of ms. Carroll gave Alice Liddell in 1864. Different in many ways from final Alice. Handlettered, illustrated by Carroll. Introduction by Martin Gardner. 128pp. 21482-6 Pa. $1.50

ALICE IN WONDERLAND COLORING BOOK, Lewis Carroll. Pictures by John Tenniel. Large-size versions of the famous illustrations of Alice, Cheshire Cat, Mad Hatter and all the others, waiting for your crayons. Abridged text. 36 illustrations. 64pp. 8¼ x 11. 22853-3 Pa. $1.50

AVENTURES D'ALICE AU PAYS DES MERVEILLES, Lewis Carroll. Bué's translation of "Alice" into French, supervised by Carroll himself. Novel way to learn language. (No English text.) 42 Tenniel illustrations. 196pp. 22836-3 Pa. $2.00

MYTHS AND FOLK TALES OF IRELAND, Jeremiah Curtin. 11 stories that are Irish versions of European fairy tales and 9 stories from the Fenian cycle — 20 tales of legend and magic that comprise an essential work in the history of folklore. 256pp. 22430-9 Pa. $3.00

EAST O' THE SUN AND WEST O' THE MOON, George W. Dasent. Only full edition of favorite, wonderful Norwegian fairytales — Why the Sea is Salt, Boots and the Troll, etc. — with 77 illustrations by Kittelsen & Werenskiöld. 418pp. 22521-6 Pa. $3.50

PERRAULT'S FAIRY TALES, Charles Perrault and Gustave Doré. Original versions of Cinderella, Sleeping Beauty, Little Red Riding Hood, etc. in best translation, with 34 wonderful illustrations by Gustave Doré. 117pp. 8⅛ x 11. 22311-6 Pa. $2.50

MOTHER GOOSE'S MELODIES. Facsimile of fabulously rare Munroe and Francis "copyright 1833" Boston edition. Familiar and unusual rhymes, wonderful old woodcut illustrations. Edited by E.F. Bleiler. 128pp. 4½ x 6⅜. 22577-1 Pa. $1.00

MOTHER GOOSE IN HIEROGLYPHICS. Favorite nursery rhymes presented in rebus form for children. Fascinating 1849 edition reproduced in toto, with key. Introduction by E.F. Bleiler. About 400 woodcuts. 64pp. 6⅞ x 5¼. 20745-5 Pa. $1.00

PETER PIPER'S PRACTICAL PRINCIPLES OF PLAIN & PERFECT PRONUNCIATION. Alliterative jingles and tongue-twisters. Reproduction in full of 1830 first American edition. 25 spirited woodcuts. 32pp. 4½ x 6⅜. 22560-7 Pa. $1.00

MARMADUKE MULTIPLY'S MERRY METHOD OF MAKING MINOR MATHEMATICIANS. Fellow to Peter Piper, it teaches multiplication table by catchy rhymes and woodcuts. 1841 Munroe & Francis edition. Edited by E.F. Bleiler. 103pp. 4⅝ x 6.
22773-1 Pa. $1.25
20171-6 Clothbd. $3.00

THE NIGHT BEFORE CHRISTMAS, Clement Moore. Full text, and woodcuts from original 1848 book. Also critical, historical material. 19 illustrations. 40pp. 4⅝ x 6. 22797-9 Pa. $1.00

THE KING OF THE GOLDEN RIVER, John Ruskin. Victorian children's classic of three brothers, their attempts to reach the Golden River, what becomes of them. Facsimile of original 1889 edition. 22 illustrations. 56pp. 4⅝ x 6⅜.
20066-3 Pa. $1.25

DREAMS OF THE RAREBIT FIEND, Winsor McCay. Pioneer cartoon strip, unexcelled for beauty, imagination, in 60 full sequences. Incredible technical virtuosity, wonderful visual wit. Historical introduction. 62pp. 8⅜ x 11¼. 21347-1 Pa. $2.00

THE KATZENJAMMER KIDS, Rudolf Dirks. In full color, 14 strips from 1906-7; full of imagination, characteristic humor. Classic of great historical importance. Introduction by August Derleth. 32pp. 9¼ x 12¼. 23005-8 Pa. $2.00

LITTLE ORPHAN ANNIE AND LITTLE ORPHAN ANNIE IN COSMIC CITY, Harold Gray. Two great sequences from the early strips: our curly-haired heroine defends the Warbucks' financial empire and, then, takes on meanie Phineas P. Pinchpenny. Leapin' lizards! 178pp. 6⅛ x 8⅜. 23107-0 Pa. $2.00

WHEN A FELLER NEEDS A FRIEND, Clare Briggs. 122 cartoons by one of the greatest newspaper cartoonists of the early 20th century — about growing up, making a living, family life, daily frustrations and occasional triumphs. 121pp. 8½ x 9½.
23148-8 Pa. $2.50

THE BEST OF GLUYAS WILLIAMS. 100 drawings by one of America's finest cartoonists: The Day a Cake of Ivory Soap Sank at Proctor & Gamble's, At the Life Insurance Agents' Banquet, and many other gems from the 20's and 30's. 118pp. 8⅜ x 11¼. 22737-5 Pa. $2.50

150 MASTERPIECES OF DRAWING, edited by Anthony Toney. 150 plates, early 15th century to end of 18th century; Rembrandt, Michelangelo, Dürer, Fragonard, Watteau, Wouwerman, many others. 150pp. 8⅜ x 11¼.   21032-4 Pa. $3.50

THE GOLDEN AGE OF THE POSTER, Hayward and Blanche Cirker. 70 extraordinary posters in full colors, from Maîtres de l'Affiche, Mucha, Lautrec, Bradley, Cheret, Beardsley, many others. 9⅜ x 12¼.   22753-7 Pa. $4.95
                                                                 21718-3 Clothbd. $7.95

SIMPLICISSIMUS, selection, translations and text by Stanley Appelbaum. 180 satirical drawings, 16 in full color, from the famous German weekly magazine in the years 1896 to 1926. 24 artists included: Grosz, Kley, Pascin, Kubin, Kollwitz, plus Heine, Thöny, Bruno Paul, others. 172pp. 8½ x 12¼.   23098-8 Pa. $5.00
                                                                 23099-6 Clothbd. $10.00

THE EARLY WORK OF AUBREY BEARDSLEY, Aubrey Beardsley. 157 plates, 2 in color: Manon Lescaut, Madame Bovary, Morte d'Arthur, Salome, other. Introduction by H. Marillier. 175pp. 8½ x 11.   21816-3 Pa. $3.50

THE LATER WORK OF AUBREY BEARDSLEY, Aubrey Beardsley. Exotic masterpieces of full maturity: Venus and Tannhäuser, Lysistrata, Rape of the Lock, Volpone, Savoy material, etc. 174 plates, 2 in color. 176pp. 8½ x 11.   21817-1 Pa. $3.75

DRAWINGS OF WILLIAM BLAKE, William Blake. 92 plates from Book of Job, Divine Comedy, Paradise Lost, visionary heads, mythological figures, Laocoön, etc. Selection, introduction, commentary by Sir Geoffrey Keynes. 178pp. 8½ x 11.
                                                                 22303-5 Pa. $3.50

LONDON: A PILGRIMAGE, Gustave Doré, Blanchard Jerrold. Squalor, riches, misery, beauty of mid-Victorian metropolis; 55 wonderful plates, 125 other illustrations, full social, cultural text by Jerrold. 191pp. of text. 8⅛ x 11.
                                                                 22306-X Pa. $5.00

THE COMPLETE WOODCUTS OF ALBRECHT DÜRER, edited by Dr. W. Kurth. 346 in all: Old Testament, St. Jerome, Passion, Life of Virgin, Apocalypse, many others. Introduction by Campbell Dodgson. 285pp. 8½ x 12¼.   21097-9 Pa. $6.00

THE DISASTERS OF WAR, Francisco Goya. 83 etchings record horrors of Napoleonic wars in Spain and war in general. Reprint of 1st edition, plus 3 additional plates. Introduction by Philip Hofer. 97pp. 9⅜ x 8¼.   21872-4 Pa. $2.50

ENGRAVINGS OF HOGARTH, William Hogarth. 101 of Hogarth's greatest works: Rake's Progress, Harlot's Progress, Illustrations for Hudibras, Midnight Modern Conversation, Before and After, Beer Street and Gin Lane, many more. Full commentary. 256pp. 11 x 14.   22479-1 Pa. $6.00
                                                                 23023-6 Clothbd. $13.50

PRIMITIVE ART, Franz Boas. Great anthropologist on ceramics, textiles, wood, stone, metal, etc.; patterns, technology, symbols, styles. All areas, but fullest on Northwest Coast Indians. 350 illustrations. 378pp.   20025-6 Pa. $3.50

MANUAL OF THE TREES OF NORTH AMERICA, Charles S. Sargent. The basic survey of every native tree and tree-like shrub, 717 species in all. Extremely full descriptions, information on habitat, growth, locales, economics, etc. Necessary to every serious tree lover. Over 100 finding keys. 783 illustrations. Total of 986pp.
20277-1, 20278-X Pa., Two vol. set $8.00

BIRDS OF THE NEW YORK AREA, John Bull. Indispensable guide to more than 400 species within a hundred-mile radius of Manhattan. Information on range, status, breeding, migration, distribution trends, etc. Foreword by Roger Tory Peterson. 17 drawings; maps. 540pp.
23222-0 Pa. $6.00

THE SEA-BEACH AT EBB-TIDE, Augusta Foote Arnold. Identify hundreds of marine plants and animals: algae, seaweeds, squids, crabs, corals, etc. Descriptions cover food, life cycle, size, shape, habitat. Over 600 drawings. 490pp.
21949-6 Pa. $4.00

THE MOTH BOOK, William J. Holland. Identify more than 2,000 moths of North America. General information, precise species descriptions. 623 illustrations plus 48 color plates show almost all species, full size. 1968 edition. Still the basic book. Total of 551pp. 6½ x 9¼.
21948-8 Pa. $6.00

AN INTRODUCTION TO THE REPTILES AND AMPHIBIANS OF THE UNITED STATES, Percy A. Morris. All lizards, crocodiles, turtles, snakes, toads, frogs; life history, identification, habits, suitability as pets, etc. Non-technical, but sound and broad. 130 photos. 253pp.
22982-3 Pa. $3.00

OLD NEW YORK IN EARLY PHOTOGRAPHS, edited by Mary Black. Your only chance to see New York City as it was 1853-1906, through 196 wonderful photographs from N.Y. Historical Society. Great Blizzard, Lincoln's funeral procession, great buildings. 228pp. 9 x 12.
22907-6 Pa. $6.00

THE AMERICAN REVOLUTION, A PICTURE SOURCEBOOK, John Grafton. Wonderful Bicentennial picture source, with 411 illustrations (contemporary and 19th century) showing battles, personalities, maps, events, flags, posters, soldier's life, ships, etc. all captioned and explained. A wonderful browsing book, supplement to other historical reading. 160pp. 9 x 12.
23226-3 Pa. $4.00

PERSONAL NARRATIVE OF A PILGRIMAGE TO AL-MADINAH AND MECCAH, Richard Burton. Great travel classic by remarkably colorful personality. Burton, disguised as a Moroccan, visited sacred shrines of Islam, narrowly escaping death. Wonderful observations of Islamic life, customs, personalities. 47 illustrations. Total of 959pp.
21217-3, 21218-1 Pa., Two vol. set $7.00

INCIDENTS OF TRAVEL IN CENTRAL AMERICA, CHIAPAS, AND YUCATAN, John L. Stephens. Almost single-handed discovery of Maya culture; exploration of ruined cities, monuments, temples; customs of Indians. 115 drawings. 892pp.
22404-X, 22405-8 Pa., Two vol. set $8.00

EARLY NEW ENGLAND GRAVESTONE RUBBINGS, Edmund V. Gillon, Jr. 43 photographs, 226 rubbings show heavily symbolic, macabre, sometimes humorous primitive American art. Up to early 19th century. 207pp. 8⅜ x 11¼.
21380-3 Pa. $4.00

L.J.M. DAGUERRE: THE HISTORY OF THE DIORAMA AND THE DAGUERREOTYPE, Helmut and Alison Gernsheim. Definitive account. Early history, life and work of Daguerre; discovery of daguerreotype process; diffusion abroad; other early photography. 124 illustrations. 226pp. 6⅙ x 9¼.
22290-X Pa. $4.00

PHOTOGRAPHY AND THE AMERICAN SCENE, Robert Taft. The basic book on American photography as art, recording form, 1839-1889. Development, influence on society, great photographers, types (portraits, war, frontier, etc.), whatever else needed. Inexhaustible. Illustrated with 322 early photos, daguerreotypes, tintypes, stereo slides, etc. 546pp. 6⅛ x 9¼.
21201-7 Pa. $5.00

PHOTOGRAPHIC SKETCHBOOK OF THE CIVIL WAR, Alexander Gardner. Reproduction of 1866 volume with 100 on-the-field photographs: Manassas, Lincoln on battlefield, slave pens, etc. Introduction by E.F. Bleiler. 224pp. 10¾ x 9.
22731-6 Pa. $4.50

THE MOVIES: A PICTURE QUIZ BOOK, Stanley Appelbaum & Hayward Cirker. Match stars with their movies, name actors and actresses, test your movie skill with 241 stills from 236 great movies, 1902-1959. Indexes of performers and films. 128pp. 8⅜ x 9¼.
20222-4 Pa. $2.50

THE TALKIES, Richard Griffith. Anthology of features, articles from Photoplay, 1928-1940, reproduced complete. Stars, famous movies, technical features, fabulous ads, etc.; Garbo, Chaplin, King Kong, Lubitsch, etc. 4 color plates, scores of illustrations. 327pp. 8⅜ x 11¼.
22762-6 Pa. $5.95

THE MOVIE MUSICAL FROM VITAPHONE TO "42ND STREET," edited by Miles Kreuger. Relive the rise of the movie musical as reported in the pages of Photoplay magazine (1926-1933): every movie review, cast list, ad, and record review; every significant feature article, production still, biography, forecast, and gossip story. Profusely illustrated. 367pp. 8⅜ x 11¼.
23154-2 Pa. $6.95

JOHANN SEBASTIAN BACH, Philipp Spitta. Great classic of biography, musical commentary, with hundreds of pieces analyzed. Also good for Bach's contemporaries. 450 musical examples. Total of 1799pp.
EUK 22278-0, 22279-9 Clothbd., Two vol. set $25.00

BEETHOVEN AND HIS NINE SYMPHONIES, Sir George Grove. Thorough history, analysis, commentary on symphonies and some related pieces. For either beginner or advanced student. 436 musical passages. 407pp.
20334-4 Pa. $4.00

MOZART AND HIS PIANO CONCERTOS, Cuthbert Girdlestone. The only full-length study. Detailed analyses of all 21 concertos, sources; 417 musical examples. 509pp.
21271-8 Pa. $4.50

CATALOGUE OF DOVER BOOKS

EGYPTIAN MAGIC, E.A. Wallis Budge. Foremost Egyptologist, curator at British Museum, on charms, curses, amulets, doll magic, transformations, control of demons, deific appearances, feats of great magicians. Many texts cited. 19 illustrations. 234pp. USO 22681-6 Pa. $2.50

THE LEYDEN PAPYRUS: AN EGYPTIAN MAGICAL BOOK, edited by F. Ll. Griffith, Herbert Thompson. Egyptian sorcerer's manual contains scores of spells: sex magic of various sorts, occult information, evoking visions, removing evil magic, etc. Transliteration faces translation. 207pp. 22994-7 Pa. $2.50

THE MALLEUS MALEFICARUM OF KRAMER AND SPRENGER, translated, edited by Montague Summers. Full text of most important witchhunter's "Bible," used by both Catholics and Protestants. Theory of witches, manifestations, remedies, etc. Indispensable to serious student. 278pp. 6⅝ x 10. USO 22802-9 Pa. $3.95

LOST CONTINENTS, L. Sprague de Camp. Great science-fiction author, finest, fullest study: Atlantis, Lemuria, Mu, Hyperborea, etc. Lost Tribes, Irish in pre-Columbian America, root races; in history, literature, art, occultism. Necessary to everyone concerned with theme. 17 illustrations. 348pp. 22668-9 Pa. $3.50

THE COMPLETE BOOKS OF CHARLES FORT, Charles Fort. Book of the Damned, Lo!, Wild Talents, New Lands. Greatest compilation of data: celestial appearances, flying saucers, falls of frogs, strange disappearances, inexplicable data not recognized by science. Inexhaustible, painstakingly documented. Do not confuse with modern charlatanry. Introduction by Damon Knight. Total of 1126pp.
23094-5 Clothbd. $15.00

FADS AND FALLACIES IN THE NAME OF SCIENCE, Martin Gardner. Fair, witty appraisal of cranks and quacks of science: Atlantis, Lemuria, flat earth, Velikovsky, orgone energy, Bridey Murphy, medical fads, etc. 373pp. 20394-8 Pa. $3.00

HOAXES, Curtis D. MacDougall. Unbelievably rich account of great hoaxes: Locke's moon hoax, Shakespearean forgeries, Loch Ness monster, Disumbrationist school of art, dozens more; also psychology of hoaxing. 54 illustrations. 338pp. 20465-0 Pa. $3.50

THE GENTLE ART OF MAKING ENEMIES, James A.M. Whistler. Greatest wit of his day deflates Wilde, Ruskin, Swinburne; strikes back at inane critics, exhibitions. Highly readable classic of impressionist revolution by great painter. Introduction by Alfred Werner. 334pp. 21875-9 Pa. $4.00

THE BOOK OF TEA, Kakuzo Okakura. Minor classic of the Orient: entertaining, charming explanation, interpretation of traditional Japanese culture in terms of tea ceremony. Edited by E.F. Bleiler. Total of 94pp. 20070-1 Pa. $1.25

matte . . . . — — n.f. braid; mat, matting